# AGAIN WITH ONE VOICE

What better way to explore the century-long history of English political reform than with the songs of the times. Covering 1768 to 1868, these compositions highlight such topics as the American Revolutionary and Civil Wars, the French Revolution, and Crimean War, and dwelling on such personages as John Wilkes, Thomas Paine, Daniel O'Connell and Napoleon Bonaparte. Scholar/singer Richard Holdstock has assembled an amazing array of 120 songs from the popular presses of the day, many of them extremely rare. and all with appropriate tunes. Throughout his thorough exploration we see the fascinating history of violence, chicanery, patriotism, and sacrifice woven in the fabric of song. This work is essential for any institutional or personal library dealing with the history of England and the struggle of the working class in general.

*Joe Hickerson, Head Emeritus, Library of Congress Folklife Center*

Dick's book is a worthy successor in spirit and outlook to Roy Palmer's *Ballad History of England*. It picks up the flame of resistance and reform, adding detail and colour to a period of history that, too often neglected, can manifestly still be heard. Especially useful are those now-unique songs from the frustratingly inaccessible, microfilm-only Madden Collection at Cambridge. Featuring a mix of original, sympathetic, and surprising musical settings, deftly arranged and notated by June Nishimoto, this is a supremely singable collection, and should enlighten and enliven our discussions and our singing in equal measure.

*Oskar Cox Jensen, Historian and Author, University of East Anglia*

There is no more exciting way of bringing historical times to life than through the songs of the people living through them. This book's selection of political reform songs of the eighteenth and nineteenth century illuminates the conditions that poor people in particular, were determined to change — sometimes at great cost to themselves. The songs have an energy and commitment fueled by anger, despair, humour and wit — what better way of meeting the ancestors who fought and improved our lives too.

*Frankie Armstrong, Godmother of the Natural Voice Singing Movement*

# AGAIN WITH ONE VOICE

## British Songs of Political Reform, 1768 to 1868

## DICK HOLDSTOCK

edited by Patience Young
music transcription by June Nishimoto

Loomis House Press
NORTHFIELD, MINNESOTA

Cover and interior design by Mark F. Heiman

Cover illustration: "Meeting at the Reformers' Tree, Hyde Park." From *Cassell's History of England, Vol. VI.* See p. 364 for more information.

ISBN 978-1-935243-80-9 (paperbound)
ISBN 978-1-935243-77-9 (hardcover)

Second printing.

Library of Congress Control Number: 2021938178

*Publisher's Cataloging-in-Publication data*

Names: Holdstock, Dick, author. | Young, Patience, editor. | Nishimoto, June, contributor.
Title: Again with one voice : British songs of political reform , 1768 to 1868 / Dick Holdstock; edited by Patience Young; music transcription by June Nishimoto.
Description: Includes bibliographical references and index. | Northfield, MN: Loomis House Press, 2021.
Identifiers: LCCN: 2021938178 | ISBN: 978-1-935243-80-9 (paperback) | 978-1-935243-77-9 (hardcover)
Subjects: LCSH Political ballads and songs—Great Britain—History and criticism. | Political participation—Great Britain—History—18th century. | Political participation—Great Britain—History—19th century. | Great Britain—History—Songs and music. | BISAC HISTORY / Europe / Great Britain / Georgian Era (1714-1837) | HISTORY / Europe / Great Britain / Victorian Era (1837-1901) | MUSIC / History & Criticism | MUSIC / Genres & Styles / Folk & Traditional
Classification: LCC ML3650.3 .H65 2021| DDC 780.942—dc23

Recordings of one verse from each song in this book are available at dickholdstock.com

# Contents

# Acknowledgements

I am grateful for the help of so many people too numerous to list here, who made it possible for this book to be published.

My dear wife, Carol Holdstock, my first editor, stuck with me and this project from its initial concept at the Vaughn Williams Library in 1993 to its final delivery to Loomis House Press in 2020. I know it would have been impossible without her. My brother, Roger Holdstock, reviewed my first attempts in 1995 and has remained a big help ever since. In recognition of my dilemma and her fascination for the book's content, Patience Young has professionally and totally edited everything and located amazing illustrations for this project. June Nishimoto has applied her brilliant skills at providing notation for all of the melodies we've had to find with adaptation to fit all 120 songs. Casey Casebeer helped find direction when it was needed most.

Over the years I have obtained advice on this project from incredibly large numbers of folkies and performers. Here are just a few of those who jump to the front of my old mind: Allan Macleod, Faith Petric, Riggy Rackin, Louisa Killen, Dave Webber, Annie Fentiman, Stan Hugill, Bill Wagman, Robert Rodriguez, Frank Harte, Ingrid and Barrie Temple, Martin Carthy, Davis Singers and Pickers, San Francisco Folk Music Club, Auburn Song Circle, Portland Folk Music Club, and Seattle Folk Music Club.

I was surprised at the number of academics from all over who gave their time to help finish this project, including: Oscar Cox Jensen, Ian Dyke, David Kennerley, Cliff Conner, Dave Gregory, Doc Rowe, James Hepburn, Malcolm Chase, Michael Scrivener, Rachel Hammersley, Richard Gault, Roy Palmer, Steve Poole, Vic Gammon, and Victor Slater.

Librarians and other custodians of songs and other resources needed to fill the gaps were: Joe Hickerson, Malcolm Taylor, Steve Roud, Martin and Shan Graeb, Esther Chadwick, Lisa Tillis, Pam Bishop, David Ingerson, Joe Offer, Qona Wright, Roly Brown, the Madden and Bodleian collections, and full assistance from Shields Library at UC Davis.

Finally, I am delighted that Mark Heiman of Loomis House Press has taken on this project.

# Foreword
by Steve Roud

It may seem a little obvious to say so, but this book is about two equally important topics—political reform, of course, but also about songs and singing. And while historians are accustomed to dealing with the former, they will often take little account of the latter, or at best take it for granted. But song was not simply a colorless medium by which the reformers got their message across; it had a resonance of its own, a social meaning, and was an integral part of the everyday experience of nearly everyone in society. And it could be extremely effective as a mode of communication. While a leader in *The Times* or a heated debate in a London coffee house undoubtedly contributed to the course of history, a successful song could reach thousands in a very short time, and not only get the message across but lodge it in people's brains and make it part of their daily lives. Modern advertisers were not the first to discover the power of a good slogan and a catchy tune.

It is also a truism to say that before the advent of recorded sound, and later broadcasting, almost everybody sang, and they sang a great deal. Around the home, in the pub, at work, in the street, in the school playground, at church or chapel, at special occasions like weddings, Christmas parties, harvest homes, and at the meetings of clubs, societies and organisations of all kinds.

But not everyone sang in the same way, or the same songs, and to a certain extent what songs you knew and performed partly defined you. While those in the tavern were merrily singing songs in praise of the good life, members of the temperance society in the school or church hall were singing, perhaps not quite so merrily, about the road to ruin that the drunkards were on. The vicar's family and servants gathered round the piano on a Sunday afternoon would be singing different songs, in a different way, than the labourer's family huddled round a meagre cottage fire.

For all levels, *song* was one of the glues which kept a community together. Because singing usually involved an audience, group solidarity or social cohesion was created and fostered in performance. This song is not just what *I* think, but what *we* think. But cohesion is also divisive—the surest way to keep your group together is to attack another group. While radicals were vocalising their "seditious" sentiments, conservatives were using patriotic verses to stiffen their resolve to fight them tooth and nail.

Songs had always been disseminated by the "oral tradition"—people picking up words and tune simply by hearing them performed—and this was especially effective for the common people. But increasingly in the period covered by this book, printed materials played a big part in song circulation. Huge numbers of song-books were published each year, tailored for all tastes and budgets, from the expensive productions with engraved music and notated piano accompaniment, down to the roughly-printed 8-page chapbooks giving just the words and sold by hawkers and in back-street shops.

But the great mass of song material reached the public on broadsides—single sheets sold by itinerant ballad-singers in the streets for a penny or less. They were cheap to print and cheap to buy, or even to be given away free. The latter was often the case in elections and when a wealthy organisation, such as the Cheap Repository Tracts, was deliberately trying to influence public opinion by using the popular mass medium.

In political debate, the broadside trade had the distinct advantage of agility—a particularly important aspect during an election or agitation over a hot topic. A candidate's latest slogan, or his reply to an opponent's attack, could be cast into verse, printed up, and sung in the streets within the hour. A shocking event, such as the Peterloo massacre, could be reported quickly and effectively, and one of the functions of the broadside was to be the tabloid newspaper of its time.

It is often said that history is written by the victors, but this is only true up to a point. It is more accurate to say that history is written by the powerful. Most of the great battles over reform were eventually achieved—universal suffrage, secret ballot, the removal of rotten boroughs, and so on—but because the successes took so long to arrive, and the reformers were so successfully portrayed as such dangerous radicals and revolutionaries, the historical record is still weighted in favour of the rulers. Indeed, we would be forgiven for getting the idea our rulers were wise in their strategy of allowing gradual controlled reform instead of outright revolution. They were the good guys.

But the songs tell a different story. Like diaries and letters, they help to bring home the lived experience, the excitement and commitment of a social and political *movement*. Every inch of progress was partly achieved, or at least accompanied by, vocal dissent, agitation, protest, against powerful forces which could turn brutal.

The songs in this book are a different way of learning about the ongoing campaigns for political reform than many official histories offer us, but they also shine a new spotlight on people's everyday lives, and the more information we have in that sphere, the better.

# Preface

This book arose out of my curiosity about why, throughout the English-speaking world, there are so many songs in the repertoires of traditional British folk music performers that admire Britain's historically accepted enemy, Napoleon Bonaparte. Many popular English songs of the 19th century had been written in praise of him. Over the years I have collected and performed quite a number of them.

After early retirement from my day job, my wife and I had an opportunity in 1992 to spend a few weeks in London. We planned to visit family and attend folk clubs and festivals. I also took time while there to search for more Bonaparte songs at the Vaughan Williams Memorial Library at the Cecil Sharp House, where I discovered the library's tremendous Broadside Ballad collection. I became hooked on the Library's microfilm records of Cambridge University's Madden Collection, containing copies of more than 30,000 broadside ballads. I left London with over 400 photocopies of broadsides and other ballads, including a handful of pro-Napoleon songs that I had never seen before, a few good drinking songs, working songs, and many working class political songs. Once these were arranged chronologically, it became clear to me that they all spoke of workers' lives and their growing commitment to amending the class-dividing political system. These ballads motivated British workers to achieve political reform through voting rights, and are excellent primary sources for learning about a volatile and significant period in British history.

My growing song collection had big gaps for topics that one would expect to have produced considerable numbers of broadside ballads. My search continued. In 1999, Oxford University's Bodleian Library placed online digital facsimiles of all its 30,000 broadside ballads, and Shields Library at my home University of California Davis acquired all twelve microfilm reels of Cambridge's Madden Collection. I then had ready access to both of these outstanding resources. From these and other, smaller broadside collections and pertinent books, most of the topic gaps were filled. The combined resources revealed the complex sentiments of working people who became more and more resolved to obtain a truly representative government. Evident in these lyrics were the depths of humiliation, strife, and hardship suffered by the working class of Britain. Armed with these ideas I determined that it was time to assemble this material into the book that you are now reading.

Often transcriptions of broadside ballads are edited and abbreviated to make them more attractive and more understandable to modern readers. Doing so sometimes misrepresents the purpose and intent of the ballads as they were first written. To avoid this, I have included all verses of lyrics, with spellings as originally printed, to show what readers saw on the original sheets. The song's source and its Roud number are listed with each entry. Following each song is my commentary, shedding light on the context, feeling, intent, and circumstances for the song, as we understand it today.

These were more than just political poems; they were all part of a singing tradition, and singing these songs today can bring us closer to those who wrote them. Some broadsides indicate the tune to which they were meant to be sung; only a quarter of those in this collection had such designations. To create a singable collection, I have paired the remaining songs with suitable melodies. My goal has been to select tunes that most street vendors of the time would have known. All but ten of the tunes clearly meet that criteria; three of those songs retain the tunes that I have always sung with their lyrics, and the remainder may have been around when the song was written—we just don't know. Tunes that were originally paired with a text are marked with a 🎵 so that you can distinguish my adaptations.

In making my tune choices I considered whether the words were similar to known songs of the time, how the melody helped convey the feeling of the words, and how well the tune fit the meter of the words. Melodies were chosen from *The News Chronicle Song Book* off mum's piano, an extensive repertoire of English and Scottish songs sung with Allan Macleod, tunes from *The Barnes Books of English Country Dance Tunes* played with Quite Carried Away, and an increasing number of recordings.

My initial quest had been to find more pro-Napoleon songs and to learn more about why they were so popular. Much on this subject has since been written by Peter Wood in *The Green Linnet,* and by Oskar Cox Jensen in *Napoleon and British Song 1797–1822,* outstanding books published in 2015. Echoing my first impulse, I am compelled here to include six songs representing pro-Napoleon sentiments, in unusual versions that are seldom heard, that were printed as broadside ballads (songs 56, 59, 60, 62, 71, and 98). All but one was written after the Battle of Waterloo, and express the enduring feelings of people who were inspired by Napoleon to fight for their own democratic reform. Their wistful tone raises the thought: if Bonaparte had prevailed, would the plight of the British working class have improved?

# AGAIN WITH ONE VOICE

# Introduction

From the late eighteenth century on into the nineteenth century, printed broadside ballads played an increasingly important role in disseminating information. They reported events affecting those afflicted by a system that maintained the deep gap between Britain's haves and have-nots. Broadside ballads were an existing economical way to produce and distribute entertainment, but as political awareness increased, they also became the best way to disperse information on events of the time that negatively affected the lives of those oppressed by the system. These ballads were printed mostly with two songs per sheet on cheap paper from a wide range of printing presses. They were distributed to street vendors who sang them on the streets of larger towns and cities, and who often traveled far and wide to find gatherings of people to buy the broadsides for a farthing or halfpenny.

Broadsides were certainly not limited to social-political issues. They included popular songs, old favorites, topical songs, and political songs calling for reform—a genre which continuously gathered momentum during the later 18th century. This turned out to be good timing because, as Steve Roud notes, "from about the 1790s to the 1860s, was the golden age for broadside song material."(Roud: 2017, 434) Frequently it became important to rush out the latest reform topic of the day, requiring the writer to quickly assemble words to fit a melody that was already popular. In their haste, many authors and type-setters often made typographical errors and other mistakes. To increase income, printers often turned to making metal stereotype copies of the hand-assembled printing forms. The stereotype plates resulted in identical copies of printed ballads appearing from presses located far from the first printer and far from the time of the story being told by the song. In some cases, there are several different versions of the same song existing in various collections. Selected for this book are what appear to be the earliest versions of songs that accurately portray the proven happenings of the time described. My source for each song is listed beneath its title.

It is not surprising that working people desired changes in Britain's ancient electoral system. In the eighteenth century, landowning voters set standards that maintained social barriers to keep workers from having any say in the governance of Britain. Then, as now, Britain's government included King, Lords, and Commons. Only the House of Commons included elected members, but usually less than 30% of its 500+ seats were contested in any election period. Members of Parliament were either returned as Knights of the Shire, with two elected from each English county and one from each Welsh county, or as representatives of various boroughs throughout the country. Boroughs were not uniform in geographical or population size. They were represented by as many as four members of Parliament, depending on one or more earlier decree. Boroughs with small electorates usually were for sale to the highest bidder and were called "Rotten Boroughs."

Electors in boroughs varied from fewer than ten to several thousand, and some major cities, including Manchester and Birmingham, had no representation whatsoever. Each borough had its own voting system with franchise varying from "The Potwallopers," where all men were enfranchised who had a family and boiled a pot, to "The Corporationers," that allowed only members of the self-perpetuating local town council, or other electors designated by an ancient decree—all of whom were required to own property. The rest of the population could not vote, including "compound householders" who paid taxes indirectly, with their rent, through their landlords. Rural workers were particularly ignored by the government.

Not only was the common man unable to vote; his interests were badly represented. The distribution of parliamentary seats was totally uneven. For example, the English County of Cornwall had just one seat fewer than the entire country of Scotland. Although members of Parliament were not paid for their positions, they frequently received substantial pensions or sinecures, that paid well for unneeded jobs. Campaigning for candidates for office usually took place at "hustings," and voting was done by signing the register book for the candidate of choice. There were many incidents of voters who were attacked by paid poll watchers or by paid enforcers because they voted the way they did.

Britain's systematic arrangements for keeping the majority of its people out of the political system were effective in maintaining the gap between rich and poor. It denied workers enough to eat, clean water, education, living wages, adequate housing, medical care, fair working hours, waste management, affordable newspapers, a fair legal system, and all the other amenities enjoyed by the haves. For the working man the Juridical system was a complete disaster, presided over by the same landed Gentry causing the problem in the first place. These sadists presided over dishing out horrible jail sentences, transportation, hanging, drawing and quartering. Getting by under these conditions was extremely difficult, and only possible when employment was steady, but totally impossible whenever the breadwinner was injured, ill or unemployed. All this was true for England and Wales, and in so many ways more so for Ireland and Scotland, where continuing enclosures stripped working people of land that they had traditionally relied upon to feed their families. Another troubling harassment occurred throughout the British Isles from the suppressive poaching laws. These laws were increasingly enforced during the period of this book, prohibiting landless people from acquiring wild game for food under penalty of death or deportation.

Workers had to contrive their own ways to improve their quality of life and feed their strong desires for political reform. That need for change is exhibited in the broadside ballads from those times.

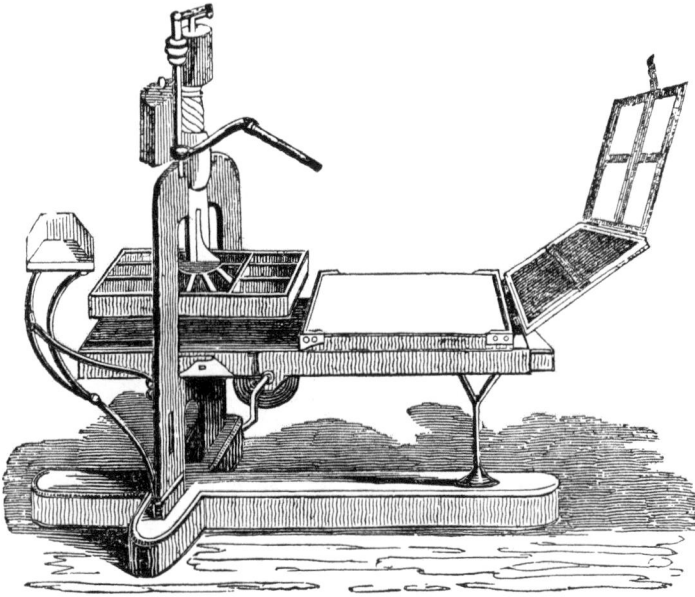

This is The Thing

John Wilkes. Engraving from a manifesto commemorating his fight
against general warrants and for the liberty of the press, 1768.

# Chapter 1
# LIBERTY: 1768–1781

*"I wish, Sir, an English Parliament to speak the free unbiased sense of the body of the English people and of every man amongst us, of every individual, who may justly be supposed to be comprehended in a fair majority."* —John Wilkes, 1776

John Wilkes, a strong advocate of political reform in Britain and America, was a key figure in the movement to realize rights and liberties for the common man. He used his satirical newspaper, *The North Briton*, to ridicule Prime Minister Lord Bute and the recently crowned George III. In its issue Number 45 (April 1763) he critiqued their aggressive takeover of Parliament by purchasing "rotten borough" seats for their allies. For this published essay, Wilkes was indicted on charges of seditious libel. Fearing the consequences, Wilkes escaped to France, but he was tried and convicted in absentia, lost his seat in Parliament, and was declared an outlaw. As word of his dilemma got out a support movement for him began to emerge throughout Britain. Five years later in 1768, Wilkes returned to England. As he approached London, he was met by throngs of people who unhitched his horses and pulled his coach by hand past houses with "45" chalked on doors, displaying signs of "Wilkes and Liberty," and with candles illuminating the windows. Broadside ballad vendors soon flooded the street market with songs that poured from the small presses supporting Wilkes and Liberty.

Wilkes ran for and won an open Middlesex parliamentary seat, but Parliament refused to seat him and sent him to prison to await sentencing for his existing libel conviction. For the next fortnight, large crowds assembled at St. George's Fields, an open space located by the prison. On May 10, 1768 a crowd of around 15,000 arrived outside the prison. The crowd chanted "Wilkes and Liberty," "No Liberty, No King," and "Damn the King! Damn the Government! Damn the Justices!" Fearing that the crowd would attempt to rescue Wilkes, troops opened fire, killing seven people.

Anger at the Massacre of St. George's Fields led to disturbances all over London. The "Wilkes and Liberty" movement, and the political broadsides that emerged from it, also became an outlet for working class anger, offering people a chance to express themselves and be heard in a public way. "The resistance of the elite pushed them to more radical expression, and violence occasionally ensued, all of which was grist for the mill of the ballad writers." (Wilson 1995: 206)

The Wilkes and Liberty Movement articulated what was then considered a radical program, calling for the common people to be fairly and equitably represented in Parliament and for lackeys of the elite ("pensioners and placemen") to be excluded from the House of Commons. Given the country's oppressive governing system, working class people were powerless to improve their dreadful conditions. Ballads reported the people's feelings as Wilkes was re-elected to and rejected by parliament three more times before he was finally seated.

At this period Britain had long led the way in the commerce of removing African people from their homes and placing them into slavery. Liverpool, Bristol, and London were the main British centers for this brutal and profitable business. In the words of William Pitt the Younger in the House Commons in 1792, "No nation in Europe... has... plunged so deeply into the guilt as Great Britain." (Thomas 1997: 235) The famous Mansfield decision of 1772, decreed by Chief Justice William Mansfield (who had also presided over Wilkes' trial), legally ended slavery on British soil. (Wise: 2005, 183) The Mansfield decision freed over 14,000 slaves living in Britain, but did nothing to limit British commerce from participating in the slave trade or to eliminate slavery in the colonies. Nor did it do anything to aid the millions of overworked, underfed, poorly housed wage slaves of the British Isles. Shortly after the beginning of hostilities in the American Revolutionary War, the Mansfield decision was invoked to convince American slaves to come over to the British side and achieve their freedom. Between eighty thousand and one hundred thousand slaves left the plantations during the war.

Working people were not alone in seeking reform; there also emerged a vigorous and largely bourgeois radical culture. Concurrent with the Wilkes and Liberty Movement, the "Society of the Supporters of the Bill of Rights" was formed to carry on the work of an earlier group called "The Real Whigs" that had worked closely with Wilkes. Society members wrote essays in defense of the American Colonies which faced increasingly repressive measures invoked by the Lord North Tory Government, and they collected money to help wipe out the huge debts incurred by Wilkes. The Society called for shorter parliaments, exclusion of pensioners and placemen from the House of Commons, and a fair and equitable representation of the people in Parliament. (Cash: 2006, 295)

Times continued hard throughout Britain, with poor harvests everywhere.

Opposition spread throughout Ireland despite, and in response to, Protestant volunteer military groups organized by the government to curb dissent. Major European powers turned against Britain and aided the Americans. America received military support from the French army and navy and financial support from France and the Netherlands. (McCullough: 2005, 293) British trade with the Colonies was lost. A great deal of parliamentary debate waged over the wisdom of continuing to pursue the war, but the will of some members of Parliament to end aggression never prevailed. Wilkes, however, was successful in his campaign of 1778 to defeat the City of London's attempt to raise a London regiment to fight in America. (Cole: 1971, 106)

# WILKES and LIBERTY,

## In Honour of No. 45.

To the Tune of, Ballance a Straw.

IN the year fixty-eight will ye Briton's be wife,
  And throw off the clouds that darken your
O will you for freedom and Liberty join,    (eyes,
To vote for our caufe that in time you may fhine.
To fave a dear country, O will you contrive,
And think of the Number of good forty-five.

Detail of broadside sheet (see song on next page)

**1**   Wilkes and Liberty: In Honour of No 45

Sir Frederick Madden's Collection of Broadside Ballads, 03:1976

*Tune: Balance a Straw; William Clark of Lincoln, 1770*

In the year sixty-eight will ye Britons be wise,
And throw off the cloud that darkens your eyes
Oh will you for freedom and Liberty join,
To vote for our cause that in time you may shine.

   To save a dear country, O will you contrive,
   And think of the number of good forty-five.

That your children forever your memories may prize,
Be careful and prudent, be cautious and wise,
Let no bribes e'er persuade ye or play a wrong game,
Least their curses forever will follow you.

Should great Ones suppress you with threats and their awes,
Remember dear Britons your country's cause
Will you stand for a man that was honest pray,
Who stood for the truth, tho' it forced him away

Since now is your time boys, I'd have you make sure
When slipp'd you may never enjoy it no more,
Tho' messengers struck to your Liberty you know
O, who was it gave them so heavy a blow.

O my good forty five, sure how just was thy cause
What a struggle thou hads't for thy country's laws
Thro' fire and sword, O how great is thy fame,
Since history for ever must honour thy name,

Now you tools of the state from the aged to youth,
Thou has fought against Liberty freedom and truth
Remember the peace that left you a cause,
And in starving the poor, don't you think it is worse.

The Wilkes and Liberty campaign told listeners to "throw off the clouds" that darkened the working men's minds to the ideas of liberty and freedom. Wilkes exiled himself for five years to France after prosecution and conviction for seditious libel for publishing number 45 of *The North Briton*, as well as a scandalous pamphlet titled "Essay on Women." Number 45 had established him as the leading critic of Lord Bute, at the time the unpopular Prime Minister from Scotland, and of the newly ascended George III. When Wilkes returned from France he immediately, unsuccessfully, tried to get elected to one of the four seats in the borough of London. The only poll in the British Isles that could count more voters was Westminster. (Cash: 2006, 207) He placed last in a field of seven candidates. Undiscouraged, Wilkes promptly announced his intention to run as a radical for one of the two Middlesex Knights of the Shire Parliamentary seats. His campaign manager was to be Reverend John Horne (Horne Tooke). On March 26, 1768, election day, Wilkes easily won a seat; the other seat was won by George Cooke. Massive numbers of people celebrated in the streets. Windows were illuminated, and the number 45 was chalked on almost every door.

Wilkes promised to turn himself in after the election, to be sentenced on the charges for which he had been convicted previously. On April 27 he was jailed, awaiting sentencing, at King's Bench Prison located in St. George's Fields in the South of London; hundreds gathered outside daily while Wilkes was there. On May 10, the day Parliament was to convene, several thousand supporters formed on St. George's Fields to escort Wilkes from prison to assume his seat in Parliament. The Government had no intention of releasing Wilkes, so soldiers were dispatched to control the crowd, which expanded during the day. The Riot Act was read, and eventually soldiers fired at the crowd; five or six protesters were killed on the spot and about fifteen wounded. (Rude: 1962, 51) The crowd dispersed through the City, and sporadic rioting took place for the next week. This incident was heavily covered by the press in Britain and the American Colonies as the "St. George's Fields Massacre."

The day after the massacre, Lord Barrington wrote to the troops that had been on duty: "I have the great pleasure of informing you that his majesty highly approves of the conduct of both the officers and men; and means that His Majesty's approbation should be communicated to them." Some weeks later the letter came into the hands of Wilkes, who sent it to the newspapers with an anonymous preface: the troops were thanked, he wrote, "for the rank and foul murders committed in these fields on the 10th of that month. My hand trembled while I copied it." (Cash: 2006, 225) On June 14, Wilkes, represented by Serjeant-at-Law Glynn, appeared before the King's Bench. Glynn had already succeeded in having the outlaw- ry charges dropped. This cleared the way for sentencing for the two libel charges. On June 18 Wilkes was sentenced to pay £500 for each offense and to serve 10 more months for the first and 12 months for the second libel. He was immediately jailed and served his full term.

Had Parliament allowed Wilkes to take the seats he won while still in jail, he would have been able to invoke Parliamentary Privilege and end his jail sentence, so after much debate on February 3, 1769, Wilkes was finally officially expelled from the House of Parliament. Though still in prison, Wilkes, acting through an organization of his supporters, once again ran unopposed for the seat from which he had been expelled. He was re-elected by a show of hands at the hustings. Parliament wasted no time passing a resolution on February 17, declaring Wilkes incapable of being elected and calling for another election.

## 2 Wilkes and Glyn: A new song

Sir Frederick Madden's Collection of Broadside Ballads, 03:1975 – Roud V38652

*Tune: Portsmouth; English Country Dance tune, printed 1701*

Brave Glyn he is our country's friend, he is sensible as fair,
His daily prayer the times may mend and brighter days appear,
Attachments, general warrants to, raised his indignant smile,
Those clouds had vanish'd long ago, when William changed the stile.

Did northern blast or southern gale again those clouds renew
Let H_____ and M_____ tell, the point from whence it strew
Unjust pathway now revers'd, now longer stands the test
The entranced need not be revers'd. my Glen you know the rest

Truth will hereafter be reveal'd, in History's faithful page,
If justice is herself conceal'd virtue sire of party rage,
While one supports another's fraud, while others sell their badges
Commerce undone proclaimed abroad, A peace in tatters and rags

This said she turn'd to the settee, where sit involved with care,
Wisest lover would not wish to see thought in a face so fair,
While moderating England's wrong, the mischief done by L____b
Her faithful hero held his tongue, And wau'd his humble state.

Le__h__m sat in thoughtful mood his head upon his hand,
While Briton's genius silent stood, to wate for his command
She started up this decreed and Britain shall be free,
Princes in petticoats did plead, Glyn, Wilkes and Liberty.

This song memorializes the legal triumphs surrounding the election to parliament of Wilkes's long-time friend John Glynn, the famous Serjeant-at-law, who had acted as Wilkes's barrister and represented him before the King's Bench. Much in this broadside ballad is obscured by time and, as with many broadsides, spellings are inconsistent; even Glynn's name is misspelled (there was in 1768 a Member of Parliament from London named Sir Richard Glyn, which may factor into the confusion.) Several names were abbreviated to avoid libel and are now lost to us.

The warrant upon which Wilkes had been arrested in 1763 named no individuals, but was a "general warrant" calling for the arrest of all persons associated with the publication of *The North Briton's* issue Number 45. In 1766 it was Serjeant Glynn, in the absence of Wilkes, who won the legal case that ended the use of this type of general warrant. In November of 1768, while Wilkes was still in prison, the by-election was held to fill the House of Commons seat vacated when George Cooke died. (Cooke had been elected to one of the Knight of the Shire of Middlesex seats the previous March, as had Wilkes.) The fall bye election proposed two candidates, Glynn and Proctor. Proctor, who had run against both Cooke and Wilkes and been defeated earlier in the year, employed a tactic frequently used in elections at the time. To disperse crowds, Proctor hired Edward Macquirk and his mob of toughs to keep Glynn supporters away from the polls. In the resulting fray, an attorney was killed. Macquirk and some of his henchmen were tried, convicted, and sentenced to be transported to North America. Glynn won the election with a wide margin, and Macquirk was taken from the transport ship and pardoned by King George III. (Cash: 2006, 236)

Brentwood Hustings, Middlesex, November 1768

## 3  An African's Appeal to the British Nation

Bodleian Library: Firth Collection b.22 (f. 90) – Roud V40899

Tune: Yorkshire; John Wainwright, 1750

Hear me, free Britons—to my plaint give ear,
My tale in many a place would force a tear:
For whilst I tread the free-born British land,
And whilst before mine eyes white freemen stand,
Vain, vain, that glorious privilege to me,
I am a slave where all things else are free.

Yet I were born, as you are no man's slave,
An heir to all that liberal nature gave;
My mind can reason, and my limbs can move
The same as yours; like yours my heart can love;
Alike my body food and sleep sustain,
And e'en, like yours, feels pleasure, want, and pain.

One sun rolls o'er us, common skies surround,
One globe supports us, and one grave must bound.
Why then am I devoid of all to live,
That manly comforts to a man can give?
To live— untaught religion's soothing balm,
Or life's choice art's;— to live— unknown the calm

Of soft domestic ease; those sweets of life,
The duteous offspring, and th' enduring wife.
To live — to property and rights unknown,
Not e'en the common benefits my own.
No arm to guide me from oppression's rod,
My will subservient to a tyrant's nod:

No gentle hand when life is in decay,
To sooth my pains, and charm my cares away;
But helpless, left to quit the horrid stage,
Harassed in youth and desolate in age.
But I was born on Afric's tawney strand,
And you in fair Britannia's fairer land.

Comes freedom then from colour? blush with shame!
And let strong nature's crimson mark your blame.
I speak to Britons — Britons, then behold,
A man by Britons snar'd, and seiz'd, and sold.
O sons of freedom! Equalize your laws,
Be all consistent — plead the negroe's cause;

That all the nations in your code may see
The British negroe, like the Briton, free.
But should he supplicate your laws in vain,
To break forever this disgraceful chain;
At least, let gentle usage so abet
The galling terrors of it's passing state,
That he may share kind heaven's all-social plan,
For tho' no Briton, yet I am — a Man.

Stockton: Printed by R. Christopher, for R.L.

This undated ballad reflects the growing movement to end slavery in Britain and its colonies. The song sheet also includes a ballad titled "The Africans Complaint" [sic] with words identical to those of the Negro's Complaint credited to William Cowper and thought to have been written in 1778. Cowper had lived and worked since 1768 with John Newton, the evangelical Christian and former captain of a slave ship, who wrote the popular hymn "Amazing Grace." Since both this song and "The Africans Complaint" plead for freedom from slavery in Britain, they may have been written before the June 1772 Mansfield Decision (below) which officially brought an end to slavery in Britain.

At the time of the Middlesex voting controversy over Wilkes, several legal cases concerning slavery were heard in London. The most far-reaching of these was of James Somerset, a slave who had sailed with his master, Charles

Steuart, from Boston to England in 1769. Steuart settled in London, where Somerset continued to do Steuart's bidding while hearing lots of talk about liberty and freedom. After two years in London, Somerset decided to gain his liberty and, probably with the help of abolitionists, was able at first to evade slave-catchers hired by Steuart.

Eventually Somerset was caught and taken to a merchant vessel where he was confined for shipment and sale in the West Indies. Two days later, on November 28, 1771, the famous humanitarian and antislavery campaigner Granville Sharp appealed to the courts on Somerset's behalf. (Pybus: 2006, 81) On a writ of habeas corpus issued by Chief Justice Lord Mansfield, Sharp obtained Somerset's release as well as a court date to consider the legality of slavery in Britain. Mansfield had also heard the many cases concerning Wilkes.

The Somerset case eventually set the precedent that slavery was not legal in Britain. Assisting Sharp and Somerset were several barristers, including Wilkes's friend and benefactor, Serjeant-at-law John Glynn. To the surprise of many, Mansfield ruled on June 22, 1772 that "though the heavens may fall Somerset was to be freed." According to Steven Wise:

> Between 14,000 and 15,000 English blacks were to be freed, three quarters of a million pounds of property [i.e. enslaved human beings] lost, 166,000 Jamaican slaves would permanently fix their eyes on England and the prudent West Indian master would henceforth leave his slave dockside when sailing for England. (Wise: 2005, 183)

Granville Sharp was a fascinating and talented character. His brother was surgeon to George III. The Sharp brothers were musicians who performed with their numerous siblings in concerts featuring the music of Handel. They performed from the deck of the family's barge that plied the rivers of the south of England. (Hochschild: 2005, 45–46) Granville later became an evangelical and studied law to aid in his quest to end slavery.

Medallion of Society for Abolition of Slave Trade in England

## 4   A New Song: Lately composed on Castle Island

Vera Brodsky Lawrence, *Music for Patriots, Politicians, and Presidents* (1975)

Tune: The Abbot of Cantebury; Watts' Musical Miscellany, 1729

You simple Bostonians, I'd have you beware
Of your Liberty Tree, I would have you take care;
For if that we chance to return to the town,
Your houses and stores will come tumbling down
Derry down, down, hey derry down.

If you will not agree to Old England's laws,
I fear that King Hancock will soon get the yaws
But he need not fear, for I swear we will,
For the want of a doctor give him a hard pill.
Derry down, down, hey derry down.

A brave reinforcement, we soon think to get;
Then we will make you poor pumpkins to sweat.
Our drums they'll rattle, and then you will run
To the devil himself, from the sight of a gun.
Derry down, down, hey derry down.

Our fleet and our army, they soon will arrive,
Then to a bleak island, you shall not us drive.
In every house, you shall have three or four,
And if that will not please you, you'll have half a score
Derry down, down, hey derry down.

Published in the *Boston Gazette* (March 26, 1770)

Not all political broadsides supported the positions of the Wilkes and Liberty faction. This one is alleged to be written by one of the British soldiers evacuated to Castle Island in Boston Harbor after the March 5, 1770 Boston Massacre. The Boston Massacre occurred on a cold, snowy night when a dispute arose between a small platoon of British troops and a group of about thirty rope-makers, sailors, and other maritime workers.

Feelings had been running high with local workers resenting off-duty soldiers working below prevailing wages, and soldiers resented being left in Boston where they were not wanted. There are many versions of how the altercation began, but there is room to empathize with both the underpaid and often unwilling troops and their colonial cousins: each was taxed and manipulated by a British government in which they had no say. Like all American seamen, their maritime workers' skills made them vulnerable to involuntary impressment into the British Navy. Whatever the actual dispute that night, the Redcoats opened fire on people in the street, wounding many and killing the alleged leader of the group, Crispus Attucks, and four others. Attucks, son of a slave father and a Natick or (Nantucket) Native American mother, had escaped from slavery twenty years earlier. Attucks had served as an able-bodied seaman and harpooner on American whaling ships most of the time since he took his freedom. His maritime skills made him especially vulnerable to impressment into the British Navy. Three days after the Massacre the bodies of those already dead were placed in separate hearses. A great procession, the largest ever held in the colonies, proceeded to the Granary Burial Ground where they were interred in one grave. To this day Attucks is honored as "the first to defy, the first to die."

Almost a year later, a trial concluded that the soldiers and their officers had acted according to their duty. The soldiers' defending attorney was John Adams, who would become the second president of the United States. Adams made the point that the tragedy was not brought on by the soldiers, but by the mob, and the mob, it must be understood, was the inevitable result of the flawed policy of quartering troops in a city on the pretext of keeping the peace. Adams went on to invoke his argument: "The plain English is, gentlemen, it was most probably a motley rabble of saucy boys, Negroes and mulattos, Irish Teagues and outlandish jack-tars. And why should we scruple to call such a people a mob, I can't conceive, unless the name is too respectable for them." (McCullough: 2001, 67)

# 5   The Harvest of Corruption
## (In the Modern Electioneering Style)

Bodleian Library: The Harding Collection, B 29(19) — Roud V30382

*Tune: Hunting Song; Henry Fielding, 1734*

Come all you tip-pling Free - men, Now to our Har - vest fly;
Haste sum-mon all the Sea - men, To join our Hue and Cry.
And a-glean-ing we will go___ a-glean-ing we will go___
a glean-ing we will go___ a glean-ing we___ will
go___ a-glean - ing we will go.___

Come all you tippling Freemen,
Now to our Harvest fly;
Haste summon all the Seamen,
To join our Hue and Cry.
    And a gleaning we will go, &c

See yonder to our Harvest Fields,
What Men of Might repair;
All blythsome, mark, how each one yields
His Lips to bless the Fair.
    And a ...

Remember, Friends, that rabble Rout,
Not worth a dozen Groats;
Who dar'd to close our Moor about,
'Till Watty cut their Coats.

'Tis they did the Lawyers hold,
To filch away our Rights;
'Twas Watty— ever firm and bold,
That crush'd the factious Wights

'Twas Watty all those Tyrants fought
Who flay'd our very Skin;
Let's thank our Stars he hither brought
The learned Serjeant Glynn.

Who will not vote for Blackett,
As Monsters must remain:
May they ne'er have a Crocket,
Nor Stool — to ease their Pain.

Within the sacred Senate Walls,
In Thunder he can speak;
Before him every Tory falls,
Nay Phipps himself will squeak.

Where'er the Voice of Watty goes,
The Bribed will it shun;
To him they seem like Summer Snows,
Or Mists, before the Sun.

To gain the Patriot Wilkes his Seat,
He like an Angel spoke;
And tho' his Eloquence was great,
It ended all in Smoke

When on the Popish Quebec Bill,
He learnedly declaim'd
Mark, how the Courtiers all sat still,
Confoundedly asham'd

What is your Phipps — with Boreas Aft
To magistratic Men?
As well the Rabble may compare
A Chatham to a hen.

Who won't at Watty's Call appear,
We heartily disdain;
His Beef, and bread and good strong Beer,
They ne'er shall taste again.
   And a gleaning we will go, &c

This ballad ridicules the electoral system that consistently ignored voters' concerns. The 1774 election involved Sir Walter (Watty) Blackett, a long-established politician famed for his corrupt and common practice of serving the electorate roast beef, bread, and good strong beer to secure their vote. In previous years the voters of Newcastle fought the proposed enclosure of their beloved common moor, where for centuries the people had grazed their cattle, grown their crops, gleaned their firewood, and held their annual fair. Blackett had refused to support the activists' struggle to keep the commons open. With help from Wilkes and his Liberty Movement in the form of legal assistance from Wilkes's friend and supporter Serjeant-at-law John Glynn, Newcastle's activist freemen had been able to keep the Newcastle town moor un-enclosed. It remains free to the people of Newcastle to this day.

Blackett and his running mate Matthew White Ridley were wealthy coal mine owners. In the past they had faced little opposition, but 1774 was different. In addition to the enclosure issue, Blackett and Ridley had refused to support a 1769 petition prepared by Newcastle freemen calling for dissolution of Parliament for refusing to seat the duly elected John Wilkes. Preparing for the 1774 election, freemen had produced a series of test articles calling for candidates to pledge to call for the House of Commons to acknowledge its mistake in expelling Wilkes from his seat, to call for shortening of the duration of parliaments, to insist on a reduction in the number of placemen and pensioners in the Commons, and to campaign for a more equal representation of the people. Blackett and Ridley refused to sign the pledge or to pursue these demands. Constantine Phipps and Thomas Delaval, running against Blackett and Ridley, supported the pledge, gaining support of the activist freemen and leading to the writing of this and at least two other anti-Blackett broadside ballads.

The 1774 election in Newcastle attracted great interest. Years later Thomas Spence, who would become a major radical activist, spoke of how much he had learned from the 1774 campaign in his hometown of Newcastle, where he was then a 24-year-old schoolteacher. More recently, Rachel Hammersley described how Wilkes in 1774 had persuaded Jean-Paul Marat, later famous as a radical journalist of the French Revolution and then resident in England, to send copies of his first political work *The Chains of Slavery* to several societies of freemen in Newcastle. His decision to publish it that year was prompted by the prospect of the forthcoming general election. His address to the electors of Great Britain, which prefaced the work, emphasized the importance of the role to be played by the electors, and offered detailed advice on the kinds of men they should choose and those they should reject. (Hammersley: 2005, 644)

In the end, good advice, clever songs, and political intrigue did not prevail against roast beef, bread, and good strong beer. The activist freemen lost their bid to influence the election's outcome. Blackett and Ridley were elected—but so was Wilkes. Blackett was the oldest member of the House of Commons when he died three years later at age 70.

# 6  To The Commons: On Meeting After The Recess

Moore, *Songs and Ballads of the American Revolution* (1905), p. 112

*Tune: Tempus Adest Floridum; Piae Cantiones, 1582*

With Christmas mirth, and Christmas cheer,
My friends pray look not glummer;
With turkey, chine, and beef and beer,
You're surely in good humor.

The folks on t'other side the wave,
Have beef as well as you, sirs;
Some chines, and turkeys too, they have,
And as they bake they brew, sirs.

What, tho' your cannon raze their towns,
And tumble down their houses,
They'll fight like devils— blood and 'oons,
For children and for spouses.

Another truth—nay, 'tis no boast,
Nor yet the lie o' th' day, sirs;
The saints on Massachusetts coast,
Gain if they run away, sirs.

For further than your bullets fly,
A common man may run, sirs,
And wheat will grow beneath the sky,
Where cannot reach a gun, sirs.

Then what are ships, and swords, and guns,
And men of bloody mind, sirs,
While, Parthian-like, who conquers runs,
Who loses,—stays behind, sirs.

Then rise my men, in merry mood,
Vote—*con-tra-di-nem cente,*
That five and five for ten are good,
And ten and ten make twenty.

Recall your ships, your troops recall,
Let friends each other nourish,
So shall old England rule the ball,
And George and freedom flourish.

"Let Britons, now sunk into tyrants and slaves!
Submit to be governed by fools and by knaves.
Not so will their kindred on this side the sea,
American Britons will ever be free."

A shortened version of this song can be found as "The Folks on T'other Side of the Wave" in *The Ballad of America* by John Anthony Scott. (Scott: 1967, 62) The present version appears in a compilation of songs gathered by Frank Moore for a Website on the American Revolution. Moore lists the song as originally written as a broadside ballad in 1776, and printed in 1777 in *The Middlesex Journal or Chronicle of Liberty*. The ballad makes well the case for discontinuing the futile and unjust British military buildup in the Atlantic colonies of North America.

The situation with the American colonies worsened after the Boston Tea Party of December 16, 1773. In March 1774, Lord North's Tory Government enacted the Coercive Acts, which were draconian measures against Massachusetts to warn the colonies against further defiance. The measures included closing the port of Boston, restricting membership in the Massachusetts legislature to appointees of the Crown, limiting town meetings to once a year, authorizing the Governor to remand colonists for trial in England, and establishing a new Quartering Act that required householders to billet British soldiers. In response, the colonies called a Congress in Philadelphia. There was little opposition in Parliament to these coercive measures, except from the London Wilkes supporters. Those speaking out against these oppressive measures included Edmund Burke, Charles James Fox, and John Wilkes himself, who was seated as a Knight of the Shire of Middlesex alongside his friend Glynn, a few months after the Coercive Acts were passed. At the same time that Wilkes was seated in the House of Commons, in October 1774, he began his one-year term as Lord Mayor of London.

When the American War of Independence began in 1775, Wilkes found a powerful source of support for his cause in the kingdom's commercial centers, whose crowded and low paid manufacturing populations responded to the fight for reform and opposition to the war. Emerging industrial cities such as Norwich, Liverpool, Manchester, Birmingham, Dudley, Wolverhampton, and even Glasgow forwarded massive petitions to Parliament in opposition to the war. It is estimated that 45,000 people signed such petitions between 1775 and 1780. As time passed, however, British merchants began to see profits from the sale of war materials, and their anti-war sentiment began to weaken.

Wilkes's first speech in the House of Commons on the subject of the American Revolution was published in the *Boston Gazette*. He rose to object to the term "rebellion" in the King's opening address to Parliament in 1775. Britain cannot win this war, he warned, not in the vast spaces of America, not against a hearty, courageous people. Do not deceive yourselves: "The whole continent will be dismembered from Great Britain, and the wide arch of the raised empire fall." His attempts to help the Americans were not lost on the colony of North Carolina, whose new revolutionary legislature in 1777 created a new county and voted to call it Wilkes County.

Boston Almanack, 1769

**7   A New Liberty Song No 44**

George C. Carey, *A Sailors Song Bag* (1976), p. 120 – Roud 9408

Tune: Female Drummer; Broadside, printed 1813

Come all you brave Americans where ever that you be
And all you well wishers to the North America—
For the wars will be over which was for to be
And we will have free tradings in North America—

Says the King unto Parlement, the parlement lets sett
Against these brave Americans their land and their trade
We will send our ships over and make them for to pay
And bring them to Subjection in North America—

O then says Lord North I think it's very right
Against those Americans to draw our swords and fight
We will send our ships over and make for them to pay
And bring them to Subjection in North America.

O then says John Wilkes, I think it is not right
Against those Americans to draw our swords and fight
For if that you do before you do return
You may depend upon it your teabinds they will burn.

The Americans they're Loyal and always very true
Unto some other country what would you have them do
For they'll tax their own land, and their Money freely pay
To cultivate their lands in North America.

There is many a brave family you very well do know
That sells their whole estate America to go
And when they come there, they their Money freely pay
To Cultivate the lands in the North America.

So here is bad luck to the King and Queen
And all the Royal family, God send them short to rain
For the wars will be over which was for to be
And we will have free trading in the North America.

This ballad from the collection of Timothy Connor seems to be of American origin although it could be from England, where many held radical views of the war. The tune common today, "Female Drummer," fits this song so well that it is used even though its origins can't be found earlier than 1813. The author or the printer used a French spelling for Parliament and the reference to the Boston tea party is confusing (tea bines were not burned, but tea was thrown into the harbor). Whatever the song's origin, it makes strong points. It supports the opinions of John Wilkes on the subject of the war. British merchants certainly preferred to keep free trading in North America; attempts at passing laws to retain British presence were never productive. To cut off British free trading in North America was a big blow to merchants.

Two other songs collected by Timothy Connor are included in this book (10 & 12). Connor was captured at sea on the Yankee privateer *Rising States* by *HMS Terrible* and was transferred to Forton Prison near Portsmouth, England as a prisoner of war. He wrote down his extraordinary repertoire of sea songs and topical broadsides, both American and British, while held at Forton from 1777 to 1779. He included this song in his collection, which was eventually edited by George G. Carey and published as *A Sailors Songbag*. Many of the songs in Connor's collection are not found anywhere else.

## 8   Britannia's Lamentation On the Devastation War

*Later English Broadside Ballads,* Vol. 1 (1975), p. 42 (Madden: 02/1002) — Roud V21859

*Tune: Chestnut; English Country Dance tune, printed 1651*

Come my sons mourn with your mother, at the me - lan - cho - ly __ news From New York and o - ther pla - ces, Where Bri-tons now do ren - de - vous, Blood and Slaugh - ter __ still con - ti - nues, While our foes Ad - van - tage take, The con - se - quen - ces of such com - mo - tion, Makes Bri - tan - nia's heart to ache.

Come my sons mourn with your mother,
At the melancholy news,
From New York and other places,
Where Britons now do rendezvous,
Blood and Slaughter still continues,
While our foes Advantage take,
The consequence of such commotion,
Makes Britannia's heart to ache.

See the stately Towns a burning,
Here the shouts and dismal cry,
Mothers with their children mourning,
While their fathers' dead do lie.
Hear the roaring cannons thunder,
See one Army run away,
The other briskly push for plunder,
In North America.

On the infant weeps the mother,
My tender babe my breasts are dry,
Your fathers killed I am starved with hunger,
While the rest around do cry,
Once I had a pleasant table,
Famine threatens now to come,
My house is changed into a stable,
This, my dears is now my doom.

View the camps in deep entrenchment,
Where the fruitful garden stood,
See the ground they fought their Battles,
Strewed with bones and stained with blood,
Nothing now but devastation
Is the prospect every way,
Kind heaven stop the desolation
In North America.

View the son pursue the father,
Brother against brother fight,
When they both was joined together
Beat their faces with sweet delight,
No power then could stand against us
But in fear would run away,
Now those foes are laughing at us,
Alas! Alas! America.

When a house is thus divided,
It seldom does continue long,
Quarrels make us poor and weaker,
While our foes grow rich and strong,
This is now the case of Briton,
Oh! gracious heaven stand our friend,
And in mercy shine upon us,
Bring these troubles to an end.

To a large extent the American War of Independence was viewed as pitting brother against brother. Prime Minister North wanted to sue for peace, but King George threatened to abdicate if he did. It appeared that everyone but the King wanted to end the war. Petitions, signed by as many British subjects as were eligible to vote, were sent to Parliament calling for an end to fighting. It wasn't only the working class — cannon fodder — that objected to the slaughter, but also the merchants and businessmen who had to contend with tremendous financial losses.

The song, described by Holloway and Black in their *Later English Broadside Ballads*, was composed in the later years of the American War of Independence (c. 1778), but the style is markedly archaic, as can be seen especially in the exhortations to 'view' the horrors of war, and the conception in stanza 5 of how civil war (here, more especially, rebellion by the son, i.e. the younger colony) breaks up the family. (Holloway and Black: 1975, 43)

# 9    Yankee Doodle: Or The Negroes Farewell to America

Boston Public Library Collection: Broadside, London: C. & S. Thompson (1775?)

Tune: Yankee Doodle; James Pike, 1730

Now far - e - well my Mas - sa my Mis - sy — a - dieu

More blows or more stripes will we e'er take from you —

Or — will me come hith - er or thi - ther me go, —

no help make you rich — by de — sweat of my brow.

Yank - kee doo - dle Yan - kee doo - dle dan - dy I vow

Yan - kee doo - dle Yan - kee doo - dle bow wow wow.

Now farewell my Massa my Missy a-dieu
More blows or more stripes will we e'er take from you
Or will me come hither or thither me go
No help make you rich by de sweat of my brow
Yankee doodle, Yankee doodle dandy I vow
Yankee doodle, Yankee doodle bow wow

Farewell all de yams and farewell to salt fish
De Bran & Spruce Beer at you all me cry Fish
Me feed upon Pudding, Roast Beef & strong beer
In Englan' old Englan' when we do get dere.
   Yankee doodle, &c.

Farewell musketo farewell de black fly
And Rattle Snake who may sting me to dye
Den Negroe go O'me to his friends in Guinee
Before dat old England he've seen'e.
   Yankee doodle, &c

Farewell to cold winter de frost and de Snow
Which cover high Hills and de Valleys so low
And dangling & ranting swearing & drinking
Taring and Feathering for seriously thinking
  Yankee doodle, &c

Den Hey! For old England where Liberty reigns
Where Negroes no beaten or loaded with chains
And if Negroe return O! may he be hang'd
Chain'd tortur'd & drowned—Or let him be hang'd
  Yankee doodle, &c

This song, using a racist parody of African speech, was written and popularized in Britain in 1775. It is now found on a web site sponsored by
the African Methodist Episcopal Church, which credits the source to documents held in The Boston Public Library. An abbreviated version of this
song is printed in Oscar Brand's *Songs of '76: A Folksinger's History of the
Revolution.*

Word of the Mansfield decision in the Somerset case, which declared an
end to slavery in Britain, quickly spread throughout the colonies, bringing hope for emancipation to those in bondage. In November of 1775,
Lord Dunmore, the Royal Governor of Virginia, offered freedom to any
slaves who would join His Majesty's troops in suppressing the American
rebellion. Thousands took advantage of this opportunity, and similar offers
from other British officers, to gain their freedom and wear the uniform
embroidered with the motto "Liberty to Slaves." In addition to the Virginia
recruits, thousands of runaways took their chances to gain liberty behind
British lines, many eventually arriving in New York City with the Redcoats.
Simon Schama quotes historians who estimate that two-thirds of the slaves
in South Carolina had run away, and that in all, between eighty thousand and one hundred thousand slaves left the plantations during the war.
(Schama: 2006: 8) Whatever their numbers, it is clear that many American
slaves saw service with the British or the Colonial forces as a hope for escape from their bonds.

A motley crew known as the Loyal Refugee Volunteers, created by the
New Jersey Loyalist Tom Ward, was partly composed of black runaways.
One particular unit of black recruits known as "Ward's Blacks" was sta-
tioned at Bergen Point on Staten Island. Formed originally to cut firewood
for the British garrison, Ward's Blacks increasingly operated as an armed
guerrilla force, making raids on the New Jersey shore under the command
of their own elected "colonel." When they successfully fought off an attack
on their blockhouse by a thousand soldiers of the Continental army led by
General Wayne, "Ward's Blacks became instant celebrities in New York and
a source of stories to sustain and inspire the black community." (Pybus:
2006, 33)

## 10 Britannia's Wish: A New Song No 33

George C. Carey, *A Sailors Song Bag* (1976), p. 96 – Roud 9401

*Tune: Bay of Biscay; Broadside, 1867*

Come lis-ten sons of Free-dom ___ Hear what tid - ing come each day Con-cern-ing of Bri - tan-nia's Child-ren ___ And trou-bles in A - mer-i-ca ___ Bri-tons a - gainst Bri-tons fight-ing ___ Blood and Slaughter swift-ly run ___ France and Spain were thus de-light-ing ___ Bri - tan - nia's mourn - ing for her sons ___

Come listen sons of Freedom
Here what tiding come each day
Concerning of Britannia's Children
And troubles in America
Britons against Britons fighting
Blood and Slaughter swiftly run
France and Spain were thus delighting
Britannia's mourning for her sons.

At Lexington the blood run spurting
The crimson stream at Bunkers hill
With clashing arms and Cannon roaring
There the British blood did spill
Besides the many sea engagements
Sullivan's Isle ah! well a day
Lament, lament each worthy Britain
The lives lost in America.

The last affair was at Long Island
Where they made their landing good
Where some hundreds we are informed
Were basely used in cool blood

But let's hope that for the future
The Quarters to each show
And as they were once friends together
Be watchful of the fatal blow.

New York ne'er got in our hands boys
If that we may believe the news
But Oh shocking is the fighting
The more we gain the more we loose
The more their beat twill be the longer
Before that trade does shine again
Kind heaven be our mediator
And let not blood be spilt in vain.

O heaven once more friendly join them
Before too deep they strike the blow
With hands and heart pray once more join them
As when they fought their Gallic foe
Let not our foes rejoice in seeing
How we do each other slay
Stop shedding blood we do beseech thee
Of Britons in America.

This is the wish of poor Britannia
Likewise each Widow Maid and Wife
Love to a Son Sweetheart or Husband
May be as dear to them as life
Give us peace and sweet contentment
And drive all trouble far away
That commerce once again may flourish
With Britain and America.

Britannia's Wish Finis

This is another anthem for peace from *A Sailors Songbag* describing something that the supporters of Wilkes understood: the colonials were Britons like themselves, and the self-determination demanded by the Americans was the same liberty that Wilkes espoused. The oppressive system that sent British soldiers to die in America to preserve Britain's trade advantage as the colonial power had also sent soldiers to St. George's Fields. Bodleian Broadside Ballads on Line has an almost identical broadside ballad entitled the "Battle of Bunker's Hill," printed by W. Wright in Birmingham (Harding B28 (266)). A few changes in most verses suggest that Timothy Connor may have altered the wording from this other broadside when he compiled his own collection of songs while a prisoner of war in Forton Prison near Plymouth. The melody "My Willie O!" is used here although it was probably of later origin.

Lexington (April 19, 1775) and Bunker Hill (June 17, 1775) in Massachusetts were the first battles of the American Revolution. On June 28, 1776 a small patriot force repelled a large British force under Clinton and Cornwallis at Sullivan's Isle at the entrance to Charleston, South Carolina, which later became the site of Fort Sumter. The British took Long Island on August 27, 1776 and New York on September 15, 1776.

Now hostilities were underway. British working people who were reeling from poor harvests, with continued lack of reliable employment and low wages, cared little for waging war with American people, who, like themselves, were seeking the freedom that they also desired. The British middle and upper classes also lost enthusiasm when the Colonial armies with their new allies began to win significant battles. Parliamentary debate waged over the wisdom of continuing to pursue the war, but the king refused to consider making peace. "The Revolution coincides remarkably with the birth of English Radicalism and helped to create the conditions for the birth of a working class movement." (Morton: 1978, 315)

John Wilkes

Chapter 2
# REVOLUTION: 1780–1789

*"I am sorry that 800 valiant English and Germans were killed in
a bad cause, in fighting against the best constitution on earth."*
—John Wilkes, speech to British House of Commons after the
Battle of Saratoga

The American Revolutionary War labored on into 1783. Working people
of Britain and America suffered from the war's effects. Americans began to
see the reality of their new governance. Sadly, the ordinary British person's
standard of living was declining, with scant hope for a remedy. As prices
climbed, income fell, and work became ever more scarce, the disillusioned
public resorted to food riots. While the business community began to see
the economic benefits of supplying the war effort, making up for earlier
losses of trade with North America, life became more unbearable for British
workers. Working class opposition to the American war was expressed in
broadside ballads, petitions, and disorderly action. Finally, in 1783, Britain
relinquished sovereignty over its former colonies in America.

While the war continued across the Atlantic, unrest festered at home. In
June 1780, a despotic maniac, Lord George Gordon, seized the moment
and led what became the most devastating riots ever to occur in London.
Gordon, an MP and recent founder of the Protestant Association, agitated
large numbers of people over a recent act of Parliament, the Catholic Relief
Bill of 1778, that enabled certain Catholics to serve under certain circumstances as officers in the British Army. He roused thousands of people to
sign his petition and their march got out of control. Over the course of
several days, hundreds of people died, prisons were emptied, and great destruction was done to persons and property. These so-called "Gordon Riots
of June 1780" marked the end of the era of Wilkes and Liberty.

In March 1782, the Tory government of Lord North was replaced by the
return to power of Lord Rockingham, well known to be a supporter of reform

and friend of the former colonies. The first act of his Whig Government was to recognize the independent United States of America, and there were consequences to be addressed. Thousands of former African slaves had been promised freedom if they left their American masters and joined the British military. After negotiations with slave owners—among them George Washington and Thomas Jefferson—many freed people were given small tracts of land in Nova Scotia. In that same year, 1782, Edmund Burke, paymaster of the new Government, with help from Christopher Wyvill, a strong reform leader from Yorkshire, was able to pass the "Economical Reform Act." This act limited distributable sinecures and pensions to save up to £72,000 per year, essentially ending the King's sustained drive to buy Parliament. Additionally, Rockingham's short-lived government passed a massive reform, relaxing control over Ireland by abolishing the most punitive restrictions contained in Poynings' Law of 1495. Catholics still could not vote, but there followed a period of novel Irish legislative freedom. This period came to be known as "Grattan's Parliament" after Henry Grattan, a major campaigner for reform in the Irish House of Commons and leader of the Patriot Party.

Only three months after taking the reins of government in March of 1782, Rockingham died. He was replaced by two short-time leaders and then in 1784 by William Pitt the Younger (Tory), who at age 24 was the youngest Prime Minister ever seated, and who would serve for almost 19 years. Right away Pitt submitted a reform act that was narrowly defeated by the Commons. The act was much like the one introduced by Wilkes in 1774 (when Pitt was only 13). In 1787 and 1789, bills to end the Test Acts, at least as they related to Protestant dissenters, were introduced and defeated by small majorities.

Meanwhile, small groups in Britain advocated adoption of the American Bill of Rights. These groups included former Wilkite members of the "Society of the Supporters of the Bill of Rights," who by then functioned as "The Bill of Rights Society." They began extracting pledges from candidates for Parliament to support reform. These reformers were effective in the Home Counties of southeastern England, but in Parliament they were easily out-voted by members who owed their seats to large landholders and "rotten boroughs." In April of 1780 a group of intellectuals, including Major Cartwright, Horne Tooke, John Jebb, Granville Sharp, and Dr. Richard Price, had formed "The Society for Constitutional Information" (SCI). The society was far from democratic, because average working men could not afford the annual subscription fee of a guinea, which was seven days' pay for a laborer of the time. "The Bill of Rights Society" remained a force for parliamentary reform until 1794.

In 1787, Thomas Paine had returned from America, spurring momentum for reform. In America, Paine's essay *Common Sense* had been sensationally influential on revolutionary thought and action. Paine returned to England to make his fortune from his innovative design for an all-steel bridge, but he soon got back into community organizing and working to advance freedom. It was said that Paine was the guest of Edmund Burke, although in later years they would become adversaries. They traveled together while scouting locations for Paine's proposed bridge. "We hunt in pairs," as Burke put it. (Hitchens: 2006, 48) Burke had long fought for the abolition of slavery and for other progressive issues of interest to Paine.

Also in 1787, fifteen years after the Mansfield Decision, the "Society for Effecting the Abolition of the Slave Trade" was formed by Thomas Clarkson and began its long journey to end slavery throughout the British Empire. This group set standards and practices still used today to organize people for social change. One year later William Wilberforce, Member of Parliament and personal friend of Prime Minister William Pitt, agreed to carry the first abolition bill through Parliament.

The penal system was straining. By the mid-1780s riots erupted in overcrowded hulks (former battle ships) holding convicts who could no longer be sent to America. Alternative destinations were considered. The government relied on limited information gathered by Joseph Banks of the Cook Expedition and decided to establish a penal colony in Botany Bay. The first convict ships set sail in 1788, starting the eventual transport of over 150,000 British convicts to Australia.

Those seeking enfranchisement for the working man in Britain during the 1780s faced many diversions and obstacles. Revolutions elsewhere, in America at the decade's beginning and in France at its end, showed that reform could succeed. But in Britain, reform became more remote. The British government had been unable to coerce American colonists to conform, but perfected its ability to intimidate and enforce compliance from the working people of Britain. It curbed civil rights, infiltrated groups with informants, inflicted extreme punishments for petty crimes, prohibited unions, denied sanitation, and deployed other deprivations to keep people in their place and without power.

## 11 The Rats and the Ferret

Sir Frederick Madden's Collection of Broadside Ballads: 11/7461 — Roud V24407

Tune: Hunting Song; Henry Fielding, 1734

At-tend a few mi-nutes I pray, And of sto-ries I'll tell you a rum 'un; I saw it my-self 'to-ther day, As I were a-goin to Lun - nun. 'Tis a-bout some old RATS in a House, Who could act and could do as they please:___ They con-trived to ex-clude___ e-ver-y Mouse, Then sat down and de-vour-ed the cheese.

Attend a few minutes I pray,
And of stories I'll tell you a rum 'un;
I saw it myself 'tother day,
As I were a going to Lunnun.
'Tis about some old RATS in a House,
Who could act and could do as they please:
They contrived to exclude every Mouse,
Then sat down and devoured the cheese.

A FERRET among them there was,
Whose zeal for the right, made him tell
Rather more then these mighty Rats chose,
So they vowed they would punish him well.
They resolved that they'd have him secured,
In a prison where all might forsake him;
And their sergeant his warrant procured,
But it puzzled him well how to take him.

Their Soldiers were now ordered out,
To surround him they came in a trice;
But soon they were put to the rout,
By his neighbors and friends Sirs, the Mice

Who with ardor pressed on to support
Their freedom, their rights and their laws,
Declaring 'twas glorious sport
To defend their defender's good cause.

The Rats now with frenzy and rage,
Found that rioting reigned with loud rattle,
Sent for Cannons and Troops to engage
In a general civilized battle.
The troops came in marching so fast,
That the Mice (wanting numbers and power),
Were forced to give in at the last,
And the Ferret was sent to the Tower.

Mate, Printer, Dover.

This ballad presents a partially disguised version of the Gordon Riots of June 1780. The names of all parties are concealed to protect the guilty, but it is understood that the rats are members of Parliament and the mice are the working class. The ferret is Lord George Gordon, who used anti-Catholic bigotry for his own aggrandizement and was the deranged youngest son of the Duke of Gordon. "The vehicle he used to project his meteoric, but short-lived, advancement was a petition opposing the 1778 Catholic Relief Bill that cynically enabled certain Catholics to serve in the army." (Wilson: 1995, 265) The ballad refers to Gordon's imprisonment in the Tower of London and the soldiers who quelled the riot.

On June 2, 1780, Lord Gordon led a crowd of 50,000 from St. George's Fields (John Wilkes' old stomping grounds) to present their petition to Parliament. Gordon had no trouble attracting a crowd for the event, but he had no idea how to stop the anger of the excited multitudes once they were gathered. As members of the House of Lords arrived, the crowd abused them: their wigs were taken, they were pelted with dirt and excrement, and they were forced to shout "no popery." Members of Commons were not treated as badly, but their coaches were covered with anti-Catholic sayings. (Hibbert: 1958, 37)

For more than a week predominantly Catholic districts of Moorfield's, Smithfield's and Wapping were sacked and burned. The numbers of demonstrators were swollen by the poor and disenfranchised, pickpockets and prostitutes, none of whom had anything to lose. They turned to tearing down prisons and releasing prisoners. Newgate, the King's Bench Prison, and essentially all prisons except the Tower of London were set in flames. Freed inmates became part of the mob, which now sought vengeance against the courts and magistrates, burning their homes and possessions.

A huge mob attacked Langdale's Distillery in Holburn and set it on fire. Hundreds of looters ran inside the burning buildings and brought out rum and gin to fuel the already delirious mob. Intense heat burst the gin vats, spreading the fire, trapping and burning many in the buildings. Poisonous unrectified gin merged with rum from broken barrels and ran into the streets. Men and women began consuming this flowing, burning liquid until they fell down with blue faces and swollen tongues. Witnesses reported seeing the bodies of women and men in the streets with their crying babies lying nearby, choking from fumes. When the militia arrived at the scene they opened fire to disperse the swarm of pickpockets who were removing what they could find from corpses. Some of this story was the subject of Charles Dickens' novel, *Barnaby Rudge.*

Gordon attempted repeatedly to quell the crowds, to no avail. As a group of militiamen, including John Wilkes, were defending the Bank of England building, wave upon wave of rioters were shot as they advanced on the bank. "Wilkes fired with determination into the packed ranks of the oncoming rioters, at the sweating, shining, faces and the rushing bodies companioned with their blue cockades, once the badge of his own supporters." (Hibbert: 1958, 102)

Gordon Riots: Catholic Massacre

Eventually, order was achieved by giving carte blanche authority to the military. Gordon was tried and acquitted for high treason, but 25 of his followers were hanged. (Cash: 2006, 363) In all, at least 700 people lost their lives in the Gordon Riots, and many hundreds more were severely wounded. Thirteen years after the riots, Gordon died while in jail for slander against Marie Antoinette. The Riots marked the end of Wilkes' leadership for Parliamentary reform, bringing to a close a period where democratic reform was synonymous with "Wilkes and Liberty."

Gordon Riots: Langdale's Distillery

## 12  A New Song: I Wish the Wars Were all Over

George C. Carey: *A Sailors Song Bag*, (1976), p. 74 – Roud 2036

Tune: *Wish the wars were all over; Casey, 1778*

Down in the meadow the violets so blue
There I saw pretty Polly milking her cow,
The song that she sang made all the grove to ring,
My Billy has left me to serve the King
And I wish that the wars were all over.

I stepped up to her and made her this reply,
And said my poor Polly what makes you for to cry.
My Billy is gone from me whom I love so dear,
The Americans will kill him so great is my fear.
And I wish that the wars were all over.

I said my dear Polly can you fancy me,
I'll make you as happy as happy can be,
No, no, sir said she that never can be
I ne'er shall be happy till my Billy I see.
And I wish that the wars were all over.

I stood amazed to hear what she said,
The small bird a singing on every tree,
The notes that she sung where nightingales notes
How the Lark and the Linnet warble their throats
And I wish that the wars were all over.

I now for my parents no longer can stay,
To seek for my Billy, I'll haste away,
To see if my Billy will make me his wife,
Free for his sake I'll venture my life.
And I wish that the wars were all over.

I now to some tailor I'll haste away,
To rig myself out in some young man's array,
Like a bold fellow so neat and so trim,
So free for his sake I'll go serve the King,
And I wish the wars were all over

This beautiful street ballad was collected in Forton, an American prisoner-of-war camp. It was popular, appearing on several broadsides of the time, and touches on themes common to many such songs. Michael Turner writes of a re-emergence of antiwar sentiment that "developed out of the general sense of unease, which swept through the nation in 1779 and 1780." (Turner: 2000, 6) The American conflict was going badly, taxes were high, and meetings on war and reform took place in many regions. This wave of protest drew strength not only from City radicalism but also from discontent in the provinces. Yorkshire took the lead under Christopher Wyvill, a conservative parson who proposed economic and parliamentary reform. Wyvill's Yorkshire County Association was an organization of country gentlemen who were bearing the brunt of taxation to finance the war. The Association wanted Government to end the expensive war, increase representation of the counties in the House of Commons, and revert to annual parliaments. (Conway: 2000, 221)

Associations formed in other counties to press for changes. These organizations became the first effective extension of modern political radicalism from the metropolitan region into the provinces. In Ireland there were growing demands for independence. Opposition leaders in parliament increased the pressure on Lord North's administration, and the Rockinghams attempted to secure extra-parliamentary support for their own scheme of budgetary reform. (Turner: 2000, 6) Rockingham did attempt to pass an early Whig Reform Bill during his short term as Prime Minister.

However, the new associations had no relevance for working people. Wyvill consistently spoke of his fear of the mobs and the ills of universal suffrage. (Thompson: 1963, 24) The workingman's view continued to be that the war pitted brother against brother.

# 13 Lord Cornwallis's Surrender

American Antiquarian Society, Thomas Ballads/152

Tune: The British Grenadiers; Edinburgh Musical Miscellany, 1738

Come all you brave Americans,
The truth to you I'll tell,
'Tis of a sad misfortune,
To Britain late befell;
'Twas all in the heights of Yorktown,
Where cannons loud did roar;
They summoned Lord Cornwallis
To fight or else give o'er.

The summons then to be served,
Was sent unto my Lord,
Which made him feel like poor Burgoyne,
And quickly draw his sword,
Say, must I give these glittering troops,
These ships and Hessians too,
And yield to General Washington,
And his bold rebel crew?

A grand council then was called,
His Lordship gave command,
Say, what think you now my heroes,
To yield you may depend—
For don't you see the bombshells fly,
And cannons loud do roar,
Count de Grasse lies in the harbour,
And Washington's on shore.

'Twas the nineteenth of October,
In the year of eighty-one,
Lord Cornwallis he surrendered
To General Washington.
They marched from their posts, brave boys,
And quickly grounded arms,
Rejoice you brave Americans,
With music's sweetest charms.

Six thousand chosen British troops
To Washington resigned,
Besides some ships and Hessians
That could not stay behind;
With refugees and blackamores,
Oh, what a direful crew!
It was then he had some thousands,
But now he's got but few.

My Lord has gone unto New York
Sir Harry for to see;
For to send home this dreadful news
Unto his Majesty;
To contradict some former lines,
That once to him were sent,
Then he and his bold British Troops,
They conquer'd where they went.

Here's a health to great Washington,
And his brave army too,
And likewise to our worthy Greene,
To him much honor's due.
May we subdue those English troops,
And clear the eastern shore,
That we may live in peace, my boys,
While wars they are no more.

The Isaiah Thomas Broadside Ballads Project of the American Antiquarian Society starts its description of this song:

> In late summer of 1781 General Cornwallis established a base for the British Army at Yorktown, Virginia, after marching north through the Carolinas with some victories and some defeats against American opposition. He was unaware of the trap being set by the confluence of the French ships and the American and French land forces that gathered around his position, outnumbering him by nearly three to one. After a siege of several weeks, he asked for a truce to settle terms for a surrender. On October 19 the formal ceremonies were held.

General Charles Cornwallis moved his army of the south to Yorktown, Virginia, to be in position to receive supplies or to enable evacuation. He had learned that he could win only small battles with very high losses since French troops were now fighting alongside Americans. His force consisted of some 6,000 Hessian and British soldiers and at least as many black and white loyalists. During the month of August 1781 many thousand blacks were employed, digging in and building up defenses at Yorktown in expectation of a siege. Reinforcements from New York City were promised. Supplies were running low, smallpox took the lives of hundreds of black loyalists, and typhus was running rampant. But Cornwallis was prepared to wait out the pending siege until those reinforcements arrived.

This all changed when a large French fleet under Admiral de Grasse entered Chesapeake Bay, cutting off escape and supplies. George Washington hastened to move his army over 400 miles from New York to join his force of 12,000 soldiers with 6,000 French troops under General Rochambeau, to attack the army of Cornwallis. Bombardment by the 41 French and American siege cannons, attrition from disease, and shortages of food and ammunition eventually led to British surrender on October 19, 1781.

The fifth stanza of this song mentions refugees and Blackamores who were present at Yorktown when Cornwallis surrendered. Britain lacked consistency on the issue of slavery, since during this time the British Army purchased 13,400 slaves to fight battles in the West Indies. Four or five thousand former slaves served as British soldiers. A substantial percentage of the British troops were near death from a variety of illnesses, but former slaves at least benefited from variolation, which is the deliberate inoculation of an uninfected person with the smallpox virus. George Washington had also ordered variolation for the American Army.

All kinds of stories have circulated about what tunes were played during the surrender of the Imperial British Army to the victorious American Revolutionary and French Armies, but none have stood the scrutiny of time. "The World Turned Upside Down" is frequently advanced as the tune that the British played. Three broadside ballads of that name are listed in the Bodleian Collection and one in the Madden Collection, but all appear to have been written after 1800. Recent writings on the surrender at Yorktown offer what is likely a more realistic and catastrophic view. Cassandra Pybus writes, "The humiliated British army marched out to a solemn drumbeat, dressed in smart new uniforms but with their colors furled and the drums covered with black handkerchiefs." (Pybus: 2006, 52)

The surrender of the British Army of Earl Cornwallis

## 14 The Dudley Boys

Palmer, *Songs of the Midlands* (1972): 88 – Roud 1131

Tune: The Dudley Boys; Pam Bishop, 1978

In the days of good Queen Bess, Ya boys, O,

In the days of good Queen Bess, Ya, — boys, O,

In the days of good Queen Bess, Co-ven-try out-done the rest.

Ya, boys, oh boys, Oh the brave Dud-ley boys.

In the days of good Queen Bess, Ya, boys, O
In the days of good Queen Bess, Ya, boys, O
In the days of good Queen Bess
Coventry outdone the rest
Ya, boys, oh boys, Oh the brave Dudley boys.

But in the times as be, Ya, boys, O
But in the times as be, Ya, boys, O
But in the times as be
We'm outdone Coventry
Ya, boys, oh boys, Oh the brave Dudley boys.

Tip'on lads they did us join, Ya, boys, O...
And we formed a strong comboin
Ya, boys, oh boys, Oh the brave Dudley boys.

We marchen into town, Ya, boys, O...
Resolved to pull the housen down
Ya, boys, oh boys, Oh the brave Dudley boys.

Toimes they were mighty queer, Ya, boys, O...
And vittle it was very dear
Ya, boys, oh boys, Oh the brave Dudley boys.

So fur to make corn cheap, Ya, boys, O…
We burned un all of a yeap
Ya, boys, oh boys, Oh the brave Dudley boys.

But the work was scarce begun, Ya, boys, O…
When sodgers came and spoilt the fun
Ya, boys, oh boys, Oh the brave Dudley boys.

We all ran down our pits, Ya, boys, O…
Frightened a'most out of our wits
Ya, boys, oh boys, Oh the brave Dudley boys.

God bless Lord Dudley Ward, Ya, boys, O…
He knowed as times been hard
Ya, boys, oh boys, Oh the brave Dudley boys

He called back the sodgermen, Ya, boys, O
He called back the sodgermen, Ya, boys, O
He called back the sodgermen
And we'll never riot again
Na boys, no boys, no the brave Dudley boys.

During the mounting British economic recession that followed America's War of Independence, British workers held demonstrations calling for lowering the prices of food, particularly bread. This song describes one such event where participants gathered in Dudley, a city in the heart of the western coal region later known as the Black Country. In this case the drastic action was "legitimized by the assumptions of an older moral economy, which taught the immorality of forcing up the price of provisions by profiteering upon the necessities of the people." (Thompson: 1966, 63) The Lord Dudley Ward who is blessed for interceding on the workers' behalf was believed to be William Ward, who served as a member of Parliament from 1780 to 1788, then moved to the House of Lords with the inherited title of 3rd Viscount Dudley and Ward. The Dudley and Ward families owned coal mines in the Dudley area.

The earliest known written version of this song dates to 1840, but it probably originated in the 1780s. The words given here in an old midland dialect are provided by Pam Bishop from Birmingham, who also wrote the melody that is shown here. Another popular song, written in 1782 by the prolific writer John Freeth, also uses the phrase "Oh the brave Dudley boys." (Palmer: 1974, 275)

## 15 A New Ballad: On the Birth, Parentage, and Education of Mr. Edmund Burke's Brat*

Bodleian Library: G.A. Warw. b.1(652) – Roud V40275

*Tune: Yellow Stockings; Daniel Wright, 1715*

Oh_____ my Ba - by my Ba - by And
Pro - vince shall vie fir its Birth\_\_\_\_ Each

oh!_____ my ba - by my dear - ee\_\_\_\_
Ci - ty it's Sta - tue shall raise - ee Each

Auch a sweet Ba - by as this\_\_\_\_ There
Pa - triot ha - rangue in the North.\_\_\_\_ Each

ne\_\_\_\_ 'er was Far nor near - ee; Each
Po - et shall sing in it's Praise - ee. Then

CHORUS

up with Se - di - tion up up, And

down with Al - leg - iance, down down - ee And

let us go back - wards and for - wards To

pull down the King and the Crown - ee

Oh my Baby, my Baby.
And oh! my baby my dear-ee
Auch a sweet Baby as this
There ne'er was Far nor near–ee;
Each Province shall vie fir it's Birth;
Each City It's Statue shall raise–ee
Each Patriot harangue in the North,
Each Poet shall sing in it's Praise–ee

CHORUS
    Then Up with Sedition, up up,
    And down with Allegiance, down down–ee
    And let us go backwards and forwards
    To pull down the King and the Crown–ee

The Embryo got with a Zest,
Grew fast to the Nation's great joy–ee
Attendance it smelt of the best.
And R\_\_\_d delivered the Boy–ee:
Republican Price then arose,
To lay his fanatical Spell on,
Some Scriptural Name would have chose,
But faltering baptized it Rebellion;
    Then up with Rebellion up, up &c

From a Fanatic's Brain it was brought,
And fed with a Pap of Sedition,
In each County, Committees were sought
To second and forward the Mission;
When a stripling to Yorkshire was sent,
Where Schooling is quite a cheap Trade–ee
On classical knowledge intent,
There Wyvil Preceptor was made–ee;
    Then up with Rebellion, up up, &c

Next Burke took the youth by the Hand,
Talk'd much of his Prowess and Parts,
Endow'd him with Forests and Lands,
Taught him Shelburne's political Arts;
To the people submissive he bow'd
Each Patriot received with a Smile,
From the Hustings he spoke to the Crowd,
And laugh'd in his Sleeve all the while.
    Then up with Rebellion, up up, &c

Now heigh for Committees and Mobs,
And heigh for Proscriptions and Brib–ee,
And heigh for Informers and Jobs,
And heigh for Lord Mansfield's fire-side –ee;
And heigh for the Conventicle Twang,
And heigh for two Quakers to-to hang, †
And Heigh for the Zeal to go further;
    Then up with Rebellion, up up, &c

Then heigh for a Scaffold and Axe,
To cut off his Majesty's Head–ee,
And heigh for a swinging round Tax,
To pay those by whom he was bled–ee;
Then down with all Order and Right,
And down with each Church with a Steeple,
Gainst Kings, Lords, and Commons we'll fight,
And a Sovereign make of the People.
Then up with Rebellion, up up, &c

\* Mr. Burke brought a Bill into the House of Commons for the Examination into the
  Expenditure of Public Money, and the Reduction of the King's Household.
† Alluding to two Quakers, Executed in America, by order of Congress

Here is a complicated song to sing. The melody is identified in *Popular Songs of the Olden Time*, where it is said to be have been written by Dean Swift as "Oh! My Kitten, my Kitten!" It was printed by Allan Ramsay in the fourth volume of the *Tea Table Miscellany* (1740) and called "Yellow Stockings." (Chappell: 1857, 603) The tune "Yellow Stockings" is played today for English country dancing. This odd song was probably not produced to attract the attention of the working people. Its intent could have been either to poke fun at Edmund Burke for picking up the torch for reform dropped by Wilkes and Wyvill, or as an indictment of revolutionary politics.

It was written during the short, but important, three-month government of the 2nd Marquis of Rockingham, the Yorkshire leader of the Whigs. One of Rockingham's first acts as prime minister was to recognize the United States as an independent nation. Burke, serving as Paymaster General in this brief government, proposed and obtained passage of the significant Economical Reform Bill. To do so, Burke built on groundwork laid by Wyvill's county associations, and he rightly timed his bill to follow the release of the report of the select committee on reform, by William Pitt the Younger. Burke's Bill eliminated a number of sinecures saving over £70,000 a year. He set his own salary as Paymaster General at £4,000, and swept away the perquisites that had enriched so many of his predecessors. Government contractors were excluded from the House of Commons, and revenue officers were disenfranchised. Although this reform bill did not include all the provisions that Wilkites and the working people of Britain sought, it did remove one major impediment to progress by diminishing the power of the throne to control Parliament.

# 16 Song of the Volunteers of 1782

Hayes, Edward, *The Ballads of Ireland*, James Duffy 15 Wellington Key, p 225

Tune: Boyne Water; James Aird, 1785

Hur - rah! 'Tis done___ our___ free - dom's won

Hur - rah for the Vol - un - teers! No laws we own,

but___ those a - lone Of our Com - mons, King, and Peers

The chain is___ broke the___ Sax - on___ yoke

From off our neck is___ tak - en Ire - land a - woke

Dun - gan - non spoke With fear was Eng - land sha - ken

HURRAH! 'tis done—our freedom's won—
Hurrah for the Volunteers!
No laws we own, but those alone
Of our Commons, King, and Peers.
The chain is broke—the Saxon yoke.
From off our neck is taken;
Ireland awoke—Dungannon spoke—
With fear was England shaken.

When Grattan rose, none dared oppose
The claim he made for Freedom:
They knew our swords, to back his words
Were ready, did he need them.
Then let us raise, to Grattan's praise,
A proud and joyous anthem;
And wealth, and grace, and length of days,
May God, in mercy grant him!

Bless Harry Flood, who nobly stood
By us, through gloomy years!
Bless Charlemont, the brave and good,
The Chief of the Volunteers
The North began; the North held on
The strife for native land;
Till Ireland rose, and cowed her foes—
God bless the Northern land!

And bless the men of patriot pen—
Swift, Molyneux, and Lucas;
Bless sword and gun, which "Free Trade" won—
Bless God! who ne'er forsook us.
And long may last, the friendship fast,
Which binds us all together;
While we agree, our foes shall flee
Like clouds in stormy weather.

Remember still, through good and ill,
How vain wore prayers and tears—
How vain were words, till flashed the swords
Of the Irish Volunteers.
By arms we've got the rights we sought
Through long and wretched years—
Hurrah! 'tis done, our Freedom's won—
Hurrah for the Volunteers!

This celebratory song speaks of winning a small degree of Irish independence with the Constitution of 1782 as well as the amendment of the hated Poynings' Law of 1495 that, since the time of Henry VII, had forbidden Irish Parliament to pass laws without prior British approval. Although the British Privy Council still reserved the right to veto Irish legislation, this was as close to independence as Ireland would come for another century.

Thomas Davis, a Protestant organizer and poet of the Young Ireland Movement, wrote this ballad in the 1840s, long after the events. The Volunteers of this song were an armed militia of some 100,000 men, primarily Irish Protestants, formed in 1778 as a defensive force to replace British regulars who had been re-deployed to the American war. The Volunteers were first organized in Belfast, hence the reference to the North. Harry Flood was a leader and tireless worker for independence within the Irish Parliament, and Lord Charlemont was commissioned by the British government to form the Volunteers. The fourth verse mentions William Molyneux, Jonathan Swift, and Charles Lucas, three Irish intellectuals who advocated Ireland's independence during the late seventeenth through mid-eighteenth century.

They mostly followed the fiery Irish politician Henry Grattan, who advocated that the Irish Parliament should declare Ireland's independence. The Volunteers had already forced Britain's Parliament in 1779 to drop trade restrictions placed on Irish commerce, as related in a 1780 broadside ballad in the Bodleian collection (Johnson Ballads fol. 382):

> If you wish now to know how our Cards we have pla'd,
> Why we took up our Clubs, and we threw down our spade;
> So dealt us all Trumps now for that very Thing,
> And so Pam* became civil as well as the King.

*The Duke of Portland Lord Lieutenant of Ireland.

In 1782, Volunteers acting in convention at Dungannon in County Tyrone pushed the Irish Parliament into declaring independence. "The Irish Protestants had won for 'Ireland' in the abstract an explicitly free and sovereign constitution, complicated only by a limitation which seemed neither a complication nor a limitation at the time: namely, the inalienable identity of the Irish Crown with that of England." (Kee: 1976, 33) But while Protestants of the North of Ireland considered this document to make Ireland free and sovereign, the Catholic majority in the rest of Ireland did not think the new independence went far enough—there were growing demands in Ireland for parliamentary reform, to check corruption and make the Irish executive (still appointed by the Crown) responsible to the Irish House of Commons. Tension also persisted because Irish politics and society were controlled by the Anglo-Irish Protestant elite, when the vast majority of the population was Catholic and excluded from public life. (Turner: 2000, 17)

Grattan demanding Irish Independence

## 17 The Countryman's Frolick; OR, Humours of an Election.

Sir Frederick Madden's Collection of Broadside Ballads: 2/1109

*Tune: King John and the Bishop; ballad tune, pre-1700*

As in West-min-ster Ci-ty I chanced to stray, Up to
Co—vent Gar-den I then took my way Got close to the hust-ings in the
nick of a fray, The peo-ple ran, knocked me down,
I up a-gain, Der-ry down, down hey der-ry down.

As in Westminster City I chanced to stray,
Up to Covent Garden I then took my way
Got close to the hustings in the nick of a fray,
The people ran, knocked me down, I up again.
Down, derry, up and Down, &c.

My fright being over I determined to stay,
On purpose to carry home the news of the day,
Adzooks! It to me was as fine as a play,
Handely pleas'd, sorely squees'd, up and Down

What hissing and groaning what shouting Huzza
Some bawling out Fox others for Hood and Wray
Being stunn'd with the noise, I no longer could stay,
Being very queer, got some beer in the town.

Such a scene of confusion I vow and protest,
I never was in such a rackeytty prest,
And bribery and corruption's all a meer jest,
Wagers lay, vote away, golden coin up, &c

What does it avail now of promising votes,
For a Devonshire kiss in an instant turn coates,
Beside lay a wager of five guineas to boot,
You'll surely win, kiss again, bring him in.

At the Star and Garter not knowing the place,
I called out no Fox but sad was my case,

For Sam House in an instant bundel'd me out of my place
Threw me in the dirt, tore my shirt, up, &c.

Then back to the country without more delay,
Well pleas'd with whole bones I safe got away,
But for the future I'll be yay and nay,
Swear black is white, wrong is right, &c.

But to add to my sorrow before I got home,
I felt for my purse, but my money was gone,
Fox or Sam House, or the devil has me quite done,
Pocket pick'd, sorely trick'd, up and down.

The poor man in this song suffered badly when he attempted to visit Westminster to observe the critically important election of 1784. His observations confirm that the practices hadn't changed since an election ten years earlier. Drinking, noise, gambling, bribery, and corruption proved too much for this countryman. Had he been able to vote, he may have been tempted to turn coat for a Devonshire kiss from Georgiana, Duchess of Devonshire, and to vote for Charles James Fox.

William Hague wrote of the Westminster election of 1784:

> From the City of Westminster came the news that Fox himself was struggling to hold his seat, despite the Prince of Wales parading through the streets in his colors and the energetic campaigning of Georgiana, Duchess of Devonshire. Twenty-three days of voting elapsed before Fox moved narrowly into second place, which would have given him one of the two seats, but the voting and the campaigning continued, in perhaps the most hotly contested constituency election of the entire century. Tens of thousands of pounds were spent on each side, vast quantities of alcohol were disbursed, dinners were held for hundreds of voters at a time, street fights between supporters of the candidates became common, 'miscreants' who attempted to vote twice were put on the ducking stool, and an unknown number of votes were cast by people who were not really voters at all. (Hague: 2004, 171)

Fox did win by a thin margin after a recount that lasted for almost a year. Also in the 1784 election, William Pitt the Younger was elected to the Cambridge University seat and asked to form a Government which now was primarily Tory. Seizing the opportunity, with the help of the seats still in control of the Crown, Pitt continued to retain control of the Government for the aristocracy for the next 17 years. As Prime Minister, Pitt again presented another bill for Parliamentary Reform in 1785. His bill proposed to buy out 36 small boroughs and transfer their MP positions to unrepresented towns and to London. The bill was defeated in Commons by 248 to 174, and with that Pitt gave up on the issue.

## **18** Transports and Old Baileys

Bodleian Library: The Harding Collection, B 28(238) – Roud 300

*Tune: Justices and Old Bailey; Broadside, 1780-1812*

Here's a-dieu to your judg-es and ju-ries_____ Jus-ti-ces and old Bai-leys al-so,_____ Se-ven years you've trans-port-ed my true love,_____ Se-ven years he's trans-port-ed you know._____

Here's adieu to your judges and juries
Justices and old Baileys also,
Seven years you've transported my truelove,
Seven years he's transported you know.

To go to a strange country don't grieve me,
Nor leaving old England behind,
It's all for the sake of my Polly.
And the leaving my parents behind.

There's the captain that is our commander
The boatswain and all the ship's crew,
There's married men too and there's single,
Who knows what we transports go thro?

Dear Polly I'm going to leave you,
For seven long years love and more,
But that time love will be but a moment,
When return'd to the girl I adore.

If ever I return from the ocean,
Store of riches I'll bring to my dear,
It's all for the sake of my Polly love.
I'll cross the salt seas for my dear.

How hard is the place of confinement,
That keeps me from my hearts delight,
Cold chains and cold irons surround me,
And a plank for my pillow at night.

How often I wished that the eagle
Would lend me her pinions to fly,
Then I'd fly to the arms of my Polly,
And in her bosom to lie.

This broadside ballad is printed in type that uses the pre-1800's long "ſ." Many other broadsides of this song in the Madden and Bodleian collections have similar words, although they were printed in a later font. It appears, then, that this might be the earliest surviving version of this broadside telling of prison transports to what we can assume was Australia. The song's sketchy description of conditions on a transport probably reflects the author's idea of what such a life might entail, rather than the memories of an actual convict. A detailed discussion by Rory Brown of this ballad and its many later versions, titled "The Transports," can be found at www.mustrad.org.uk.(Brown: 2006, 176)

The proposal to colonize Botany Bay with convicts was formally drawn up in an unsigned document titled "Heads of a Plan for Effectually Disposing of Convicts" and presented to Pitt's cabinet in August 1786. Its intent was clear: "The proposed colony would serve as a remedy for the evils likely to result from the late alarming and numerous increase of felons in this country, and more particularly in the metropolis." (Hughes: 1988, 66) The first 669 convicts of the 150,000 who were eventually transported to Australia arrived in Botany Bay in January 1788. It was soon clear that poor soil made the Bay unsuitable for settlement, so the first colonists moved north and established the colony at Port Jackson (now Sydney). The term "Botany Bay" stuck as the destination, although the region of the Bay itself was never used as a penal colony.

The Landing of the Convicts at Botany Bay

## 19 The African's Complaint

Bodleian Library: Firth Collection b.22(f. 90) – Roud 13891

*Tune: Stuttgart; Christian F. Witt, 1715*

Forc'd from home, and all its plea-sures, A - fric's coast I
left for - lorn, To in - crease a stran - ger's trea - sures
O'er the rag - ing bil - lows borne.

FORC'D from home, and all its pleasures,
Afric's coast I left forlorn,
To increase a stranger's treasures
O'er the raging billows borne.

Men from England bought and sold me,
Paid my price in paltry gold,
But tho' theirs, they have enroll'd me —
Minds are never to be sold.

Still in thought as free as ever,
What are England's rights? I ask:
Me from my delights to sever,
Me to torture, me to task?

Fleecy locks, and black complexion,
Cannot forfeit nature's claim;
Skins may differ, but affection
Dwells in white and black the same.

Is there, as ye sometimes tell us,
Is there One who dwells on high?
Has He bid you buy and sell us,
Speaking from His throne, the sky?

Ask Him if your knotted scourges,
Or your blood-extorting screws
Are the means which duty urges
Agents of His will to use?

Hark!—He answers—wild tornadoes
Strewing yonder sea with wrecks;
Wasting towns, plantations, meadows,
Is the voice with which He speaks.

He foreseeing what vexations
Afric's sons should undergo,
Fix'd their tyrant's habitations
Where His whirlwinds answer—No.

By our blood in Afric wasted
E'er our necks receiv'd the chain,
By the miseries that we tasted
Crossing in your barks the main.

By our sufferings since ye brought us
To the man-degrading smart,
All sustain'd with patience, taught us,
Only by a broken heart.

Deem our nation brutes no longer,
Till some reason ye shall find,
Worthier of regard and stronger
Than the colour of our kind.

Slaves of gold, whose sordid dealings
Tarnish all your boasted powers;
Prove that you have human feelings,
E'er you proudly question ours.

STOCKTON: Printed by R. CHRISTOPHER, for R.L.

William Cowper wrote these lyrics at the request of the Society for Effecting the Abolition of the Slave Trade. Originally included in a collection of poems, they were also widely distributed as a street ballad. The last verse of the song delivers a telling judgment: the lust for gold is a greater source of degradation to the slaver than captivity was to the slave.

The Society was formed in 1787 by Thomas Clarkson, a recent theological student; Granville Sharp, another Anglican; and nine Quakers. As a citizen's movement, it was remarkably successful in gaining public support and organizing for political action. Employing for the first time techniques that are used in today's political campaigns, the Society periodically printed five hundred to a thousand copies of what the minutes referred to as "a letter to our friends in the Country" to inform them of the state of the business. "The Committee agreed on a piece of text that was to be hand delivered to every donor living in greater London, appealing for another contribution at least as big as the last. This may have been history's first direct mail fundraising letter." (Horchschild: 2005, 128) What activist group today does not publish such a newsletter, print or electronic?

Soon after the Society was formed, William Wilberforce was recruited to be the abolitionist movement's spokesman in the House of Commons. In 1789 he introduced a bill to abolish the slave trade, timed to follow a huge Privy Council report on slavery. Despite all the work done by the Society for Effecting the Abolition of the Slave Trade and by Wilberforce, the matter was stalled by Parliamentary inaction. "Procrastination, that most polished vice of British politics worked its morphic spell." (Schama: 2006, 261) This was a bitter pill for the activists to swallow, but their energy eventually prevailed.

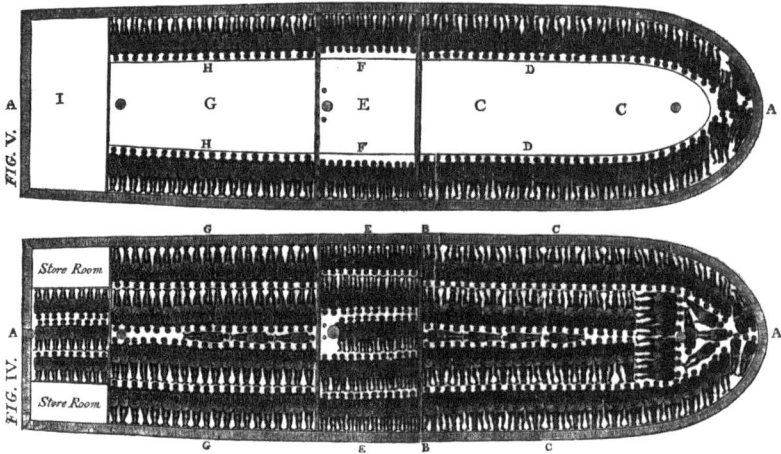

Diagram of a Slave Ship

## 20 The File Hewer's Lamentation

Wilson, *The Songs of Joseph Mather* (1862): 1

Tune: The Miller of Dee; Village Opera, 1729

Or - dained I was a beg - gar And have no cause to swag-ger, ___ It pier - ces like a dag - ger To think I'm thus for - lorn. ___ My trade or oc - cu - pa - tion ___ Was ground for la - men - ta - tion, Which makes me curse ___ my sta - tion, And wish I'd ne'er been born. ___

Ordained I was a beggar.
And have no cause to swagger;
It pierces like a dagger—
To think I'm thus forlorn.
My trade or occupation
Was ground for lamentation,
Which makes me curse my station,
And wish I'd ne'er been born.

Of slaving I am weary,
From June to January
To nature it's contrary—
This, I presume is fact.
Although with a stammer,
Our Nell exclaims I clam her,
I wield my six-pound hammer
Till I have grown round-backe'd.

I'm debtor to a many,
But cannot pay a penny;
Sure I've worse luck than any;
My traps are marked for sale.
My creditors may sue me,
And curse the day they new me
The baliffs may pursue me,
And lock me up in jail.

As negroes in Virginia,
In Maryland or Guinea,
Like them I must continue—
To be both bought and sold.
While negro ships are filling
I ne'er can save a shilling,
And must, which is more killing,
A pauper die when old.

My troubles never ceased,
While Nell's bairn time increased;
While hundreds I've rehearsed
Ten thousand more remain;
My income for me, Nelly,
Bob, Tom, Paul, Bet, and Sally,
Could hardly fill a belly,
Should we eat salt and grains.

At every week's conclusion
New wants bring fresh confusion,
It is but mere delusion,
To hope for better days,
While knaves with power invested,
Until by death arrested,
Oppress us unmolested
By their infernal ways.

A hanging day is wanted;*
Was it my justice granted
Poor men distressed and daunted
Would then have cause to sing—
To see in active motion
Rich knaves in full proportion,
For their unjust extortion
And vile offences swing.

---

* Our criminal laws were cruel at that time. In London alone, in 23 years following
1750, 678 persons were executed for various crimes. Legislators did not see the
value of the schoolmaster. No wonder Mather wished to improve the world by stran-
gling the knaves.

This song was written by Joseph Mather from Sheffield (1737–1804). According to Roy Palmer, Mather couldn't read but he authored a large number of topical songs, only two of which have been found as printed broadsides. (Palmer: 1988, 25) Fifty-five of Mather's songs were collected in an 1862 book edited and annotated by John Wilson. Many of his songs reflect his own struggles to feed his wife and their five children on a journeyman file-maker's wage. "It would be impossible now to understand the influence Mather exercised over the minds of his fellow workmen, without some acquaintance with their moral, social, and political condition. His influence wether [sic] well directed or not was powerful, because in him the artisans recognized a champion of labor." (Wilson: 1862, 11)

Several songs from these times compare the British wage slave's situation to that of African slaves throughout the western world. It is thought that slaves were housed and fed, while that was rarely the case for the wage slave in Britain. In this song we get a view of the plight of a skilled working man, who clearly was not doing well.

File Cutters

Thomas Paine

Chapter 3
# PAINE: 1789–1795

> *"It is over the lowest class of mankind that government by terror is intended to operate, and it is on them that it operates to the worst effect. They have sense enough to feel they are the objects aimed at; and they inflict in their turn the examples of terror they have been instructed to practice."* —Thomas Paine, *Rights of Man*

The songs in this chapter emphasize the immense impression that the French Revolution and the philosophies of Thomas Paine made on the working people of the British Isles. News of the storming of the Bastille on July 14, 1789 spread quickly throughout Britain, deeply affecting popular sentiment. Through his writings, Paine inspired people to pursue the ideals emerging in the Age of Enlightenment and to remain committed to political reform. Meanwhile, attempting to rid the country of the radical political reform movement, the Pitt Government presided over a plague of libel, sedition, and treason trials. These draconian trials were highly publicized and fearfully followed by the population of Britain as they approached war with France. Then there was the recovery of George III from his first bout of mental illness, which was announced in April of 1789.

On November 4, 1789, the 101st anniversary of Britain's so-called Glorious Revolution, Richard Price, economist and Unitarian minister of Newington Green, delivered a "Discourse on The Love of Our Country" that echoed the thoughts of thousands:

> I have lived to see the rights of men better understood than ever, and nations panting for liberty, which seemed to have lost the idea of it. I have lived to see thirty millions of people, indignant and reso-lute, spurning at slavery, and demanding liberty with an irresistible voice. After sharing in the benefits of one Revolution, I have been spared to be a witness to two other Revolutions, both glorious. And now, methinks, I see the ardor for liberty catching and spreading,

a general amendment beginning in human affairs, the dominion of kings changed for the dominion of laws, and the dominion of priests giving way to the dominion of reason and conscience. (Bartel: 1965, 45–46)

Disagreeing with this perspective, Edmund Burke authored *Reflections on the Revolution in France,* which was published November 1, 1790 and became the bestselling, semi-official ruling class response to the French Revolution. Will and Ariel Durant describe Burke's severe criticism of Price: "Clergymen he felt should mind their business, which is to preach Christian virtues.... Aristocracy is desirable, for it allows a nation to be ruled by trained and selected minds.... Monarchy is good because it gives a psychological unity and historical continuity helpful in the difficult reconciliation of order with liberty." (Durant: 1975, 514)

At first, public opinion appeared to favor Burke's position. The tide changed with the publication of Paine's *Rights of Man* in March 1791 (with a second volume in 1792), written for the working man. On the Glorious Revolution of 1688, Paine criticized Burke, saying, "I am contending for the rights of the living, and—Mr. Burke is contending for the authority of the dead over the rights and freedom of the living." (Paine: 1791, 1)

The first volume of *Rights of Man* includes three points taken from The Declaration of the Rights of Man and of Citizens (1789) by the National Assembly of France:

I. Men are born and always continue free and equal in respect to their rights. Civil distinctions, therefore, can be founded only on public utility.

2. The end of all political associations is the preservation of the natural and imprescriptible rights of man; and these rights are liberty, property, security, and resistance of oppression.

3. The Nation is essentially the source of all Sovereignty; nor can any individual or any body of men be entitled to any authority which is not expressly derived from it. (Paine: 1791, 117)

*Rights of Man* became an immediate success. It was distributed among working people throughout Britain and ultimately to all of Europe and North America, and it helped shape the thinking that inspired the ascendancy of the working man. It provided points for political discussion groups that sprang up throughout Britain for many years to come. (Nelson: 2006, 221) By 1802, over 500,000 copies of *Rights of Man* had been sold, many as abridged editions for sixpence each.

In July of 1791, a so-called "Church and King" riot took place in Birmingham, targeting religious dissenters and radicals. Dissenters' chapels were burned to the ground, including the home of Joseph Priestley, a Unitarian minister who was also the chemist who discovered oxygen. In September of that year, the young Irish lawyer Wolfe Tone's *Argument on*

*Behalf of the Catholics of Ireland* was published in Dublin. It was rapidly noticed by Belfast intellectuals who invited Tone to meet with them. "The Society of United Irishmen" was formed in Belfast in October 1791, and one month later it was established in Dublin. Founding members included Wolfe Tone, Thomas Russell, William Drennan, William Sinclair, Henry Joy McCracken, and Archibald Hamilton Rowan, who were soon joined by Napper Tandy. Seeing their new organization as "a regeneration of the Irish nation, they adopted their seal designed by Drennan, which was a harp with the motto, I am new strung and shall be heard." (Curtin: 1994, 246) It was not long before Government saw the danger of Paine's book, and the publisher and the printer were soon arrested for sedition. Paine was indicted for treason, but at the last minute escaped to France, where he had been chosen to serve in the general assembly by several different districts. (Hitchens: 2006, 56)

Meanwhile, also in 1792, Corresponding Societies formed in cities and towns throughout Scotland and England, where excerpts from *Rights of Man* were read and discussed. These new societies operated under egalitarian principles. The "London Corresponding Society of the Unrepresented Part of the People of Great Britain" (L.C.S.), founded in 1792 by Scottish shoemaker Thomas Hardy, relied upon a membership subscription of a penny a week, catering to a different class of person than the Society for Constitutional Information (S.C.I.) that had been founded in 1780 with its annual subscription of one guinea. These new societies were structured to enable hundreds of small groups to meet separately throughout England and Scotland and keep in touch through correspondence. Groups soon existed in most cities and towns, numbering over 100 societies, with a nominal membership of over 10,000 and with strong ties to the United Irishmen. The membership of each group was kept small to avoid infiltration by government spies.

As Corresponding Societies spread, a counter-organization emerged in 1792 under the leadership of John Reeves, calling itself "The Association for the Preservation of Liberty and Property against Republicans and Levelers." This organization obtained considerable support from the government, magistrates, and men of property. It amassed evidence against radicals and was responsible for numerous bonfires throughout the country where Paine was burned in effigy.

On January 21, 1793 King Louis XVI was guillotined. On February 1, 1793 war between France and Britain began when the French Convention declared war on both England and Holland. In April 1793, although Britain was gearing up for yet another war, four major happenings regarding reform occurred:

> 1. "Friends of the People," a moderate upper-class reform movement which included several members of Parliament, issued an "Address to the People" calling for moderate political reform.

2. Major Cartwright of the Society for Constitutional Information objected to the address's weak stance on reform, causing controversy among reform leaders. (Cone: 1968, 127)

3. Charles Grey submitted a resolution for Parliament to take up the reform issue, losing on a vote of 282 to 41. (It took thirty-nine more years before Grey's Parliamentary Reform Bill of 1832 was eventually passed.)

4. A minor bill was passed by the Irish Parliament known as the Catholic Relief Act of 1793, which had been urged on by Henry Grattan. (Hague: 2004, 359) The act gave Catholics the right to vote but only for Protestants, since Catholics still could not take a seat in Parliament.

The Scottish Friends of the People, founded in 1792 to advocate for parliamentary reform, convened a first British Convention in Edinburgh in December of that year, attended by over 150 delegates representing more than 70 societies from 35 towns and villages. The convention approved a petition to Parliament calling for reform and agreed to meet again the following April. (Bewley: 1981, 48) Although the Edinburgh Convention was peaceful and care had been taken to avoid potentially seditious statements—the Society of United Irishmen sent an address of fraternity with Scottish nationalistic aspirations but it was not well received—its success was reason enough for Henry Dundas, Pitt's Secretary of State, to look for ways to prevent the spread of its influence. Thomas Muir, vice chair of the convention who had invited conversation with the Irish, was indicted for sedition under Scottish law on January 2, 1793. While he awaited trial, two more conventions were held in Edinburgh in April and in November with London Corresponding Society representation. Three leaders of these meetings, Reverend Thomas Fitch Palmer, Maurice Margarot, and William Skirving, shared the same fate as Muir and were indicted for sedition.

The subsequent convictions in January 1794 of these four leaders of the Edinburgh conventions led to an immediate resurgence of many branches of the Corresponding Societies, leading an estimated 2,000 people to attend a joint L.C.S. and S.C.I. general meeting at London's Chalk Farm on April 14, 1794. Resolutions were passed accusing the Government of high treason for the tyranny of the judiciary in Scotland. (Barrell: 2000, 189) On that same day Pitt's wartime Government embarked upon a plan to put an end to dissent, starting with suspending habeas corpus. Just three days after the Chalk Farm meeting, a small number of demonstrators shouted "Down with George," "No Pitt," "Bread," and "Peace" as the King's entourage progressed toward the opening of the Houses of Parliament, and a thrown stone fractured a window of the royal coach. Urged on by the Government, the press cited this as evidence of a plot to kill the King. A great deal would be made of this so-called "pop-gun" incident.

Between May and July of 1794, thirteen leading activists of five reform societies were rounded up and held without charge or trial in the Tower of London. It wasn't until October 6 of that year that an indictment of high treason was brought against twelve of them. Expecting to get an easy conviction, the State decided to try Thomas Hardy first, but the Government couldn't make the charges stick when faced with the sterling defense presented by radical lawyer Thomas Erskine, who had earlier defended Thomas Paine. Hardy was acquitted on Guy Fawkes Day (November 5) and soon charges were dropped against the remaining radical reformers. Release of the "twelve apostles of reform" sparked a revitalization of the reform movement. Throughout the country, societies continued to grow and mass meetings were held, culminating in an enormous meeting chaired by a young Irish intellectual, John Binns, at Copenhagen Field (Islington) on October 26, 1795. This time it was acknowledged that over 200,000 attended. Speakers called for Parliamentary reform, a change of ministers, and Peace with France. (Turner: 2000, 83)

Another set of charges was brought against three other members of the London Corresponding Society regarding the "pop-gun" incident, alleging that it had been a plot to assassinate King George III with a poison dart fired from an air gun. The members were arrested near the end of 1794, and in December 1795 one more was also indicted for the same crime. All four were acquitted of treason in May 1796 on the grounds that the chief witness against them was dead.

Pitt called for stronger measures to suppress dissent. He proposed—and Parliament passed—the "Two Acts of Coercion" on December 18, 1795. The "Seditious Meetings Act" was to be in effect for three years: meetings of more than fifty people now had to be licensed by local magistrates (a direct response to the mass meetings sponsored by the L.C.S.), and public lectures were also to be regulated. The "Treasonable Practices Act" (later made permanent by the Treason Act of 1817), whose preamble referred to the attack on the king's coach, widened the definition of treason to include plans to harm the king, help invaders, or coerce Parliament. Spoken words came within the scope of this Act. (Turner: 2000, 83)

Britain was fighting on two fronts, battling both France and the Parliamentary reform movement. Government hired 22,000 Hanoverian and Hessian soldiers to fight in the lowlands of Holland under Prince Frederick, Duke of York and Albany, who was the blundering second son of the King. At home, Pitt and Dundas battled to prove the treasonous nature of the growing Parliamentary reform movement. At first it appeared that the government would succeed on both fronts. But by 1795 things began to slide: the French were gaining in the lowlands of Holland, Britain was losing control of the Mediterranean, the reform movement showed more militancy, and harvests were persistently poor. People continued to read the banned *Rights of Man*. It was no wonder that Pitt's government was looking for a way to end the war.

## 21 The Tree of Liberty

Sir Frederick Madden's Collection of Broadside Ballads: 8/5135.

Tune: The Moreen; Neale's Collection, 1787

The great Reformation approaching we hail,
'Gainst statesmen and priests Truth and Reason prevail.
Triumphant the Planters of Liberty see,
Preparing the soil of the globe for the tree.
    All shall yield to Freedom's fair tree,
      Bend to thee
      Blest Liberty;
   Heroes are they now planting thee,
   And all their great names immortal shall be.

Away with the Splendor and pomp of a court,
Our toil shall no longer the baubles support;
No longer the slaves of a statesman and King,
Inspired by the Muses of Freedom we sing.
    All shall yield, etc.

Ye Britons, for courage in battle renowned,
For freedom and riches— Alas! Empty found!
Triumphant ye came from the field and the main,
To be conquered and plundered by statesmen again.
   Then repair to, etc.

Ye Trees of Corruption, in Courts ye abound;
The fruits ye produce are a curse to the ground;
In the soil where ye flourish no others can grow;
But now see the axe at your roots aim the blow.
   All shall yield, etc.

May Heaven guard the People and Armies of France,
And crush all their foes wherever they advance.
An end to the councils of Traitors combined—
The downfall of Tyrants— and Peace to Mankind.
   All shall yield, etc.

How great in the ages to come, and how dear,
Your names and your conquests, great heroes, will appear.
With raptures they'll read, and your actions review,
While under the shade of the tree raised by you.
   All shall yield, etc.

Sold, Wholesale and retail by Citizen T. G. Ballard,
No 3. Bedford Court, Covent Garden,
— where may be had variety of Patriotic Publications.

Those most dedicated to Parliamentary reform were united to plant the "tree of Liberty" and defend it from statesmen and priests. This song is a celebration of what British progressives saw as the ultimate birth of liberty for the world. Throughout the American and French revolutions, many songs were written on the theme of the tree of liberty. American references were to large elm trees where messages (broadsides) would be posted to alert citizens of upcoming actions in the struggle against British oppression. This song advances the broader worldview of freedom exemplified by its beginnings in the French Revolution, declaring republican sentiments aiming the (metaphorical) axe at the roots of corruption, which will be replaced by the tree of liberty. The French people and their armies will take down tyrants and bring ultimate peace to all mankind.

The recovery of George III from his first bout of mental illness was announced in April of 1789. His recovery meant that Prime Minister Pitt did not have to call for establishing Regency of the despised Prince of Wales. This led to wide celebration and perhaps the highest level of public acclaim for William Pitt. (Hague 2004: 267)

## 22  Edmund Burke: To The Swinish Multitude

Bodleian Library: The Harding Collection, B 5(97) – Roud V38876

*Tune: King John and the Bishop; ballad tune, pre-1700*

Ye base SWINISH herd, in the Style of Taxation,
What would you be after, disturbing the Nation?
Give over your grunting— be off to your Stye,
Nor dare to look out if a king passes by.
    Get ye down, down, down—keep ye down

Do you know what a King is? By Patrick I'll tell you –
He has power in his pocket to buy you and sell you;
To make you all Soldiers, or keep you at work –
To hang you, and cure you for Ham and Salt Pork!
    Get ye down, &c.

To be sure I have said, but I spoke it abrupt,
That the State is DEFECTIVE, and also CORRUPT;
But remember I warned you with Caution to peep,
For Swine at a Distance 'tis needful to keep.
    Get ye down, &c.

The State, it is true has grown fat upon SWINE,
And the Church's weak Stomach on TYTHE PIG can dine;
But neither, ye know, when they roast at the Fire,
Have a right to find Fault with the Cook, or enquire.
    Get ye down, &c.

And now for the Sun, or the Light of the Day,
It doth not belong to a PITT you may say;
I tell you be silent, and cease all your jars,
Or he'll charge you a Farthing a piece for the STARS.
   Get ye down, &c.

What know ye of Commons, of Kings, or of Lords,
But what the dim Light of Taxation affords?
Be contented with that— and no more of your rout,
Or a new Proclamation shall muzzle your SNOUT.
   Get ye down, &c.

Here's myself and his DARKNESS, and HENRY DUND-ASS;
SCOTCH, ENGLISH, and IRISH, with Fronts made of Brass;
A cord platted three-fold will stand a good pull,
Against SAWNEY, and PATRICK, and old JOHNNY BULL.
   Get ye down, &c.

To conclude then— no more about Man and his Rights,
Tom Paine and a rabble of Liberty Lights;
That you are but State Swine, if you ever forget,
We'll throw you alive into the horrible PITT!
   Get ye down, down, down—keep ye down

This satirical ballad, if not authored by Thomas Spence, surely contains his spirit. Spence was a writer, philosopher, and leader of what became some of the more radical reformers before and after his death in 1814. The song appears to have been written after Burke and Paine completed their books on the French Revolution, and when many were protesting Prime Minister Pitt's new taxes on all manner of things. New taxes were consistently being raised to pay the interest on the loans incurred by Britain during the American Revolution. It also seems to be written before 1792, when "Pitt began to rectify this by removing, albeit prematurely, taxes on female servants, candles, and carts and wagons." (Hague: 2004, 306) This tongue-in-cheek song catches the widespread contempt for Burke's views that the educated nobility and clergy were the protectors of the under classes, and that education would be wasted on the masses. He had written: "Along with its natural protectors, and guardians, learning will be cast into the mire, and trodden down under the hoofs of the swinish multitude." (Burke: 1790, 92)

The sixth verse refers to Pitt's hated window tax that landlords used to justify boarding up or removing tenants' windows to cut down on property taxes. Burke, says the songwriter, tells the swinish multitude not to make a fuss or he and Pitt will initiate taxes for observing the stars. The seventh verse refers to the gruesome three: Burke, the Irishman, against Patrick; Pitt, the Englishman, against John Bull; and Home Secretary Henry Dundas, the Scot, against Sawney.

## 23  God Save Great Thomas Paine

Wilson, *The Songs of Joseph Mather* (1862): 56

Tune: God Save The Queen; Thesaurus Musicus, 1744

God save great Tho - mas Paine, His "Rights of Man" to ex-plain
To e' - ry soul. He makes the blind to see What dupes and
slaves they be, And points out li - ber-ty from pole to pole

God save great Thomas Paine,
His "Rights of Man" to explain
   To e'ry soul.
He makes the blind to see,
What dupes and slaves they be,
And points out liberty
   From pole, to pole.

Thousands cry "church and king"
That well deserve to swing,
   All must allow;
Birmingham blush for shame,
Manchester do the same,
Infamous is your name,
   Patriot's vow.

Pull proud oppressors down,
Knock off each tyrant's crown,
   And break his sword;
Down with aristocracy,
Set up democracy,
And from hypocrisy
   Save us good Lord.

Why should despotic pride
Usurp on every side?
   Let us be free;
Grant freedom's arms success,
And all her efforts bless
Plant thro' the universe
   Liberty's tree.

Facts are seditious things
When they touch courts and kings
  Armies are rais'd,
Barracks and bastilles built,
Innocence charged with guilt,
Blood most unjustly spilt,
  Gods stand amaz'd.

Despots may howl and yell,
Tho' they're in League with hell
  They'll not reign long;
Satan may lead the van,
And do the worst he can,
Paine and his Rights of man
  Shall be my song.

Another song by Joseph Mather from Sheffield (see No. 20) shows support for Tom Paine's *Rights of Man* and reflects the republican sentiment immediately understood by working people.

For Paine, the American experience was central. He became aware of Whig and republican ideas early in life, participated in the radical transformation of those ideas in America, and transmitted democratic republican ideology back to Britain. The United States, in Paine's view, supplied a model of the benefits of government, based on the rights of man, where hereditary rule had been rejected and the "productive classes" had come into their own. (Wilson: 1988, 184)

When Paine returned to England from America in 1787, he commuted between London and Paris to observe the beginnings of the French Revolution. The first volume of *Rights of Man* was released in March 1791, the second in 1792. By 1793 over 200,000 copies—including thousands of cheap abridged versions—had been sold. The Society for Constitutional Information "voted its thanks to Paine for his most masterly book... which stated political truths so convincingly as to accelerate the reform spirit" (Cone: 1968, 107) and took responsibility for its distribution. The popularity of the book undoubtedly owed much to growing scorn for Burke's *Reflections on the Revolution in France.*

The majority of middle and upper class reformers dissociated themselves from Paine's doctrine, and the government brought charges of sedition against him in May of 1792. That same month the first "Royal Proclamation against Seditious Writings and Publications" was enacted. Paine's trial was scheduled for December by which time he was back in France, never to return to England. Tried in absentia, he was found guilty, outlawed, and his book was banned.

## 24   A New Song: By Phelemy Freebairn

*Northern Star*, November 1792

*Tune: Larry Grogan; James Oswald, 1760*

Ah - rah   Pad - dy   my   joy____   what
ne - ver   can   thrive,   if   you

makes you   so   shy   To   take   up   with   your   pro - test - ant
both   do   not   strive__   To   live   on   good   terms   with   each

Bro - ther,   your   Bro - ther.   Sure you   o - ther, each   o - ther.

Arrah Paddy my, joy
What makes you so shy,
To take up with your protestant brother, your Brother;
Sure you never can thrive,
If you both do not strive
To live on good terms with each other, each other.

You foes long have prided,
To see you divided,
That they with more ease might oppress you, oppress you.
But when they once find
You together have join'd,
I'll be bound, they'll be glad to caress you, caress you

Then your rights will be granted,
And all that you wanted
To fit you for every high station, high station.
At Assizes and Election
You'll shine in perfection—
Oh then you'll be a bright nation, bright nation.

But if by a sad blunder,
You still keep asunder,
Those blessings can never attend you, attend you.
Till you go to your graves,
You shall live and die— slaves—
And if you die such fools, d— I mend you, d— I mend you.

Castle Street Lishures, Nov. 20, 1792

This song was published in Samuel Nielson's weekly *Northern Star* newspaper during the first year of its publication. *Northern Star* was the voice of the Belfast United Irishmen, who advocated that "the public-will was indivisible,—thus they sought to eradicate sectarian tensions in Ireland, the persistence of which they attributed to the illiberal machinations of a 'divide and rule' imperial policy." (Curtin: 1994, 15)

Though their organization was centered in Belfast, many United Irishmen lived in Dublin. Their intent was to fight for all men's rights, whether Protestant or Catholic. *Northern Star* covered intelligence from France and the continent, drawing on newspapers and other communications arriving daily from the Freeport of Hamburg, and it printed full texts from British meetings of reform clubs. *Northern Star* had support from elements of both the Belfast and Dublin business communities who filled every edition of the paper with paid advertising.

Archibald Hamilton Rowan, on behalf of the United Irishmen, addressed the December 1792 Scottish Friends of the People Society's Reform Convention in Edinburgh. "We greatly rejoice that the spirit of freedom moves over the face of Scotland—from a conviction of the union between virtue, letters, and liberty, and now rises to distinction,—for a reform in Parliament—with the unity and energy of an embodied nation!" (Ellis & Mac a'Ghobhainn: 1989, 60)

## 25 The Dispersion of the British Convention

Sir Frederick Madden's Collection of Broadside Ballads: 08/5147 — Roud V41368

*Tune: Sit Down Neighbours All; Charles Morris, 1786*

In the good town of E-din-burgh a woe-ful thing be-fell, sir,
and if you will at-tend to me, the oc-ca-sion I will tell, sir,
the things which hap-pened there, caused each pen-sion-er to won-der,
And turn up his eyes, as a duck does in thun-der
Bow, wow, wow, Down with the swine and rab-ble bow, wow, wow

In the good town of Edinburgh, a woeful thing befell, sir,
And if you will attend to me, the occasion I will tell, sir;
The things which happened there, caused each pensioner to wonder,
And turn up his eyes, as a duck does in thunder.
    Bow, wow, wow;
    Down with the swine and rabble, bow, wow, wow.

A set of hair-brained fellows, met upon a daring plan, sir,
No less than to discuss the rights and liberties of man, sir;
But no man of sense would e'er listen to their babble, sir.
For almost all belonged to the GRUNTERS OR THE RABBLE, sir.
    Bow, wow, wow, *etc.*

To reform our constitution, these same fellows did intend, sir,
When every placeman knows this truth, that 'tis too good to mend, sir;
And the magistrates have proved they had an infamous intention,
Or else they never would have dared to call themselves convention,
    Bow, wow, wow, *etc.*

Still further to evince their horrible design, sir,
They called each other Citizen, and that increased their crime, sir;
When if their conversation to their nature they would suit, sir,
Instead of Fellow Citizen, they'd grunt out Brother Brute, sir.
   Bow, wow, wow, *etc.*

Nay, more; in every thing they did, to seem as bad as France, sir;
They framed their committees of instruction and finance, sir;
But if instruction were to spread, how horrible was that, sir!
Good lord; why the rabble might begin to smell a rat, sir.
   Bow, wow, wow, *etc.*

Then they said, that a man, sir, in any rank or station,
Had a right by his vote to a share in legislation;
And that when from the pockets of the poor the money went, sir,
They had a right to ask in what manner it was spent, sir.
   Bow, wow, wow, *etc.*

Then they talked as if our tax had become a grievous weight, sir,
And that sinecure places did no service to the state, sir;
But if it be but justice to pay men for doing something, sir,
'Tis generous, I'm sure, to pay men for doing nothing, sir.
   Bow, wow, wow, *etc.*

Then they wished too that all enmity 'twixt nations should be o'er, sir,
That the sword should be sheathed, and that blood be no more, sir;
But what man in oppression could possibly go further, sir,
Than to take away the bread of those who live only by murder, sir.
   Bow, wow, wow, *etc.*

So mad at last were they become, that I am almost sure, sir,
They thought that the rich were no better than the poor, sir!
And at length they had scattered quite a panic through the city.
By appointing FOUR men on a secret committee.
   Bow, wow, wow, *etc.*

The magistrates alarmed at this, and rousing one and all, sir;
With all the myrmidons of power, set off to attack the hall, sir;
And they never would have suffered them to come to such a pass, sir,
But they had not yet received their orders from Dundas, sir.
   Bow, wow, wow, *etc.*

But as soon as master Harry had sent his orders down, sir,
Up rose at his command, all the rulers of the town, sir;
And some profanely whisper, that on entering the room, sir,
These tools of power shed an unsavory perfume, sir.
   Bow, wow, wow, *etc.*

Indictments on each friend of freedom followed close behind, sir,
The judges very kindly taught the juries what to find, sir;
Though this indeed was useless, for I'll venture to assure ye,
They had taken care enough before to pack a proper jury.
   Bow, wow, wow, *etc.*

Objections were repelled, brought in any former shape, sir,
For SEDITION was the crime, and not a simple RAPE, sir;
And at length this dire fancy for reform to allay, sir,
They decreed a trip for fourteen years to Botany Bay, sir.
   Bow, wow, wow, *etc.*

Thus every method has been tried to quench this daring spirit, sir;
May both magistrates and judges meet with that reward they merit, sir;
For each method they've pursued, that all honest placemen ought, sir,
And if poor freedom be not stabbed I'm sure it's not their fault, sir.
   Bow, wow, wow, *etc.*

Printed for T Spence No 8 Little Turnstile Holburne;
Patriotic Bookseller, and Publisher of Pigs Meat.

This clever, biting parody of "The Drummer and the Cook" was written by Thomas Spence to protest the Pitt Government's war against working class enfranchisement. Three conventions for parliamentary reform met in Edinburgh within a year, and Henry Dundas, Pitt's Home Secretary, brought charges of sedition against leaders of all three, using ancient Scottish law.

The first was a Scottish Friends of the People Society's Reform Convention, held in Edinburgh December 8, 1792, gathering over 150 representatives of some seventy Scottish societies. The eloquent young attorney, Thomas Muir, vice president *pro tem* of the convention, introduced an address of solidarity that had been sent from the United Irishmen. But the convention, concerned only with reform, voted to consider this Irish statement as somewhat treasonous. Seeking to avoid potentially seditious statements, the convention resolved to petition Parliament for peaceful reform, taking the French oath "to live free or die" and agreeing to reconvene in April 1793.

This second convention in Edinburgh was held less than three months after France declared war against Britain. Chaired by the Unitarian minister, Thomas Fitch Palmer, this meeting was less well attended than the first. The convention adjourned until November when it was hoped that delegates of the London Corresponding Society and the United Irishmen could attend. Before the third Scottish convention was called to order in November 1793, leaders of the first two conventions had been tried and convicted for sedition. They were sentenced to transportation to Australia—Muir for fourteen years and Palmer for seven.

The third convention, of the British Convention of the Delegates of the People Associated to Obtain Universal Suffrage and Annual Parliaments, was attended by 180 delegates from reform societies in Scotland, England, and Ireland. Leaders of this convention were arrested, and its delegates were dispersed. Trials of key participants in the third Convention resulted in speedy convictions and sentences of fourteen years' transportation. William Skirving of the Scottish Friends of the People and Maurice Margarot of the L.C.S. were tried together, and Joseph Gerrald of the L.C.S. was tried a month later.

While Thomas Muir and the Reverend Thomas Fitch Palmer were held on hulks awaiting their transportation, Charles James Fox, leader of the opposition in Parliament, dined with them, in a gesture of sympathy and disgust for Government repression. "Fox remarked that Scotland could no longer be regarded as a free country and that England was going the same way." (Turner: 2000, 78) On February 13, 1794, *The Surprise* sailed from Woolwich carrying Scottish Convention activists Muir, thirteen months after his arrest; Palmer, a leader of the second Scottish Convention held in April; Margarot, an L.C.S. delegate to the third convention; and Skirving, delegate of the Friends of the People. Sailing with the convicted activists were 60 female convicts under the age of forty. (Bewley: 1981, 103)

Pitt was determined to ignore petitions and organized demonstrations, and to purge dissent. Four weeks after *The Surprise* sailed, Parliament suspended habeas corpus and proceeded to fulfill Fox's prediction by arresting all of the leaders of both the London Corresponding Society and the Society for Constitutional Information.

*Illustrious martyr in the glorious cause*
*Of truth, of freedom, and of equal laws.*

Thomas Muir

## 26 A new Song, called
## The French Kings Blood Crying for Vengeance

Bodleian Library: Firth Collection b.22(f. 89/1) – Roud V30541

*Tune: The Poacher; Broadside, 1780-1812*

Come here you tender Britons,
And Listen to this deed,
Hear how those cruel Frenchmen
Have caused their King to bleed;
Their lands full of pollution,
Sprinkled with scarlet die,
Shun such a flood of Christian blood,
Doth loud for vengeance cry.

Black clouds hang over Paris,
Where dreadful horrors reign,
These indicate vast thunder
From Portugal and Spain;
From Austria and from Russia,
And from Prussia more renowned,
As they draw near Demourier,
He'll tremble at the sound

If these are not sufficient,
Brunswick and Holland too,
With the warriors of Great Britain,
Will turn out such a crew;
Our fleet of floating batteries,
So warlike and so grand,
We'll never retrench from the French,
Till they purify the land.

Look out you bold convention
And make more Demouriers,
For soon you'll have such volleys
Come thundering in your ears;
They'll stupefy your senses,
In time for mercy cry,
Your King you've killed, his blood you've spilled,
For which vengeance loud doth cry.

Wretches! What could induce you
To sacrifice your King?
Was it to make all Europe
Destruction on you bring?
Your fate is sure and certain,
You've nowhere now to fly,
Now down you must, by all you're curst,
Destroyed King and Country.

Could you not spare your Monarch?
You wild blood-thirsty crew!
Great George's royal Britons
You ruffians will pursue;
In vain they'll run for shelter
Under your idol tree,
Her blossoms fade while you degrade,
Yourselves and liberty.

I'll say no more at present,
The tragedy's too deep,
Think of your Queen and Princess,
In prison how they weep;
You've made a blot in history,
By your infernal rage,
The combined drum beats come, come, come!
To lop you up the stage

This ballad attempted to rouse public support for what was expected to be a short war with France and compassion for the death of its king. It was written in 1793, between January 21, when King Louis XVI was guillotined, and October 16, when Queen Marie Antoinette suffered the same fate. Dr. William Maxwell from Kirkconnel, a friend of Robert Burns, was on the scaffold when Louis XVI was executed. "He soaked his handkerchief in the tyrant's blood to send back to Scotland as a souvenir." (Ellis & Mac a'Ghobhainn: 1989, 54) On January 24, 1793, Britain dismissed the French ambassador, and on February 1, France declared war on England and Holland.

By this time the name of General Charles Francois Dumouriez (referred to in the ballad as Demourier) was well known in Britain. Four months earlier, at the Battle of Valmy, the French Revolutionary Army under Generals Dumouriez and Kellerman had successfully routed an 80,000-man army of Prussians, Austrians, French émigrés and assorted German armed forces who had entered France. Then on November 6, 1792 at the Battle of Jemappes, Dumouriez defeated 14,000 Austrian troops to take Belgium. Following this acquisition, revolutionary France notified England of its resolve to force open the outlets of the river Scheldt. England had long benefited economically from ancient treaties that enabled Holland to control traffic to Antwerp on the Scheldt. Pitt's response to this ultimatum was a swift but undelivered statement: "England will never consent that France should arrogate the power of annulling... treaties..." This undelivered message also included an offer to support recognition of the revolutionary government of France, provided it return to its pre-war frontiers. (Hague: 2004, 325)

Dumouriez, though popular in France, was later suspected of diverting military funds for his own profit. He went on to lose an important battle on March 18, 1793 at Neerwinden against the army of Archduke Charles of Austria. Facing the probability of the guillotine, he defected to the allies. He was eventually given a pension by Great Britain in 1800, where he served as a consultant to the British Army, never returning to France.

The Guillotine

## 27 The Pop-Gun Plot Found Out: Or, Ministers in the Dumps

Sir Frederick Madden's Collection of Broadside Ballads: 8/5134

*Tune: Goddesses; Country Dance Tune, 1650-1701*

In these days of alarm, when our wise Administration,
For the benefit, they say, and the honor of the nation.
Have discovered such base plots, that the man must want his reason,
Who could not see strong symptoms of the symptoms of high treason?
　Hum.hum,hum,&c.

A society of Democrats, called London Corresponding,
They a convention meant to call, which set us all a wond'ring;
They meant to change, I dare affirm, deny it if they can sir,
Our glorious constitution for their Mad Rights of Man, sir
　Hum.hum,hum,&c.

Our sapient Heav'n-born Minister ne'er dreamt of the harm, sir,
That was so near approaching till the meeting at Chalk Farm, sir,
Then each independent pensioner and placemen, one, and all, sir.
Combin'd the system to support, for fear that it should fall, sir,
　Hum.hum,hum,&c.

State Warrants soon were issued, the Traitors to discover,
And a committee appointed which hum'd one another,
Then before the Privy Council, to hear what they would say, sir,
These Citizens were carried; but the order of the day, sir, was.
   Hum.hum,hum,&c.

But sure how hair will stand on end when once I do begin, sir,
The dreadful story to relate of our most gracious King, sir,
How that poison'd arrow, by some plebeian hand, sir,
In his most sacred guts was intended to be cram'd, sir
   Hum.hum,hum,&c.

But, ah the dark design! – what a blessing for the nation! —
Was happily discover'd while 'twas in contemplation:
For had it pierced his Royal paunch, he surely had been dead, sir
Tho' possibly he'd not been hurt if it had struck his head, sir,
   Hum.hum,hum,&c.

Confusion horror, dire dismay, seiz'd ev'ry Loyal breast, sir,
Till le Maitre Smith, and Higgins were each put to the test, sir,
Whose innocence appear'd so clear, the man must have a thick
  skull
Who could not see it was meant for to deceive poor Jack Bull.
   Hum.hum,hum,&c.

'Tis true there was something made that looked like a pop-gun,
Invented, as they say, by that d— n'd informer Upton:
But how a wretch like him, with a new invented harmless thing,
Could frighten a whole nation, to me it is astonishing,
   Hum.hum,hum,&c.

But Treason with the Minister— curse on his vile hypocrisy!
Is Hubbab'd about— but his aim is at Democracy;
Well knowing that its glorious light will soon dispel the evil
That we've too long been troubled with, and chase it to the devil
   Hum.hum,hum,&c.

But Britons, be not dup'd by such base insinuations;
For those that cry stop "thief!" are the rogues that rob the nation
Of their treasure and their liberty— soon the times will alter,
And they will be rewarded with a G—l—ine or h–lt–r,*
   As sure as a Gun, &c.

*Guillotine or halter

The London Corresponding Society held a meeting on April 14, 1794 attended by 2,000 at Chalk Farm (now within the Camden Town district of London) where enthusiastic speeches calling for Parliamentary reform were delivered. The wartime Parliament was alarmed, and on that same day passed a bill to suspend habeas corpus. According to some sources, this enabled the Government to arrest as many as 200 members of L.C.S. and S.C.I. over the coming weeks and hold them initially in the Tower of London without charges or bail. Thirteen were interrogated by a secret committee of Parliament on October 6, and all except one were formally indicted, becoming the "twelve apostles" to face charges of developing a conspiracy to commit high treason. (Bewley: 1998, 165) High treason in this case was plotting against the crown and was subject to the penalty of being hanged, drawn, and quartered.

This song concerns the so-called "pop-gun" incident that took place three days after the Chalk Farm meeting, when a stone was thrown at the King's carriage. It reflects the commonly held view that the Government was hypocritical in its attempts to discourage public support for parliamentary reform by making up the bizarre story about a plot to assassinate the King. On September 29, many daily newspapers carried lengthy accounts of what the *Oracle* in its headline described as a "Horrible Project to Assassinate the King of this Country." (Barrell: 2000, 445)

Release of this fake news months after the incident occurred was timed to shortly precede the October 6 indictment of the seven members of the London Corresponding Society (L.C.S). and five members of the Society for Constitutional Information (S.C.I). The government's case relied upon a government spy, Thomas Upton, who alleged that the L.C.S. had plotted to shoot a poison dart at the King using a popgun disguised as a walking stick. Peter Lemaitre and George Higgins, members of the General Committee of L.C.S., were arrested, followed a few days later by two more members, John Smith and Anthony Beck. All four were artisans or booksellers. They were held in custody for eight months until, on the scheduled day of their trial, the Government dropped all charges due to the alleged death of its primary witness, Thomas Upton. Yet another individual, Irish physician Dr. Robert Thomas Crossfield, was charged, tried separately for conspiracy, and acquitted one week before the trial date of Lemaitre, Higgins, and Smith.

The song confirms that—all things considered—those who cry "stop thief!" are the rogues that rob the nation's people of the treasure of their liberty.

## 28 True Reformers

Wilson, *The Songs of Joseph Mather* (1862): 37

Tune: Fathom the Bowl; S. Baring-Gould, 1794

Come ye patriots bold, whose affections are cold
Toward tyrannical monsters' laws,
Let's true friendship display, and commem'rate the day
That our brethren escaped from their foes:

When bloodhounds of state were most insatiate
For the lives of brave Hardy and Friends,
Heaven lent her kind aid to those mortals betray'd,
And redeemed them from ruffians and fiends,

When arraigned at the bar, Hardy alone like a star,
Though opposed by the infamous Ross;
But alas to be brief, his poor wife died with grief—
Ah who can compensate his loss.

Consolaton to Muir, may his heaven be secure—
Schirving's, Palmer's, Yorke's, Margrot's, and P—'s;
Let's not Gerrald forget, nor the least patriot,
Whose characters admit of no stain.

'Twould be cruel to o'erlook Erskine, Gibbs, and H. Tooke,
Who defeated their wicked design;
May Thelwell and the rest with good Juries be blest,
And their souls through eternity shine.

Into ruin we sink, England's now on the brink,
By its infernal wise men's exploits;
Swift destruction to all who our lives do enthrall
And invade constitutional rights.

This song, another by Joseph Mather from Sheffield, commemorates the acquittal of Thomas Hardy on the charge of Treason and covers other events of these times. Considering that Mather relied on his daughter to help him to read, it illustrates how broad the dissemination of news of these extraordinary events was to locations as far from London as Sheffield.

Undeterred but disturbed by the deportation of the "martyrs" of the Edinburgh meetings, the London Corresponding Society continued pursuing political reform and holding meetings. They held a combined meeting attended by over 2,000 at Chalk Farm on April 14, 1794. Other well-attended meetings were soon held in London, Sheffield, and Halifax. E.P. Thompson, speaking of these times, writes: "This was the harvest, not only of persecution, but also of rising prices and economic hardship." (Thompson: 1966, 131)

This song names many of those imprisoned or transported for their L.C.S. reform efforts and celebrates that Thomas Hardy was judged innocent. Mather includes hopes for a similar outcome for famous pamphleteer John Thelwell, whose trial did not end until December 15, 1794. Both Thomas Erskine, defense council for the reformers, and prosecutor Sir John Ross are mentioned. The third verse refers to the death of Mrs. Lydia Hardy who was with child when her husband was imprisoned in the Tower of London. An L.C.S. publication states that crowds celebrating a naval victory over the French (the Glorious First of June) attacked Hardy's house. Lydia escaped but died soon afterwards in childbirth. Her child was stillborn, the sixth infant death for the couple.

The song mentions Horne Tooke, who with John Wilkes in 1769 founded "The Society of Gentlemen Supporters of the Bill of Rights." Tooke was the second to be tried for treason. Tooke's trial lasted six days, but the Jury only took eight minutes to arrive at a not guilty verdict. The third and last of the prisoners to be tried was John Thelwall, who was also acquitted, after whom all those originally arrested were set free.

Treason trials at that time rarely took more than a day. Hardy's trial took nine very long days with the court often sitting until midnight. Anticipating a guilty verdict, the Lord Mayor called up troops to prevent rioting. But on November 5, Guy Fawkes Day, the jury, after deliberating for three hours, returned a verdict of not guilty. This was greeted with widespread relief and satisfaction all over the country. "Hardy turned to the jury and spoke for the first time during his trial, 'My fellow countrymen, I return you my thanks.' Rejoicing crowds carried Hardy and his attorney Erskine home. They took Hardy's coach along a circuitous route, stopping to cheer in strategic places such as Carlton House and St James's Palace. The Government had overplayed its hand." (Bewley: 1998, 171)

## 29 Serjeant Kite's Invitation to the Swinish Multitude. To be Shot at for Sixpence a Day

Sir Frederick Madden's Collection of Broadside Ballads: 08/5148

Tune: Old Sir Simon the King; Humphry Salter, 1683

Come rouse my good fel - lows to arms, ___
For won - der - ful sums we will pro - mise

And ___ fol - low the sound of the drum,
Which we pos - si - bly nev - er will pay;

If you'd cut a fine fig - ure in sto - ry,
But of this my brave com - rades be cer - tain;

In - list in my re - gi - ment, come.
You'll be shot at for six pence a day.

But of this my brave com - rades be cer - tain;

You'll be shot at for six pence a day ___

Come rouse my good fellows to arms, And follow the sound of the drum,
If you'd cut a fine figure in story; Inlist in my regiment, come:
For wonderful sums we will promise, Which we possibly never will pay;
But of this my brave comrades be certain; You'll be shot at for sixpence a day.
   But of this my, &c

Away with you, silly poor blockheads Who talk of the blessings of peace,
I'll prove to you peace is no blessing, So give over prating and cease;
For war is the only true blessing; Its war brings the soldiers in play,
'Tis war gives the brave an occasion, To be shot at for sixpence a day.
   Shot at &c.

In peace should you chance to be hungry, In vain for some victuals you'll call,
But war gives the soldiers in battle, A breakfast of powder and ball;
And if once you eat this provision, You'll never be hungry again,
For it fills a man's stomach at once, And soon puts an end to his pain,
    When he's shot at, &c.

Peace makes a man idle my boys, And to prove it is wond'rous easy,
For in peace a man's sure to get rich And riches will make a man lazy;
But follow my standard, brave boys, And laziness soon will decay,
For nobody ever got rich, That was shot at for sixpence a day.
    Shot at, &c.

If you live you may chance to grow old, And with it old age will bring trouble,
When you'll fold up your arms and look grave, And exclaim that long life is a bubble,
But be bold, my brave fellows be bold, Drive the cares of old age far away,
For very few ever grew old, Who are shot at for sixpence a day.
    Shot at, &c.

Instead of base sitting at home, At ease with your children and wives,
I lead you to fight against men, Who you never saw before in your lives.
When your captains will gain all the glory, And you all the toil of the fray,
The time now's to catch at the honour, To be shot at for sixpence a day.
    Shot at, &c.

Written to a popular old melody, this satirical song reminds those who consider enlisting that, although they may not survive, they will be paid the immense sum of sixpence a day. Now at war with France, Britain needed to raise its own army and navy to replace the Hessians and Hanoverians that Pitt had originally hired to fight in the lowlands of Holland. "God and King" movements began the propaganda necessary to convince young men to join up. This ballad fueled the other side, leaving little question about how exciting it would be to join an army. The Admiralty's press gangs were out to abscond with those who were needed to man the fleet. The introduction of Pitt's 1795 tax on hair powder became the source of jokes that "enlistment was the fate widely and very easily predicted for barbers and hair dressers." (Barrel: 2006, 163)

According to the late Piers Mackesy, "The state of the army in 1793 was deplorable, in both quality and numbers, and it was to remain short of offensive force throughout the wars." (Dickinson: 1989, 155) Manpower shortages reflected apathy and dissent on the merits of the war, and it became necessary to establish quotas for each county to supply soldiers.

## 30  Lock Jaws: A Ballad

Sir Frederick Madden's Collection of Broadside Ballads: 08/5132

*Tune: Ye Warwickshire Lads and Lasses; Charles Dibdin, Sr., 1769*

Ye Westminster Lads and ye Lasses,
See what in our Parliament passes:
Be dismal and dumb for instead of your Laws,
Billy Pitt is to give you a pair of Lock'd Jaws!
A pair of Lock'd Jaws,
Instead of your Laws;
Billy Pitt is to give you a pair of Lock'd Jaws!

In the middle of our horrible disasters
He lays on this worst of all plasters;
He takes from us bread:—Aye, this is the cause,
We've no use for our Teeth, for he locks up our Jaws!
A pair of Lock'd Jaws!
And Famine's the cause,
We've no use for our Teeth, for he locks up our Jaws!

To his crew he gives Sinecure Places,
To support him in all of our disgraces;
He crams with our Bread their monstrous craws,
While the people are doomed to a pair of Locked Jaws
A pair of Lock'd Jaws,
To feed their dam'nd craws;
For the craws of all craws are the Ministers craws!

Ye Guinea-pigs, Pittites, and Tories,
Ne'er chouse us with rascally stories;
Ye powder your heads while we live upon Straws,
And are doom'd by this Bill to a pair of Lock'd Jaws!
A pair of Lock'd Jaws,
Or to live upon Strawrs
We are doom'd by this Bill to a pair of Lock'd Jaws!

To grant every Turncoate's pretensions
We'er saddled with Places and Pensions;
And while on our loaves they lay their sharp Paws,
To starve us at once they lock up our Jaws!
They lock up our Jaws!
With their terrible paws;
And starve us at once they lock up our Jaws!

We are told of alarms and of terrors
As a screen for the ministers errors;
So, this measure will hide all his criminal flaws,
For, to stifle our clamour, he locks up our Jaws!
A pair of Lock'd Jaws
Will screen all his flaws;
And, to stifle our clamour, he locks up our Jaws!

He persists in his scandalous measures,
And squanders our Blood, and our Treasures:
The Swine have long liv'd on upon mere hips and haws;
Nay, that is too good; so he Locks up our Jaws!
He Locks up our Jaws,
E'en denies hips and haws
And gives to the swine a pair of Lock'd Jaws!

Our Billy compar'd is to no man,
Nor Frenchman, nor Grecian, nor Roman:
He's so full of his tricks, when our purse-strings he draws;
But the trick of all tricks is to lock up our Jaws!
He locks up our Jaws!
When our purses he draws,
And to pilfer our Money he locks up our Jaws!

With Pop guns and Plots he confounds us:
With Barracks and Camps he surrounds us:
By arts such as these the people he awes.
And, back'd by his Red-coats, he locks up our Jaws!
He locks up our Jaws!
While the Bayonet awes,
His Barracks are built, and he locks up our Jaws!

Ye Westminster Lads, and ye Lasses,
Who see what in Parliament passes,
Be steady and firm, or the'll pair down your claws,
For ever be dumb, or now open your Jaws.
All open your Jaws,
Or they'll pair down your claws;
For ever be dumb, or now open your Jaws

This song is a protest against Two Acts of Coercion, the Treasonable Practices Act and the Seditious Meetings Act that passed with a large majority and received royal assent on December 18, 1795. These Acts were designed to stop opposition to Pitt's Government. "He had to protect himself and his administration from political failures, and guard against criticism from George III and the Portland Whigs." (Turner, J: 2000, 84)

After release of the "Twelve Apostles" late in the previous year, momentum for reform built toward what was claimed to be the biggest political meeting yet, held on October 26, 1795 in the fields near Copenhagen House in Islington. L.C.S. sources estimated that 300,000 attended the meeting. (Barrell: 2000, 553) John Binns, a twenty-two-year-old Irishman who had arrived from Ireland just one year before, presided. The gathering remained peaceful and resolved to demand Parliamentary reform, removal of the present ministry, and peace in place of starvation, want, and misery. But the size of such gatherings alarmed the authorities, and the government used a phony ploy to justify passage of these two highly draconian laws.

The melody used for this song, "Ye Warwickshire Lads and Lasses," was first used in the 1769 Jubilee celebration of William Shakespeare.

*A LOCK'D JAW for JOHN BULL*

## 31 Billy is Sick of the War: By Mr. Dyke

Sir Frederick Madden's Collection of Broadside Ballads: 02/0961

*Tune: Oh Dear, What Can the Matter Be; The British Lyre, 1792*

CHORUS: O dear, what can the rea - son be? Dear, dear,
what can the rea - son be? O dear,
what can the rea - son be? Bil - ly grows sick of the war.
VERSE: He pro - mised he'd beat all the French in short time, sir,
Make them have a King, pun - ish them for their crimes, sir,
In - stead of that he sits at home drink - ing wine, sir,
All po - wers are de - clin - ing from war.

CHORUS

O dear, what can the reason be? Dear, dear, what can the reason be?
O dear, what can the reason be? Billy grows sick of the war.

He promised he'd beat all the French in short time, sir,
Make them have a King, punish them for their crimes, sir,
Instead of that he sits at home drinking wine, sir,
All powers are declining from war.

   O dear, what can the reason be, &c.

He promis'd what great things he'd do for the nation,
But damn it, what makes him so fond of taxation,
Good people blame him, both in high and low station,
And say he's asham'd to make peace.

   O dear, what can the reason be, &c.

He said that the French never should Holland take, sir,
The French march'd o'er ice, thousands fled o'er the lake, sir.
My lords, the sweet virgin was in a mistake, sir,
And now he's asham'd to make peace.

    O dear, what can the reason be, &c.

The hectoring Duke of Brunswick first led the way, sir,
Next the King of Prussia came in British pay, sir,
But for fear Black Bess should take his kingship away,
He was forc'd with the French to make peace.

    O dear, what can the reason be, &c.

Now Spain and Germany they have a peace sign'd, sir,
Left Billy in the lurch, raving in his mind, sir,
Why did not they ask his leave, they are unkind, sir,
He despairs now his end, but can't gain.

    O dear, what can the reason be, &c.

There's Black Bess of Russia has sent her fleet here,
For which assistance the British will pay full dear,
But all politicians do now at the farce swear,
And wish for the blessings of peace.

FINAL CHORUS
We all the reason now guess, sir, Now all the reason do guess, sir,
O all the reason do guess, sir, Why Billy's grown sick of the war.

This broadside claims to have been written by Ian Dyke, and is clearly a parody of "What Can the Matter Be?" It is, however, similar to many other songs written at the time by Captain Charles Morris. It tells of "Billy" Pitt's struggles to retain support for Britain's war against revolutionary France. The ballad sheet has the year 1795 handwritten on it, but this may have been added later. Reference is made to the losses of the Duke of Brunswick, who had retreated from the French after the cannonade of Valmy in September of 1792. Pitt's friend, William Wilberforce, had offered an amendment to the king's speech at the opening of Parliament on December 30, 1794 to negotiate with France for peace. (Hague: 2004, 365)

1795 was a disaster for Britain's hopes to retain the first coalition of nations then fighting the French Republic. In January, crossing the ice that held the Dutch fleet in its grip, the French re-occupied Austrian Netherlands and established the Batavian Republic. In May, Prussia signed the peace of Basle, ceding to France territories on the left bank of the Rhine. In June—because his Italian wife told him to—Charles IV, the pathetic King of Spain, signed another treaty of Basle with France, eliminating Britain's sea power in the Mediterranean. (Durant: 1975, 114) Terrible financial shortages, mounting opposition at home, and poor harvests caused Pitt to look for new tax schemes to finance an unpopular war. From 1795 on, Pitt was secretly, and sometimes overtly, looking to end hostilities with the revolutionary government of France. (Hague: 2004, 375)

"Black Bess" in the song was a nickname given to Catherine the Great of Russia. She had maintained a squadron of warships with the British Navy in the Channel from the beginning of the war. But much changed when she died in December 1796 and was succeeded by her son Paul I. (Hague: 2004, 385)

William Pitt

## 32 A New Song

Sir Frederick Madden's Collection of Broadside Ballads: 08/5151

*Tune: Brighton Camp; Thomas Skillern, 1799*

In these disastrous dismal days of Riot, Law, and Libel,
When men almost suspect the right they have to read the Bible;
I'll venture here to sing the truth, may you approve the strain,
And as the way to please you most, I'll strive to give you Paine.

There was a man whose name was Paine, a man of Common Sense,
Who came from Philadelphia here, his knowledge to dispense;
He taught that man had equal Rights, as equal sons of nature
Deriv'd by universal grant by heaven's legislature.

He taught that on the people's will all lawful power depended,
That governors were for the good of the govern'd intended;
And many other wholesome truths, all form'd on reason's plan,
He wrote within a little book, and called it "Rights of Man".

The nation soon approv'd the book, they read and understood it,
But certain rogues whom I name not, with jealous aspect view'd it;
And many a courtly sycophant its page with terror traces,
For if each man should have his right, the rogues would lose their places.

Then Billy Pitt he raised a cry—a cry of consternation,
Which rous'd the roguish and the weak throughout the British nation;
That Church and State were tumbling down, and ruin hover'd o'er us,
The Lords and Parsons stretch'd their throats, and join'd the horrid chorus.

Like Quixote, that renowned knight so fam'd in Spanish tale,
And full as mad stept Edmund forth, equipt in courtly mail;
He from the treasury took a spear, 'twas tipped with gold and pointed,
And on his arm he bore a shield, giv'n by the Lords anointed.

Thus armed with pow'r, he thought divine, he rush'd into the battle,
And on the little stay-maker most furiously did rattle;
He threw his darts sublime about, and rav'd of plots and treason,
But Freedom's Champion stood unhurt, for he was clad in reason.

When courtiers found his arguments could not be overturn'd,
They cunningly concluded he by proxy should be burn'd;
In every town through this good realm, poor Paine was executed,
And what their malice could not reach, the faggot has confuted.

Though buried with the dead he lies, by loyal undertakers,
His spirit still pervades the land and never will forsake us;
We'll drink a bumper o'er his tomb — a tribute of affection,
And wish the sleeping Rights of Man — a speedy RESURRECTION.

This broadside ballad was written after Tom Paine's 1792 conviction, in absentia, for treason. The eighth verse refers to the bonfires used by "Church and King" mobs to burn Paine in effigy. The typeface for this ballad sheet uses the old "ſ" symbol, implying that it was printed before 1800. Only the last verse of this song appears to have been written after his June 9, 1809 death. Perhaps this really refers to the multiple, metaphorical deaths from the bonfires.

Although there had been a time when Paine and Burke were on friendly terms, this ballad describes them in figurative combat. While Paine was burned in effigy in England, France accepted him as a hero. Arriving there in 1792, he was soon appointed to the Assembly. Paine's Assembly vote of January 1793, to spare the life of King Louis XVI, made him a victim of Robespierre's reign of terror; he was imprisoned from December 1793 to November 1794. (Nelson: 2006, 260) It took the guillotining of Robespierre and the intervention of the American Ambassador, James Monroe, for Paine to be released from prison. While confined, he finished his last major work, *The Age of Reason,* which criticized organized religion but recognized the existence of a Supreme Being. Its first of three volumes was published, in both France and Britain, in 1794. (Nelson: 2006, 267)

Shortly after Napoleon Bonaparte, as First Consul, seized power from the Assembly in 1799, his police began to harass Paine. He wanted to return to America, but it wasn't until the election of Thomas Jefferson (1801) and the Treaty of Amiens (1802) that he felt safe to do so. He arrived to a cold reception in Baltimore, but after some time Jefferson helped Paine to acquire a small pension, enabling him to live out his last years on his farm in relative obscurity.

THEOBALD WOLFE TONE.

Chapter 4
# INSURRECTION: 1796–1799

*"I knew Ireland could not of herself, throw off the yoke, I sought for help wherever I could find it."* —Wolfe Tone at his Court-Martial, November 10, 1798

By 1796 Britain had been at war with the French Republic for three years. Concurrently, the British battles for political reform were moving toward infectious insurrections. In fact, the two conflicts became intertwined. In those early days of the Republic, France offered aid to all peoples striving for their liberty. (Weber: 1997, 34) Remembering France's earlier support for the American Revolution, British reform groups like the United Irishmen sent representatives to France, seeking help to overthrow their government and to reform their own inflexible system. An impressive number of British activists obtained access to France through the free Port of Hamburg, including Tom Paine, Wolfe Tone, Napper Tandy, and Archibald Hamilton Rowan. Thomas Muir became involved in 1798, after escaping his transport to Australia. Later, other representatives of the United Irish, such as aristocrat Lord Edward Fitzgerald and activist Arthur O'Connor, met with French representatives elsewhere on the continent.

Plans for French support of the British insurrection relied on massive numbers of British workers to come forward and join with French forces, who would provide ample armaments. This could not be done as long as the Royal Navy's blockade of all French shipping remained intact. To remove the blockade, a complete Strike of the Royal Navy was to be instigated. Once the Royal Navy was curtailed, the plan was to first invade Ireland, where the United Irish were sure that thousands of Irish were ready to join in and throw off their chains. Similar invasions were to follow in Wales, Scotland, and England, where the people were said to be crying for reform. These plans relied upon careful timing, excellent communications, and full support of the people. However, plans went awry and failed miserably, due to extremely poor timing, violent storms, ineptitude at sea, overestimation of support, and Napoleon Bonaparte.

After many false starts and delays, an enormous and well-armed French invasion fleet set sail from Brest in the bitter cold of December 12, 1796 with 43 vessels and 14,450 troops. The highly successful young French General Lazare Hoche was in charge of the expedition. General Grouchy was also on board. Wolfe Tone sailed with the fleet on the *Indomitable*. After skirting storms and the British blockade, some of the fleet arrived at Bantry Bay on December 22 during an easterly gale. Most of the fleet held off till December 30, but were never able to land. Only a handful of this invasion force, including Generals Hoche, Grouchy, and Tone, made it back alive to France.

Two months later, on February 22, 1797, the French landed an invasion force of 1,400 men under the command of Chef de Brigade William Tate, who spoke no French, at Fishguard on the coast of Wales. Tate had served in the American army during the War of Independence. The orders for this invasion were unclear, and few of the soldiers assigned to this expedition had received any training. There was no sign of locals waiting to join with the invasion force, and within 48 hours the French surrendered to the local militia before leaving the point of landing.

Although the timing was off, a highly motivated British Navy went on strike at Spithead on April 15, 1797. The striking sailors had not been paid or granted shore leave for two years, and their wages had not increased since the reign of Charles II. They demanded an end to oppressive usage, short rations, unwholesome food, excessive cruelty, and arbitrary punishment. The strike quickly spread from Spithead to Plymouth, the Nore, and eventually the North Sea Fleet at Yarmouth. Some concessions were won at Spithead, but strikers at the Nore were dealt with harshly, with 29 leaders hanged on the yardarm on June 30. The Great Mutiny is an important chapter in the fight for reform, since much of the Navy consisted of quota men from all areas of Britain and Ireland. Each county was required to send quota men, who often were skilled and literate craftsmen and merchants. Many a night was spent on board ship reading aloud excerpts of readily available cheap copies of *Rights of Man,* with lively discussions on how its contents impacted the lives of sailors. Given that able-bodied seamen working on a man-of-war were harassed, humiliated, and disdained, they eagerly accepted Paine's ideas of freedom and equality. The quota men were a substantial cross-section of the working people of Britain, with a disproportionate percentage from Ireland. Their immediate embrace of the notion of achieving empowerment within the British Navy against great odds shows that the battle for reform was still alive. The word "strike" was coined at this time, because as ships joined the action, they *struck* (lowered) their yardarms to make it more difficult to quickly return to sea. Another signal of a ship's crew joining the strike was to fire a gun and raise the red battle flag; the red flag has continued to represent rebellion ever since. For nearly a month, due to the strike, the British were unable to blockade the French navy, thus leaving the door open for France to invade Ireland. But the French, though elated by Britain's embarrassment, nevertheless failed to exploit it. Despite their repeated promises of aid, the French appeared unable or unwilling to deliver. (Curtin: 1994, 262)

In May of the following year, convinced that French aid would not materialize, Ireland exploded into major violent uprisings against British rule. Though plans were formulated for coordinated rebellion nationwide, they fell apart when almost all United Irish leadership were arrested and ultimately held in Fort George, Scotland. These arrests left only a few leaders, including Edward Fitzgerald, to cope with thwarted plans, broken commitments, and failed communications. The leaders' arrests reduced the insurrection to a number of isolated and almost aimless outbreaks. (Wells: 1986, 137) The most successful battles took place in County Wexford, but that campaign ended at the battle of Vinegar Hill on June 21, where Irish regiments of the British Army ruthlessly crushed the disorganized, under-equipped patriots. In Wexford an image of Catholic massacre and plunder lived on in the hearts and minds of the Irish people. Many Protestants regarded it as a "popish rebellion," and political principle and religious prejudice forbade them from aiding or abetting such a conspiracy.

But France had not given up on Ireland. Three French expeditions sailed to Ireland in 1798, at the urging of radicals including Wolfe Tone, Napper Tandy, and Thomas Muir, the Scottish organizer who had recently arrived in France after escaping from Australia. On August 23, not long after the Irish rebellion had been put down, a small French force of 1,150 experienced troops on board four frigates under General Humbert, who had independently financed this venture, landed in Killala on the west coast of Ireland. Humbert's expedition, though late, garnered considerable support from the Irish population. It was able to win several small skirmishes as it crossed half the country before it was stopped at Ballinamuck by a large force of British troops under General Cornwallis. There the French were taken as prisoners of war, while the Irish were cut down by the hundreds. A second expedition, under the command of Napper Tandy on board a corvette equipped with 270 Frenchmen and a large supply of weapons, arrived in Rutland on September 16 and left immediately upon realizing that the enterprise was hopeless. The third expedition, under the command of General Jean Hardy, included Wolfe Tone and approximately 3,000 men. On October 12 they were intercepted by a British squadron off Tory Island. French losses were 425 killed and wounded and 1,870 captured. (von Pivka: 1980, 67)

Wolfe Tone was among the prisoners taken. He was eventually taken to Dublin, where he pleaded guilty to the charge of hostility to the King and was sentenced to die by hanging. He cheated the hangman by slitting his own throat. He survived, but one account claims that he was told by a surgeon that to move or to speak would be fatal. He replied, "that was the most welcome news you could give me," and died at once.

Many voices were raised, on many fronts, for reform and fair representation. Those voices come down to us, today, in the song sheets of the people.

The Wreck of the French Ship *Le Droits d'Homme* (see page 137)

## 33 The New Irish Drum

R. Wilson, *Paddy's Resource* (1798): 12

Tune: Beggar Boy; Dancing Master, 1650–90

The Fourteenth of July lets never forget,
When Frenchmen espoused fair Liberty's cause—
The Sons of *Hibernia* remember it yet,
And boldly call out *for a new code of laws.*
Praised—Heaven be praised,
The glorious day of UNION is come;
To shake the foundation of vile usurpation,
And tyrants to frighten with LIBERTY's drum

By the tools of oppression, we long were divided,
Superstition and prejudice made us' oft bleed—
But when *all* in friendship are firmly UNITED,
From discord and bigotry then we will be freed.

UNION, UNION, NATIONAL UNION,
Will banish corruption from the *Irish* shore;
So pleas'd and delighted, all parties UNITED,
Religious dissentions will then be no more.

Hail to the bright day may all Irishmen say,
When the sons of old PADDY like brothers will be,
Each face sweetly smiling no tongue e'er beguiling,
But dancing and singing the sweet *gramachee*.
Liberty Liberty — O! sweet Liberty!
Rally the Sons round thy favourite TREE;
The *Green Flag* extend it. Come let us defend it,
*UNITED, determined to die or live Free.*

With taxes and tithes we have long been oppressed,
Placemen and pensioners for to support,
The hard earned pence of the labouring poor,
Is squandered away by an English Court
*Ireland, Ireland* — slumbering *Ireland*!
Under proud England how long will you groan?
Arise from your trance, turn your eyes toward *France*,
And by her example let's tyrants disown.

We oft have been told — but I'm sure It's a lie,
That *England* ought our mistress to be;
Tho' our island is small, yet we are not afraid,
To fight for ourselves our Country for to be Free.
Thunder, thunder *Irish* thunder!
These vile herd of miscreants we'll frighten away —
The *Shamrock* we'll raise it, all nations will praise it,
We will fraternize on that glorious day.

This song appeared in a 1798 New York version of a collection of Irish songs "compiled for the People of Ireland" entitled *Paddy's Resource: Being a Select Collection of Original and Modern Patriotic Songs.* Another book by the same name with the same purpose had more songs in it and was printed in 1796 in Philadelphia, which was then the capital of the United States. The song calls for the Irish people to throw in their lot with the Republic of France.

The idea of encouraging France to assist the United Irishmen to overthrow the British yoke had gained impetus in April 1794, when the radical Irish Reverend William Jackson, an agent on behalf of France, met with Archibald Hamilton Rowan, Wolfe Tone, and others to assess the revolutionary climate in Ireland. The meeting took place in Rowan's cell in Dublin's Newgate Prison, where he was imprisoned for seditious libel after returning from Scotland (see No. 25). At the meeting, Wolfe Tone assumed the task of writing a treatise for the French Assembly, outlining how the Irish people would welcome and join with the French to drive out the British. Tone's document was to be sent by ordinary mail to France via the free port of Hamburg, but on information leaked to authorities by Jackson's English companion, John Cockain, it was intercepted by Dublin Castle. As a result on this betrayal, Jackson was sentenced to death, Rowan escaped to France, and Tone escaped to America. By 1795, a small but vocal contingent of United Irishmen were living in Philadelphia, where Tone and Napper Tandy were joined by Rowan, who had fled France during the Terror. (Weber: 1997, 39)

From the United States, Tone arrived in France on February 2, 1796, under the alias "James Smith," to advocate for a French expedition to Ireland. "He had the support of Pierre Adett, French Ambassador to the States, and brought the hastily revised treatise that had been written in Ireland two years earlier. He had no formal accreditation from the United Irishmen." (Elliott: 1989, 281) Fortunately, enough contact already existed between the United Irish and the French government to assure trusted communication.

The United Irish Crest

## 34 The Tenders Hold, "Or Sailors Complaint"

B. T. Bennett, *British War Poetry in the Age of Romanticism* (1976): 122

Tune: Vicar of Bray; The Quaker's Opera, 1714

Whilst lands - men wan - der, though con - trolled,
Oh, view the ten - der's loath - some hold

And boast the rights of free - men,
Where droops your in - jured sea - men;

Dragged by op - press - ion's sa - vage grasp

From e - ve - ry dear con - nect - ion, Midst pu - trid air, oh,

see them gasp, Oh, mark their deep de - ject - ion

Whilst landsmen wander, though controlled,
And boast the rights of freemen,
Oh, view the tender's loathsome hold
Where droops your injured seamen;
Dragged by oppression's savage grasp
From every dear connection,
'Midst putrid air, oh, see them gasp,
Oh, mark their deep dejection.

Blush then, oh, blush, ye pension host
Who wallow in profusion
For our foul cell proves all your boast
To be but mad delusion.

If liberty be ours, oh say
Why are not all protected?
Why is the hand of ruffian sway
'Gainst seamen thus directed?
Is this your proof of British rights?
Is this rewarding bravery?
Oh shame to boast your tars' exploits,
Then doom those tars to slavery.

When just returned from noxious skies
On winter's raging ocean,
To land the sun-burnt seaman flies
Impelled by strong emotion.
His much loved mate, his children dear,
Around him cling delighted,
But lo the impressing fiends appear
And every job is blighted.

Thus from each soft endearment torn
Behold the seaman languish,
His wife and children left forlorn,
The prey of bitter anguish.
'Reft of those arms whose vigorous strength
Their shield from want defended
They droop, and all their woes at length
Are in a workhouse ended.

Mark then, ye minions of a court
Who prate at freedom's blessing,
Who every hell-born war support,
And vindicate impressing.
A time will come when things like you,
Mere baubles of creation,
No more will make mankind subdue
The work of devastation.

Seamen's anger over impressment, the newly enacted quota system, and long-standing grievances ignited the mutiny which would erupt throughout the fleet. The Navy had not received a raise in pay since the reign of Charles II. Most sailors had not been paid at all for the previous two years. Desertions were so common that shore leaves had not been granted for two years. Inhumane punishments, including flogging with the cat-o'-nine-tails, were dealt out by drunken, sadistic officers for the smallest offense. Crooked merchants teamed up with corrupt Navy pursers to provide short weighted, poor quality provisions to increase their personal profits.

The need to maintain huge navies at this time was complicated by losses from disease and desertion. It is estimated that of the 103,660 deaths recorded during the Napoleonic Wars, 82% resulted from disease, 12% from shipwreck or accident and only 6% from enemy action. Additionally, 113,273 men deserted. (Lloyd 1967: 87)

## 35 The Shan Van Vocht

T. Moylan, *The Age of Revolution* (2000): 22 – Roud 6529

Tune: Shan Van Vauch; P. W. Joyce, 1841

O the French are on the sea, says the Shan Van Vocht;

O the French are on the sea, __ Says the Shan Van Vocht.

O the French are in the bay, __ they'll be here with-out de-lay,

And the O-range will de-cay, Says the Shan Van Vocht

O the French are on the sea, Says the Shan Van Vocht;
O the French are on the sea, Says the Shan Van Vocht.
O the French are in the bay, they'll be here without delay,
And the orange will decay, Says the Shan Van Vocht.

And their camp it shall be where? Says the Shan Van Vocht.
Their camp it shall be where? Says the Shan Van Vocht.
On the Curragh of Kildare, the boys will all be there,
With their pikes in good repair, Says the Shan Van Vocht.

Then what will the yeomen do? Says the Shan Van Vocht.
What will the yeomen do, Says the Shan Van Vocht?
What should the yeomen do, But throw off the red and blue.
And swear they'll be true, to the Shan Van Vocht.

And what colour will they wear? Says the Shan Van Vocht.
What colour will they wear, Says the Shan Van Vocht.
What color will be seen, where our fathers' homes have been,
But our own immortal Green, Says the Shan Van Vocht.

And will Ireland then be free? Says the Shan Van Vocht.
Will Ireland then be free? Says the Shan Van Vocht.
Yes! Ireland shall be free, from the centre to the sea;
Then hurra! for liberty! Says the Shan Van Vocht.

The Shan Van Vocht is that "grand old woman," signifying Ireland. The origin and date of this popular and often quoted song are not known, but it is generally considered to have been written in anticipation of what became the aborted French liberation of Ireland in the later 1790s. However, according to Zimmerman, the first printed version was in *The Nation* issue of October 29, 1842. (Zimmerman: 1967, 133)

This version from Moylan states that "the French are in the bay" but it doesn't say which bay. It could refer to any of the three major French attempts to land a force to aid the United Irish to liberate Ireland. The first attempt sailing from Brest in December of 1796 was the *Armee Francaise en Irlande,* led by Lazare Louis Hoche, the French general who had defeated the revolt in the Vendee; sailing with the fleet was Theobald Wolfe Tone, who sailed as an Adjutant General of the French Army. "The fleet included 43 vessels, 17 of which were ships of the line, 14,450 troops, and more artillery, arms and ammunition for the Irish than Tone could have ever hoped for." (Elliott: 1989, 323)

"It was likely that British intelligence had been forewarned of Hoche's original plan to land at Galway. British Admiral Sir Edward Pellew, sailing the *Indefatigable,* spotted the French leaving Brest and sent word to the blockade fleet under Admiral Colpoys that the French were out to sea; however, in spite of the warning, Colpoys let them slip by." (Dugan: 1965, 37) Acting on sealed orders that were to be opened only after the fleet was at sea, Hoche changed course to sail for Bantry Bay. To confuse the British Naval blockade, his fleet sailed south through a difficult strait in foul weather where they lost several vessels and thousands of men. Hoche sailed on the *Fraternité*, a separate ship from that carrying Wolfe Tone and most of the other senior officers. Hoche's and several other vessels were blown out to the mid-Atlantic, preventing communication with the rest of the fleet and leaving General Grouchy to try to fill his shoes.

Extreme weather and poor seamanship wreaked further havoc. On December 22 the damaged fleet, now under Grouchy, anchored sixteen ships in, and nineteen outside, Bantry Bay. There was much talk about attempting a landing in the mighty storm that persisted for more than a week. Caution eventually prevailed, when Grouchy finally ordered the fleet to sail back to Brest. Only fifteen of the original 43 ships which had sailed in December returned to port.

## 36 The French Invasion

S. Jones, *The Last Invasion of Britain* (1950): 269

Tune: St. Matthew Passion Chorale; J.S. Bach, 1727

Ho,   Bri-tons give at-ten-tion to   what I   have to   say

How   Pro-vi-dence did   fa-vour us   and   mer-cy   did   dis-play;

How   we   were saved in   Pem-broke-shire From   dan-ger of the   Gaul,

When   they at-temp-ted   to   land here With   mus-ket, sword, and   ball.

Ho, Britons, give attention
To what I have to say,
How Providence did favour us
And mercy did display;
How we were saved in Pembrokeshire
From danger of the Gaul,
When they attempted to land here
With musket, sword, and ball.

It was in February,
The three-and-twentieth day,
The French they came to Fishguard
To take our lives away.
Full fourteen hundred of them bold
Did land on British shore,
Such dreadful sight was ne'er beheld
In Pembrokeshire before.

Lord Cawdor sent his loyal men
Rode bold to Fishguard town,
And Major Ackland likewise,
To keep the Frenchmen down.
Lieutenant-Colonel Colby
Rode like a valiant knight,
And for his king and country
Determined for to fight.

And worthy Captain Ackland,
To him praise is also due,
He and his men proved loyal,
Being willing and so true,
And Colonel Knox together,
In full career they went
To face the bloody Frenchmen,
Whose hearts did then relent.

Esquire Chiles of Begelly,
He mustered before day;
And being a loyal subject,
He marched us all away.
He rode himself before us
Upon his gallant steed,
And so to Fishguard town we went
To face the French with speed.

The country folks they gathered
To Fishguard from all parts,
And like loyal men were willing
To try their skill and hearts;
With hooks and knives and pitchforks
To oppose the enemy,
And for their king and country
Courageously would die.

The Frenchmen they desired
The British force to know
Before they did surrender,
They gave a fatal blow.
Two of our countrymen
Courageously did go.
They thought to meet them as their friend,
But met them as their foe.

In answer to the Frenchmen,
Lord Cawdor to them said,
That they were four thousand—
On battle all were bent;
And hundreds more were coming,
Increasing from all parts,
Who solemnly there did declare
To fight with all their hearts.

It was on Friday evening
That they gave up the field;
It was a pleasant sight to see
So many forced to yield.
'Tis not our men, or strength of arms,
But Providence, we own,
Did fight the battle for us
And keep the Frenchmen down.

When they found out our forces
They saw it was in vain
For them to stand engagement—
The case was made so plain.
Twelve hours they did desire,
And would surrender then.
Lord Cawdor he allowed it,
And so did all his men.

God bless our king and country
With plenty, joy, and peace,
And may all French and Spanish
From Britain ever cease.
Likewise all our noblemen—
Bless them with counsel wise
For to be loyal to their king
And face their enemies.

This patriotic Welsh song extols the virtue and military acumen of the proud yeomen of Pembrokeshire, under the command of the bold Lord Cawdor, who expelled the French invasion army from Wales in February 1797. The song exaggerates the role of the Welsh yeomanry but, as stated, providence carried the day. According to E. H. Stuart Jones, this ballad was "transcribed from the dictation of an old man, who used to sing it, by the daughter of Mr. Olive, formerly of the Pear Tree Inn, Jeffreyston, near Tenby." (Jones: 1950, 269) Today the local militia continues to sing the praises of the great defeat of the French Army on the shores of their homeland.

Two months after Hoche's abortive attempt to land at Bantry Bay, the French did land 1,400 men at Fishguard in Wales under the command of an ageing former United States officer, William Tate, from North Carolina. As part of the grand plan envisioned by Wolfe Tone and General Hoche, this small French force was to have been landed in Wales as a concurrent diversion from Hoche's expedition. Tate's expedition suffered like Hoche's, with one delay after another, and was not ready to embark before the few survivors of Hoche's forces had returned to France. Although the diversionary advantage was lost, Tate and his men finally set sail on February 13, 1797.

Tate's expedition was also a convenient means to expel undesirables from France: his force included released convicts, royalists, disruptive regulars, and British prisoners of war recruited earlier by Wolfe Tone. Tone wrote: "saw the Legion Noire reviewed about 1800 men. They are the banditti intended for England and sad blackguards they are." (Thomas: 2007, 60) France welcomed the opportunity to rid itself of such unsavory characters while at the same time testing the revolutionary spirit of the Welsh people.

Tate's French expedition landed at Fishguard on February 22. Once on shore, this undisciplined ragtag army proved impossible for Tate to control. The first night ashore they harassed local cottagers, stole food, and got drunk on bottles of wine that had washed ashore from a recent shipwreck. It is rumored that the next morning local villagers crowded on nearby hills to observe the landing site. The tall black hats worn by local women were said to look like British military helmets to the French, who began to pressure for immediate surrender. Support from the locals was not likely after the antics of the previous night, so the indecisive crew wavered until the local militia arrived, and Tate surrendered.

French Landing at Carregwasted, February 22, 1797

## **37** The Genius of Britain

C. Firth, *Naval Songs and Ballads* (1907): 279 – Roud V18992

*Tune: Plymouth Sound; Broadside, 1777-1844*

The ge - nius of Bri - tain went ho - ver - ing round, For she

feared that fair Free - dom was fled; But she found to her joy that she

was not quite gone, But re - mained with the fleet at Spit - head.

Re - joiced at the news to the Char - lotte she flew, Where fair

free - dom was heard sat en - throned: They all manned the Yards as the

god - dess came in. For — Bri - tain and Free - dom they owned.

The genius of Britain went hovering round,
For she feared that fair Freedom was fled;
But she found to her joy that she was not quite gone,
But remained with the fleet at Spithead.
Rejoiced at the news to the Charlotte she flew,
Where fair freedom was heard sat enthroned:
They all manned the Yards as the goddess came in.
For Britain and Freedom they owned.

The fleet hailed the goddess with three hearty cheers
As she stood on the Charlotte's gangway,
She dropped a sad tear as she looked on her sons
Who so long neglected had lay;
She was led to the cabin fair freedom was there,
True loyalty sat by her side;
Britannia down in a transport of joy:
"All hail to my heroes she cried."

Every ship in the line sent two seamen so brave,
Whom the goddess received with a smile:
They assured her that if they were treated like men
They would still guard her favorite isle.
"Go on my brave sons in the steps you now tread,
Be virtue your guide and your guard,
And god who rules over the land and the sea,
Will your honest endeavors reward."

The Genius of Ireland came in with her harp,
She saluted fair freedom with tears,
They manned the yards to welcome her over,
And every ship gave three cheers,
Success to the seventeen united bright stars,
Let their praise echo round every shore,
And the fifteenth of April will ne'er be forgot
Till Britannia and freedom's no more

This song, written at the Spithead anchorage near Portsmouth during The Great Mutiny of 1797, was also used during the trial of participants in the Strike at the Nore. The *Queen Charlotte*, a 100-gun man-of-war, became the gathering point for two representatives from each of the seventeen vessels that had first joined the strike, referred to as the seventeen bright stars. The song relates the goddess's visit to sailors, where she meets fair freedom, the mythical muse Britannia, and the Genius of Ireland with her harp.

Only 15 percent of the British Navy were volunteers. Quota men comprised as much as 12 percent. These reluctant conscripts, taken from the cities and towns all over Britain, were often educated enough to be able to read the most popular book of the time. They, like the French sailors at Brest and the Dutch at Texel, spent hours between decks reading and discussing Tom Paine's *Rights of Man*. With this background, it was hardly surprising that "A Humble Petition" begging for payment of back pay was drafted by the men at Spithead, the great anchorage of the Channel Fleet just off Portsmouth. (Lloyd: 1967, 87)

On March 7, 1797, copies of "A Humble Petition" were signed by the crews of each ship at the anchorage and returned to the committee on the *Queen Charlotte*, and then forwarded to two of the sailors' best friends in high places: Admiral Howe, who in 1794 had commanded the naval battle of the "Glorious First of June," and Charles James Fox, leader of the opposition in Parliament. The petitions sent to Fox were intercepted by Government agents, so the loyal opposition never saw them. Several weeks later, Howe showed the petition to a member of the Admiralty Board, and a decision was made to send the Channel Fleet back to sea under Admiral Bridport who had just returned to port on March 30. "The Admiralty believed that the best way to control discontent was to order the fleet to sea."(Wells 1986: 85) The Admiralty's order to sail was "telegraphed" to Bridport using the Navy's semaphore system on April 15, and he gave the order to sail that day.

There was no turning back; strike was inevitable. Ships' crews were to watch for a signal from the *Queen Charlotte*. A single cannon shot followed by the raising of the Blood Red Flag would be the sign to start the strike. Instead, the action began quietly on each ship with boats launched from the *Queen Charlotte* and the *Royal George* circulating within the fleet. In the boat from the *Royal George* was Valentine Joyce, a former radical publisher from Ireland, and now the principal leader of the seamen. The boats hailed each ship's crew, advising them that all officers were permitted to remain on board, and that the men were to obey all orders except an order to sail, until the grievances cited in the "Humble Petition" were met. Each crew was to pick two delegates and send them to a meeting of a fleet committee that evening on *Queen Charlotte*. (Dugan: 1965, 92)

The *Queen Charlotte* Laying at Spithead

## 38 British Tars Rewarded

Sir Frederick Madden's Collection of Broadside Ballads: 2/1010 — Roud V22857

*Tune: O'Donnell Abu; Joseph Haliday, 19th C.*

The tars of old England have long toiled in vain,
From the time of King Charles down to this present reign,
But their royal master their wages doth raise,
So join, British sailors, in King George's praise.
The fleet of Lord Bridport, the terror of France,
Petitioned the throne that their pay might advance,
Their petition was granted each petition redressed,
In the heart of each seaman great George he is blessed.

No longer neglected no longer forlorn,
Brave seamen will wander, dejected our scorn;
Their petitions are granted, each grievance made known,
Soon met with redress at the foot of the throne.
Cheer cheer British seamen, your sails now unfurl,
Against our proud foes soon defiance we'll hurl,
Our toils are rewarded advanced is our pay,
Success to those seamen whom gained us the day.

Adieu pretty Nancy of Portsmouth, adieu,
When your William is absent, I pray then be true,
To fight for our King, and our country we go,
Our toils are rewarded we'll face the proud foe.
Farewell to our children, farewell dearest wives,
We don't leave you distressed, though we venture our lives,
Our pay is advanced which you shall receive,
Then dry up each tear, girls, and cease for to grieve.

Then my boys hoist your sails, to old England adieu.
No longer oppressed, to you will prove true,
You shall find that a tar is both grateful and brave,
We'll die but our King and our country we'll save
Three cheers lads, three cheers lads, we lose sight of land,
In defense of our country we'll join heart and hand,
And when we return boys, we'll drink, dance and sing,
With wives and with sweethearts, so God save the King.

The Great Strike dragged on until the sailors' favorite admiral, "Black Dick" Howe, who had received their petition weeks earlier, was sent to negotiate with the men of the Channel Fleet at Spithead. All their grievances were heard, and a list of approximately 75 of the most abusive officers, with Admiral Colpoys at the top, was presented to Howe. In the meantime, the fleet at Plymouth joined with the men at Portsmouth, sending delegations and petitions of support. The Nore sent men to observe the Spithead negotiations.

Howe proceeded with open negotiations with the men. While this went on, Bridport was receiving urgent messages from the Admiralty to set sail, because their inaccurate intelligence had told them that the French fleet had set sail for Ireland from Brest. It was not, however, until Sunday, May 14th that agreement was finally reached to remove some 114 officers, and the remaining issues were partially resolved. The next day a major celebration of unity in the fleet was held with Lord and Lady Howe as the guests of honor. (Manwaring: 1935, 115) The outcome was lauded by the press and this popular broadside on the subject was widely distributed.

## 39 The Muse's Friendly Aid

C. Gill, *Naval Mutinies of 1797* (1913)

Tune: Fathom the Bowl; S. Baring-Gould, 1794

The Muse's friendly aid I must invite,
Likewise a pen that's taught itself to write,
No wit I boast, but am by fancy led
To search the deep caverns of my hollow head,
If Attic rhyme Apollo there has stored,
I'll here deposit all her favorite hoard.

In days of yore when rich and poor agreed,
Poor served the rich and rich the poor relieved.
No despotic tyrants then the womb produced
But mutual all, each loved, and none abused,
But now how dreadful is the scene reversed,
We're blest with birth, but with oppression cursed.

The theme I treat on is our royal tars,
Whose god like spirits rival even Mars,
From their supineness now their souls are roused
To rod and yoke no longer are exposed.
But all alike, each swears he will be true,
And tyrants ne'er their former course renew.

At Spithead first their noble blood was fired;
Each loved his King, but one and all aspired;
To serve each other was their full intent,
And if insulted were on mischief bent,
But still their country's cause they would maintain,
Against the rebels or the power of Spain.

Then at the Nore the lions boldly roused
Their brethren's cause at Spithead they espoused.
Each swore alike to King he would be true,
But one and all the tyrants would subdue,
Their gallant hearts the chains of bondage broke
Not to revolt, but to evade the yoke.

In Yarmouth next old Neptune reared his head,
Awake my sons, the watery monarch paid—
The torpid vapours from your souls remove—
Inspire yourselves with true fraternal love.
Unto the Nore repair without delay,
There join your brothers with a loud Huzza.

The worthy god's advice the heroes took,
Each broke his chains and off the panic shook
Unto the Nore their gallant ships they steered,
Whilst brethren cheered them as each ship appeared.
Oh Britons free, usurp no tyrant sway,
Protect your tars, and then they'll you obey.

This ballad was found in papers taken from the 64-gun man-of-war *Repulse* that had arrived from Yarmouth during the last days of the strike at the Nore. According to correspondence from the Public Records office at Kew, Richmond, Surrey, this ballad was used as evidence against the Nore mutineers and was entitled "An Insidious Song."

Two delegates had been selected from the fleet anchored at the Nore, given £20 to cover the cost of their journey, and sent to observe the strike negotiations with Admiral Howe at Spithead. These delegates returned on May 18th with news of the settlement that had been reached four days earlier. When the Spithead agreement was read at the Nore, resolving only some of the petition's concerns, it was greeted with jeers. Richard Parker, the newly appointed chief spokesman of the fleet at the Nore, allegedly said, "You've brought three pennyworth of ballads for our twenty pounds." (Dugan 1965: 196) Parker was a good choice as spokesperson for the Nore; he had previously served as a naval officer, and later taught school before he was sent as a quota man to become an able-bodied sailor.

A new list of sailors' grievances was drafted at the Nore. The eight articles in this new petition included, in addition to all things granted at Spithead, concerns that had not been conceded there: the granting of shore leave, stipulation that no officer expelled from a ship for bad conduct would be returned for service on another ship, and more equitable distribution of prize money from resale of captured enemy vessels. These demands were strengthened when, on May 19, delegates of twelve ships from the fleet at Yarmouth joined the delegates of twenty ships at the Nore in signing the new petition. (Gill: 1913, 389)

The sailors at the Nore did not fare as well as those at Spithead. They were accused of ingratitude for the concessions made to the sailors at Spithead, and of disloyalty at a crucial time when an invasion of Britain was imminent. The government spread rumors that the mutineers were planning to sail up the Thames to shell the city of London. The Admiralty cut rations and stirred public opinion against the strikers. A five hundred-pound reward for the capture of Richard Parker was posted in Sheerness. Parker had also resisted proposals by some of the men to defect with the ships to France. The end rapidly arrived on June 15 as, one by one, the ships raised the white flag of surrender. Richard Parker himself then surrendered and was taken the next day to Maidstone jail, where government agents interrogated him.

His court-martial started on Thursday June 22. He was found guilty on Monday June 26 and sentenced to death on June 30, 1797.

RICHARD PARKER.

## 40 President Parker

Roy Palmer, *The Oxford Book of Sea Songs* (1986): 166 – Roud 1032

Tune: President Parker; Palmer, 1824

Ye gods a-bove pro-tect the wi-dow, and with pi-ty look on me.

Oh help me, help me out of trou-ble and out of all ca-la-mi-ty,

For by the death of my dear Par-ker fate to me has proved un-kind;

Though doomed by law he was to suf-fer I could-n't e-rase him from my mind.

Ye gods above protect the widow, and with pity look on me.
Oh help me, help me out of trouble and out of all calamity,
For by the death of my dear Parker fate to me has proved unkind;
Though doomed by law he was to suffer I couldn't erase him from my mind.

Brave Parker was my lawful husband, my bosom friend I loved so dear;
And at the moment he was to suffer I was not allowed to come near.
In vain I asked in vain I strove, ay, three times o'er and o'er again;
But still they replied, "You must be denied, and must return on shore again."

I thought I saw the yellow flag flying, the signal for my husband to die.
A gun was fired as they required when they hung on the yard so high.
I thought I saw his hand a-waving, bidding me a last farewell;
The grief I suffered at this moment no heart can paint, no tongue can tell.

My fainting spirit I thought would follow the soul of him I loved most dear;
No friend or neighbor would come near me to ease me of my grief and care.
Then unto the shore my Parker was brought, most scornfully to be laid
   in the ground,
And for to get my husband's body an artful scheme I quickly found.

Indeed of night when all was silent, and many thousands fast asleep,
I and three more went to the shore and to his grave did quietly creep.
With trembling hands we worked with shovel and digged his body from
   the cold clay,
And there I had a coach a-waiting to carry to London his body away.

And there I got him decently buried, and then the doleful task was done;
I soon did finish the doleful task that his imprudence had begun.
Oh farewell, Parker, thou bright genius, thou were once my only pride;
Though parted now it won't be long till I am laid down by your side.

Ye gods above protect the widow, and with pity look on me.
Although my Parker was hung for mutiny there were worse men in the
    wars than he.
All you who hear my tender ditty do not laugh at me in disdain,
But look on me with an eye of pity, for it is now my only claim.


This is the best known of all the songs of The Great Strike, telling of Ann McHardy Parker's ordeal. Things were very rough for the mutineers at the Nore after their surrender. Parker was brutally interrogated by government agents at the Kent County gaol in Maidstone. His court-martial started on June 22, he was found guilty on June 26, and he was sentenced to death on June 30. In all, 29 men from the Nore were hanged, and many more were flogged or deported to Australia.

Before Richard Parker's death, his wife Ann had traveled to London and daily petitioned the Queen for leniency for her husband, but her pleas fell on deaf ears. She somehow managed to arrive in Rochester on the night of June 29, and there she found a market gardener who took her down the Medway to Sheerness at the break of dawn. Three times she attempted to get close enough to speak to her husband before he jumped to his own death, cheating the hangman of satisfaction. That night, Mrs. Parker exhumed his body from his tidewater grave with the help of three other women, and smuggled it to London where she obtained a Christian burial for him at the chapel of St. Mary Matfelon, Whitechapel, the original of which had been the headquarters of Wat Tyler's mutinous encampment in the peasants' revolt of 1381. St. Mary Matfelon was destroyed in the bombing of World War II.

It would be many years before true reforms were instituted in the British Navy.

## 41 The Battle of Blorris Moor

Trinity College J.D. White Collection: OLS X-1-532 no 163

*Tune: Adieu Sweet Lovely Nancy; Harding B17(175a), 1796-1853*

As - sist now, you Mu - ses, and grant me no ex - cus-es,

Con - cer-ning a few ver-ses, it's trea-son I am sure,

By the deeds of Col-onel Bar - ber, we dare in - sist no far-ther:

He's a per - fid - i-ous vil - lain who be - trayed us, I am sure.

Assist now, you Muses, and grant me no excuses,
Concerning a few verses, it's treason I am sure,
By the deeds of Colonel Barber, we dare insist no farther:
He's a perfidious villain who betrayed us, I am sure.

They were lads of good behaviour, no heroes could be braver,
Until O'Brien and Lynch deceived us and swore our lives away;
For the sake of cursed gold in store, those perjured villains swore,
And left us bleeding in our gore on the 29th of May.

Belfast may well remember when tyrants were in splendour;
All in their pomp of grandeur, they bound us to a car,
With our infantry advancing and our cavalry a-prancing,
And glittering arms glancing, all in their pomp of war.

The hills and dales were crowded, from every part surrounded,
The streets were strongly guarded most shocking for to see;
Our drums did loudly rattle, like Tartars going to battle,
Or like lambs led on to slaughter, bleeding for liberty.

They held a consultation to find some information,
And in his exultation, the Colonel he did say:
This day you shall be rewarded, and with the guilt you ne'er will be
    charged,
And your pay shall be enlarged on, if you make a discovery.

A few moments we stood a-musing, our senses began confusing;
Smiling we refused him, and made him this reply:
We own we did the harm against the laws of arms,
And our souls you cannot harm—we have but once to die.

Altho' we are young and tender, to you we will not surrender,
And Hibernia's bold defenders we will always constant prove;
We own we are united, and by death we'll not be affrighted,
But in hopes to be requited by Him who rules above.

When we received our sentence, we knelt down to repentance,
Looking for our acquaintance, and for mercy we did call;
They formed a hollow square, and the guard stood front and rear,
And our breasts we did prepare to receive the deadly balls.

Their guns they then presented, and our tender hearts they entered,
Which makes our friends lament for to see our destiny,
To see those heroes four lie bleeding in their gore,
On the plain who dyed all o'er, most shocking for to see.

To search the learned pages and number the outrages,
And all the learned sages of genuine wit and skill,
It's not the want of education but the want of toleration,
With grief and vexation I must drop my trembling [quill].

Membership in the United Irishmen peaked in Belfast and Dublin by 1797. By then much of their activity was well known to a huge cadre of government informers imbedded throughout their ranks. Informers revealed that recruitment was spreading even to the Monaghan Militia, recently deployed to Belfast along with the Scottish Reay Fencibles, and identified four Irish soldiers who were ringleaders in recruiting soldiers into United Irishmen. These ringleaders were court-martialed, sentenced to death, and summarily shot. "Thousands of soldiers were summoned to witness the executions and then marched past the bullet-riddled bodies of their unfortunate comrades." (Curtin: 1994, 172) The words to the song imply that the bodies of the four slaughtered were left to rot in their gore for at least 13 days after being slaughtered. This incident was one of hundreds of atrocities that were intended to deter hopes and plans for the French to help throw off the yoke of English oppression.

This sad dirge imagines the feelings of the men killed in this incident. A significant side story is the demise of the *Northern Star* newspaper, the printed voice of the United Irishmen. Proving that they got the intended message when marched past the four bullet-riddled bodies, a group of Monaghan Militia went on to attack and destroy the *Northern Star* presses; the edition of Monday May 15–Friday May 19, 1797 was its last. The paper did not rise again until the Chartist Movement in 1837 named its paper "*The Northern Star*" in tribute to the United Irish.

Ballads of this style spread the word throughout Ireland, exposing many horrors against those dedicated to the cause of freedom. Nancy Curtin says,

> The message of the ballads was simple. Ireland was ruled by tyrants. Only a union of Catholic and Protestant could overthrow these oppressors. The record of government travesties against the people was vividly exposed. The French were allies in the cause of Irish liberty and would offer timely assistance to Irish patriots. The choice was between freedom and slavery. (Curtin: 1994, 200)

Scottish Reay Fencibles

## 42 Edward

R. Wilson, *Paddy's Resource* (1798): 119

Tune: When Bidden to the Wake or Fair; William Shield, 1782

What plaintive sounds strike on my ear!
They're Erin's deep-ton'd piteous groans,
Her harp, attun'd to sorrow drear,
In broken numbers joins her moans.
In doleful groups around her stand
Her manly sons (her greatest pride),
In mourning deep, for by the hand
Of ruthless villains Edward died.

Th' assassin horde had him beset,
As slumbering on a bed he lay,
Arise, my Lord, Swan cries, up get,
My prisoner you I make this day.
Unaw'd our gallant chief up steps,
And in his vengeful hand he takes
His dagger keen—quite hard it gripes,
Then to the savage crew he speaks

"Come on who dare—your courage shew,
Gainst Erin's steady children's chief,
Your burthen'd soul at single blow
I'll from your body soon relieve."
Fear-stricken at his manly form,
The blood-stain'd tribe, save Swan, back drew;
Who from our chieftain's potent arm
Receiv'd a stroke that made him rue.

Aloud he shriek'd, then Ryan came
Unto his aid with trembling steps;
Mean caitiff Ryan, lost to shame,
With deeds most foul was full your cup.
Like vivid lightning at him flew,
With well-aim'd point, our hero sweet,
The dastard's blood he forthwith drew,
And left his bowels at his feet.

So wide the gash, so great the gore,
That tumbling out his entrails came:
Poor grov'ling wretch! you'll never more
Attempt to blast unsullied fame;
A baser death should you await,
The hangman's rope—not Edward's hand,
The gallows-tree should be your fate,
Your life deserv'd a shameful end.

Next came on Sirr, half dead with fear,
Deep stain'd with crimes his guilty mind,
He shook all through, by Edward scared,
Like aspen leaf before the wind;
With coward step he advanc'd slow,
Dreading to feel our Edward's might,
Tho' eager for to strike a blow,
Yet fearful to appear in sight.

Assassin-like, he took his stand,
Behind the door—and there he stood,
With pistol charg'd in either hand,
So great his thirst for Edward's blood;
Upon his brows stood imp of hell,
Within his heart a devil foul,
Dire murder dire, and slaughter fell,
Had full possession of his soul

His bosom friend suggested then.
A bloody deed—a devil's act
An hell-fram'd though… ARISE YE, MEN,
Revenge, revenge the horrid fact.
Sound, sound aloud the trump of war,
Proclaim that Edward's blood is spill'd!
By traitor's hand, by coward Sir,
Revenge! Revenge! for Edward's kill'd.

According to Paul Weber, Lord Edward Fitzgerald, a Protestant aristocrat and dedicated radical, had joined fellow aristocrat and United Irishman Arthur O'Connor to meet with French government representatives in Hamburg, Germany, and Basle, Switzerland in May 1796. They had made contact with General Hoche and helped to foster the December 1796 attempted invasion at Bantry Bay. Hoche actually dealt with O'Connor and Wolfe Tone separately, and those two only met in France after most plans were laid. (Weber: 1997, 49–51) After the aborted 1796 French invasion, O'Connor was to go again in 1798 to the continent as emissary of the movement to arrange a new invasion and revolution in Ireland.

United Irishmen's plans to launch a full-scale rebellion in concert with a French invasion were thrown a devastating blow when on February 28, 1798 O'Connor was arrested at Margate in Kent, just prior to embarking to coordinate with the French. The government rounded up most of the United Irishmen leadership as they met at Leinster on March 12. Fitzgerald was able to escape, and as commander of the United Irish Forces in Dublin, he then set the date of May 23 for the revolution to commence. Fitzgerald correctly assumed that spies had already reported to government security forces at Dublin Castle that over 100,000 oathbound members were awaiting orders to begin the fight. Tired of waiting for word from France with most of the country under martial law, and knowing government would strike any moment, the revolution could no longer wait.

Fitzgerald moved among safe houses in Dublin until he was fingered by an informer, Francis Magan, for a £1,000 reward. (Bartlett: 2004, 29-30) Major Henry Sirr, with a small detachment of yeomen, broke into Fitzgerald's room on May 19, just four days before the revolution was to start. Fitzgerald fought the intruders, killing one, but he was felled with two bullets. He died in jail, but not before the rebellion had begun.

## 43 Father Murphy: Or the Wexford Men

Sir Frederick Madden's Collection of Broadside Ballads: 12/8638 – Roud 3020

*Tune: Boulavogue; Maidin Domhnaigh, 1802*

You Roman Catholics throughout this nation, Of no persuasion I speak but thee, Keep fresh in date the year nine-ty eight, Since we lost the pride of our coun-try, I mean that he-ro, brave Fa-ther Mur-phy, that for your sake fought for li-ber-ty. When vio-lent pitch caps most la-ce-ra-ting on your heads were placed in this coun-try.

You Roman Catholics throughout this nation,
Of no persuasion I speak but thee,
Keep fresh in date the year of ninety-eight,
Since we lost the pride of our country,
I mean that hero, brave Father Murphy,
That for your sake fought for liberty,
When violent pitch caps most lacerating
On your heads were placed in this country.

On Whit Sunday we got uneasy
To break the chains of our country,
We took up arms to defend God's garments,
And raised the green flag of liberty.
The Caernarvon Cavalry we did oppose them,
The first lieutenant we took down,
And Captain Donovan, that rode before them,
He never went back to Caernarvon town.

On Oulart Hill we first showed our valour,
Where nine hundred of the north Militia on the ground did bleed,
With deadly risk and fame advancing,
To Enniscorthy we marched with speed;
The loyal townsmen gave their assistance,
We'll die or conquer, they all did say,
And the Hessian Cavalry made no resistance,
And along the pavement the footmen lay.

Our trumpets sounding, with valour bounding,
Our drums a-beating and our men reviewing,
Like triumphant heroes that feared no danger,
We marched for Wexford in the afternoon.
On the Rocks we took up headquarters,
Early next morning at eight o'clock,
The British army sallied out their forces,
Our guns men gave them a woeful shock.

We took the town, and we drank like topers,
We fought the soldiers and cavalry,
The troops retreating with dread and danger,
They dare not face our artillery.
We marched to Ross, and got intoxicated,
We fought three battles on the one day,
First in the morning we did them storm,
At the second volley they ran away.

When reinforcement came down upon us,
Just in the evening, with fire and smoke,
We were forced to leave them, the town then blazing,
On our retreatment burned Scullabogue;
In Carrick we for some time waited,
We were preparing for Gorey town,
In Tubberneering we feared no danger,
Our Irish heroes they cut them down.

Our guns at Gorey like hail did shower,
Our pikemen did rally all round the field,
Their cavalry they made no resistance,
The foot soldiers they lay on the green,
We marched to Comer, and fought the soldiers,
We travelled round through the Colliery,
They stole our guns, which left us disarmed,
We lost our lives in Kilkenny.

If we had conduct to march on forward,
And not returned back to Gorey town,
We would have saved the lives of ten thousand heroes
That died in Arklow—God rest their souls.
It was by their means Father Murphy was taken
On our retreat towards Castlemore,
He was brought to Tullow and used severely,
This blessed priest they burned him sore.

Here's a health to you, brave County Wexford,
Throw off the yoke and to victory come,
Let no man think we gave up our arms,
For every man has his pike and gun.
So now my friends, the time is approaching,
All in one body we will appear;
We'll be commanded by some pious teacher,
Like Father Murphy and his Shelmaliers.

Without leadership from United Irishmen in Dublin and Belfast, the rebels were out of touch with each other throughout the country. The result was chaotic. The signal to start the revolution on May 23 was that the Dublin to Belfast Stagecoach would be stopped. (Curtin: 1994, 258) This was only partially accomplished, so the revolution could not proceed as planned. It became impossible to stem devastating reprisals from government forces who acted on well-documented intelligence of United Irish plans in Dublin, Belfast, and their adjacent territories.

Oddly, in 1798, Dublin Castle suffered from a complete lack of information on the extent of support for the revolution in County Wexford. (Bartlett: 2004, 65) The support should have been predicted because of the years of provocation by the predominantly Protestant militia of Wexford, known to be excessively violent. There was also the North Cork Militia, assigned to the area and well known for "pitch cap" torture methods. Even so the explosion of resentment and sectarian violence in Wexford matching the violence shown by the Government forces was not anticipated.

This broadside ballad presents a sectarian interpretation of the fighting, demonstrating how small, local acts could escalate and sweep people into unexpected action. Father John Murphy, curate of the chapel of the tiny village of Boolavogue, was one of many people who were reluctantly drawn into a spontaneous uprising. As late as the morning of May 26, "Father Murphy previously advocated the surrender of arms, only to be swept into the field in a wave of warm sympathy for unfortunate parishioners." (Wells: 1983, 140) Later that day a brief skirmish occurred when Murphy and some forty parishioners were confronted by a group of twenty volunteer cavalrymen from Camalin, a nearby village. The cavalrymen had burned down a house while searching for weapons. Incensed parishioners fought the cavalrymen, killing two, including the lieutenant in charge. This encounter led to massive reprisals and the burning of Father Murphy's chapel as well as 170 houses. Seeking strength in numbers, the people of Boolavogue joined with others at nearby Oulart Hill, where they became part of a group of 1,000 patriots. The raggle-taggle group, including Father Murphy, went on to win several battles, each time adding more people to their band. This went on until June 21 when they were finally attacked by a large government force at their camp on Vinegar Hill. Father Murphy was among those able to escape from that battle. Many gave in but Murphy believed they could maintain the revolt until what they considered to be the imminent arrival of the French. (Wells: 1983, 144) Father Murphy was ultimately separated from the rebels and on July 2 he was captured, taken to Tullow, and condemned to death for treason by a military tribunal. He was hanged, decapitated, and his head was impaled on a spike to warn other traitors to the Crown. Yet many survivors of this tragedy fought on in small guerrilla-style bands for another five years.

Father Murphy

## 44 Rouse, Hibernians

O' Bradaigh, *Songs of 1798* (1982): 20

*Tune: Willie was a Wanton Wag; Aria Di Camera, 1727*

Rouse, Hi-ber-nians, from your slum-bers! See the mo-ment just ar-rived
Im-per-ious ty-rants for to hum-ble Our French bre-thren are at hand.
Vi-va la, U-ni-ted he-roes, Tri-um-phant al-ways may they be,
Vi-va la, our gal-lant bre-thren They have come to set us free.

Rouse, Hibernians, from your slumbers!
See the moment just arrived
Imperious tyrants for to humble
Our French brethren are at hand.

> CHORUS
> Vive la, United heroes,
> Triumphant always may they be,
> Vive la, our gallant brethren
> They have come to set us free.

Erin's sons, be not faint-hearted
Welcome, sing then "Ca ira"
From Killala they are marching
To the tune of "Vive la."

To arms quickly, and be ready,
Join the ranks and never flee,
Determined stand by one another
And from tyrants you'll be free.

Cruel tyrants who oppressed you,
Now with terrors see their fall!
Then bless the heroes who caress you,
The Orange now goes to the wall.

Apostate Orange, why so dull now?
Self-willed slaves, why do you frown?
Sure you might know how Irish freemen
Soon would put your Orange down.

This song tells of the French squadron that eventually landed at Killala Bay on the west coast of Ireland in August of 1798. Though ill-prepared, Catholic residents of Connacht rallied to join in the fight for Ireland's liberation and to end the Orangemen's influence. According to Zimmermann, "this song was found on a scrap of paper thrown from the pocket of the mother of Dougherty, a United Irishman killed in autumn of 1798 at Delgany in County Wicklow." (Zimmermann: 2002, 160)

The invading squadron was under the command of General Jean Joseph Amable Humbert, a veteran of campaigns with the recently deceased General Hoche who had led the first French fleet to Ireland two years earlier. Humbert was one of the few survivors of the wreck of the French battleship *Le Droits d'Homme*, following that earlier attempt to land in Bantry Bay. Tired of waiting for the contentious United Irishmen to reach consensus, Humbert financed his own expedition and took off, landing without opposition in Killala on his birthday, August 22. "He broke open his sealed orders for *the March and Operations for General Humbert*. To his surprise they were for an invasion of England." (Dugan: 1965, 414) In Killala he soon doubled his army with willing, starving, Irish recruits. Communication was a big problem, since only a few of the French spoke even a little English and most of the Irish spoke only Gaelic; however, they rapidly arranged to march inland.

At Castlebar on August 26, Humbert outflanked a British force of more than 10,000 under General Gerard Lake, and most of the British retreated in terror. Two hundred of Lake's militia joined Humbert after the battle. When news of this defeat reached General Charles Cornwallis, the King's high commander in Ireland, he feared another Yorktown and marched over 20,000 men toward Castlebar. Aware of the British advance, Humbert took his army to Sligo on another lightning march, hoping to link up with a second French invasion group whose plans to land further north did not bear fruit.

On September 8, Cornwallis's enormous army surrounded Humbert's small force near Ballinamuck. He tried to surrender his entire army, but Cornwallis accepted only the surrender of the 844 Frenchmen. After disarming the Irish the King's men butchered about four hundred of them where they stood and hunted the rest down on horseback. (Dugan: 1965, 419)

## 45 Tone's Grave

E. Hayes, *Ballads of Ireland, v. 1,* (1919): 233 – Roud 9313

Tune: Bodenstown Churchyard; Thomas Davis, 1845

In __ Bo - dens-town Church yard there is __ a green grave,

And wild - ly a - long it the win - ter winds rave,

Small shel - ter, I ween, __ are the ruined walls there,

When the storm sweeps down on the plains of Kil - dare.

In Bodenstown Churchyard there is a green grave,
And wildly along it the winter winds rave;
Small shelter, I ween, are the ruined walls there,
When the storm sweeps down on the plains of Kildare.

Once I lay on that sod—it lies over Wolfe Tone—
And thought how he perished in prison alone,
His friends unavenged, and his country unfreed—
"Oh, bitter," I said, is the patriot's mead.

For in him the heart of a woman combined
With a heroic life, and a governing mind—
A martyr for Ireland—his grave has no stone—
His name seldom named, and his virtues unknown.

I was woke from my dream by the voices and tread
Of a band, who came into the home of the dead;
They carried no corpse, and they carried no stone,
And they stopped when they came to the grave of Wolfe Tone.

There were students and peasants, the wise and the brave,
And an old man who knew him from cradle to grave,
And children who thought me hard-hearted; for they,
On that sanctified sod, were forbidden to play.

But the old man, who saw I was mourning there, said,
"We come, sir, to weep where young Wolfe Tone is laid,
And we're going to raise him a monument, too—
A plain one, yet fit for the simple and true."

My heart overflowed, and I clasped his old hand,
And I blessed him, and blessed every one of his band;
"Sweet sweet! 'tis to find that such faith can remain
To the cause, and the man so long vanquished and slain."

In Bodenstown Churchyard there is a green grave,
And freely around it the winter winds rave—
Far better they suit him—the ruin and gloom
TILL IRELAND, A NATION, CAN BUILD HIM A TOMB.

Thomas Osborne Davis, author of this popular broadside, was a famous revolutionary Irish writer, organizer, poet, and chair of the Young Ireland Movement of the 1840s. Born in 1814, he lived and wrote more than four decades after the death of Tone. It is said that he wrote this song after seeing Tone's unmarked grave. The lyrics call for restoring the grave to make a place for commemorating this hero. His words appeared on many broadsheets and in many books, encouraging the construction of the site where annual commemorations of Wolfe Tone's life are held today.

Wolfe Tone, a founding member of United Irishmen, had been instrumental in negotiating plans with the French. He had sailed with Hoche's failed expedition to Bantry Bay in 1796. In the fall of 1798, he was on board the newly renamed 74-gun French ship *Hoche*, flagship of Commodore Bompard's very professional fleet of eight frigates, wearing the French uniform of *chef de brigade*. General Jean Hardy, leading the expedition, commanded the 3,000 experienced troops on board, and they carried many field guns. The fleet set sail from Brest on September 6, 1798, heading to Tory Island, intending to reinforce Humbert who had landed at Killala in mid-August.

Off Tory island on October 12, they encountered British ships as well as foul weather, and in this battle many of the French vessels were damaged. Tone's commander asked him to leave in a fast frigate with dispatches to France. But Tone replied, "Shall it be said that I fled while the French were fighting the battles of my country?" (Jones/2: 1950, 223) He stayed with the *Hoche* and, after two hours of severe losses, the fleet surrendered to the British and he was taken prisoner.

Tone was sent to Dublin in chains, where he was court-martialed and sentenced to death. The military court refused him the right of a firing squad and sentenced him to be hanged. The night before he was to be hanged, he attempted to take his own life by cutting his throat with a knife he had concealed. He didn't die immediately from his wound, but one legend says that he died a week later, after learning that the civil courts had suspended his sentence.

Francis Burdett

Chapter 5
# WAR: 1800–1815

*"Government was guilty of the oppression of an enslaved and impoverished people."* —Francis Burdett

War against France pressed on, despite growing resentment by the increasingly impoverished British working people. Thanks to Francis Burdett, William Cobbett, and the mythical General Ludd the battle for working class freedoms persisted through the long war years, and another step was taken toward abolishing slavery in the British Empire. The sham of a separate Irish government came to an end, and a short peace with France paused years of battle against Napoleon. This era ended with yet another war, this time against the United States.

Prime Minister Pitt was bent on curbing dissent from Ireland and in 1800, his government applying economic pressure and he himself promising to work for Catholic enfranchisement, forced the Irish Parliament to dissolve. On January 1, 1801, the Union Act went into effect, dissolving the modern parliament of Ireland—which had existed only since 1782—and forming the United Kingdom. Ireland received 102 seats in the House of Commons and 45 in the House of Lords. Pitt also attempted to deliver his commitment for enfranchisement but the King defeated his efforts. Instead of contesting the King's hostility, Pitt and his veteran cabinet resigned, having presided over more than seventeen of the most turbulent years in the status quo's struggle to prevent democratic reform.

King George then appointed Henry Addington, a vocal opponent of Catholic enfranchisement, as Prime Minister. Weary of Britain's war against France, Addington sent Lord Cornwallis, of Ireland and Yorktown fame, to Amiens to negotiate a peace treaty, signed on March 25, 1802. When the French representative arrived in London bearing the signed treaty, the common people unbridled the horses and pulled his carriage by hand through the streets, shouting "Vive la Republique Francaise! Vive Napoleon!" The English upper class flocked to Paris, excited to see the fashions and splendor of the victorious Bonaparte court. Wounded and rejected British sailors and soldiers were dumped back on the impoverished streets to fend for themselves. Most of the sailors who were promised prize money never received a penny. Wheat prices were two and a half times higher than when the war began, and wheat continued to set the standard of living for the common people. High prices and the General Enclosure Law of 1801 enabled farmers and their landlords to line their pockets and influence the ever increasing enclosures of land, which deprived the poor of the common ground that had sustained them for centuries, making land and agriculture objects of speculation.

With the Peace of Amiens, France and Britain would work together. British radicals realized that they could not expect help from the French Republic to achieve reform. Now reform was up to the remaining faithful, whose efforts were still plagued by poor planning, bad luck, and government informers. Innocent, even distinguished citizens were caught up in sweeps made possible by the suspension of habeas corpus. Conspiracies and attempted uprisings were put down. Colonel Despard was hanged along with six other United Britons on February 21, 1803 while up to 20,000 witnesses looked on. (Conner: 2000, 254) Robert Emmet was hanged, drawn, and quartered on September 20.

But a little over a year after peace was signed, Britain realized that Cornwallis's deal to cede Malta to the French was a bad move; war resumed with France on May 18, 1803. Parisian sojourners rushed back to London and out went the press gangs to replenish depleted ranks. Addington soon resigned and Pitt agreed to serve again as Prime Minister. Napoleon set his sights on crossing the channel and taking Britain before she could gear up for a solid war effort. In desperation the British government raced to reassemble its navy and army. The common people, wanting nothing of wars that resulted in slaughter and famine, were bombarded with broadside ballads painting Bonaparte as the tyrant to end all tyrants with his sword pointing at the heart of the British Lion. The "Warning Drum" resounded from every street corner, as everyone learned that the French "have horns," "they were digging a tunnel to get at the English maidens," and that they would come and "drink old England dry." The propaganda began to work, and while Bonaparte built his invasion fleet, England made ready for the attack.

By August of 1805, Bonaparte had incurred huge debt assembling a massive invasion force. He needed the Spanish Navy to distract the Royal Navy in order to knock out the British blockade, but he had to wait for Admiral Villeneuve and the Spanish fleet to arrive. The combined fleets were now months overdue, and the newly formed Russian-Austrian alliance threatened France from the north. On August 26, Napoleon reluctantly gave up the idea of invading England. Fifty-four days later, on October 21, off Spain's Cape Trafalgar, the combined fleets of France and Spain were destroyed by the British Navy led by Admiral Horatio Nelson. For a time, the people of Britain breathed easier and modestly supported the war effort.

Prime Minister Pitt's untimely death in January 1806 meant important changes in Parliament. The incoming Grenville and Fox Ministry of All the Talents (Bi-Party Coalition Government) brought more abolitionists into the cabinet, enabling William Wilberforce and Charles Fox to advance the abolitionist campaign in the Commons, while Lord Grenville advocated it in the House of Lords. On March 25, 1807, an Act for the Abolition of the Slave Trade was passed, 283 to 16. Fully ending slavery in the British Empire would take another 26 years, but this Act reflected the temper of the new Parliament.

Countering Britain's blockade of the French coast, in 1806 Napoleon established the Continental System, an all-European trade embargo against Britain. Heightened unrest throughout Britain led to major recession by 1810. Massive unemployment, high grain prices, and shortages of other commodities resulted in widespread starvation and food riots. In this financial crisis, the ideals of reform threatened to re-emerge. Imprisoned for seditious acts were John Gale Jones of the London Corresponding Society, who spoke up for the starving majority; Sir Francis Burdett M.P., who called for Jones's release; and William Cobbett, publisher of the *Weekly Register*, who published Burdett's speech.

The Luddite movement emerged in 1811 in Nottinghamshire, Yorkshire, Lancashire, and Cheshire. The mythical General Ned Ludd broke into textile factories and smashed the new wide-frame looms operated by non-apprenticed labor who turned out shabby work. When America's President James Madison declared war on Britain in June of 1812, trade and the working people were further devastated. In the next year over 12,000 troops were diverted from both war efforts to quell the Luddite movement, but not before considerable damage was done to manufacturers.

In October 1813, Napoleon was defeated by the combined armies of Austria, Prussia, and Russia at Leipzig. The French lost nearly 75,000 men; the opposition, 54,000. When Napoleon's marshals refused to continue fighting, he abdicated by signing the Treaty of Fontainebleau on April 13, 1814 and was then banished to the Mediterranean island of Elba. The Treaty of Paris, signed May of 1814 with relatively lenient terms for the French, returned the Bourbon monarch to the throne. Once again, wealthy British admirers of all things French flocked to the continent. Caroline, the Princess of Wales and estranged wife of George IV (now the unpopular Regent) tried to visit Napoleon on Elba. "The emperor in the middle of public works and reconstruction, was unable to receive her appropriately and asked her to defer the little visit." (Lean 1970: 114)

The American "War of 1812" ended when the Treaty of Ghent was signed on December 24, 1814. Its biggest battle was fought after the war was officially over. Andrew Jackson's American troops stunningly defeated the British army at New Orleans on January 8, 1815. Over 2,000 British troops were killed, while only thirteen Americans perished.

The wars, for a time, were over, but the workers lost out again with enactment of dreadful Corn Laws.

## 46 A New Song: Pitt and the Union

Bodleian Library: The Harding Collection, B 14(314)

*Tune: Casey's Jig; James Aird, 1788*

Come neigh-bors at-tend while I tell you a sto-ry,
of a cun - ning young blade whom they call Bil-ly Pitt,
Who, gull - ing John Bull of his cash and his glo - ry,
On a no - ta-ble scheme to re-pair them has hit.
This Bil - ly long time to pre-vent our u-ni - ting,
And lo - ving o - ther had hung up the boys,
Now he flat - ters him-self that be-cause we've done fight - ing,
An U - nion he'll car - ry with-out a - ny noise.

Come neighbours attend while I tell you a story,
Of a cunning young blade whom they call Billy Pitt,
Who, gulling John Bull of his cash and his glory,
On a notable scheme to repair them has hit.

This Billy long time to prevent our uniting,
And loving each other had hung up the boys,
Now he flatters himself that because we've done fighting,
An Union he'll carry without any noise.

But why should our isle be united to Britain,
With debt overwhelm'd and with taxes assess'd,
Why because as of late by the Clerk he has written,
They may take our all from us and leave us the rest.

Good neighbours a tempest appears to be brewing,
And hark the wind whistles a terrible squall,
Shall Irishmen then be involved in the ruin
By putting their backs to a tottering wall.

Says the Clerk to ensnare you, your wealth is transcendent!
But with Ireland for this to an Union agree?
We know that before we became independent,
United with England no riches had we.

The Clerk he informs us the Romans and Sabines
United, some thousands cen'tries ago!
But the latter rememb'ring the flames of their cabins,
And rapes of their daughters would fain have said no.

The Sabines United thus laid the foundation,
Of the power, the grandeur, the greatness of Rome;
And thus for the sake of a "separate" nation,
Must Ireland Unite to be beggar'd at home.

Seven provinces also we're told by the Clerk
United and broke from the oppression of Spain;
But the parallel here leaves us all in the dark,
For they never returned to th' oppressors again.

Arrah paddy beware, there's snake in these offers,
For, Billy can gild, whilst he poisons the pill;
And tis sure do you see when he emptied your coffers,
He'll send them all back for the boys to refill.

Let England and Europe still wrangle, but neighbours
What has our little island to do with the strife?
Let Paddy enjoy the fruits of his labours,
And Billy may fight all the days of his life.

Let traitors the rights of their country surrender,
And barter their love and their virtue for gold;
But the sons of Hibernia strong do defend her,
As they ne'er be bought, so they ne'er will be sold.

Then neighbors uniting in bonds of affection,
Prepared for the worst for the best let us hope,
And may he who'd betray us to foreign subjection,
Like Judas receive his deserts on a rope.

Dublin, December, 1798

This Dublin broadside ballad, dated December 1798, tells of Ireland's objection to losing its limited independence. Ireland had its own Parliament since 1297, but it became subservient to England's Parliament with the passage of Poynings' Law in 1495. Then, in 1652, Cromwellian laws disenfranchised all Catholics in Ireland. Ireland's Parliament continued, with limited powers, until a major reform was enacted in 1782. In 1793 the Irish Parliament passed the Catholic Enfranchisement Act that allowed Catholics to vote for members of Ireland's Parliament but continued to disallow them to be seated as members.

The Irish rebellion of early summer 1798 convinced Pitt to abolish the five-century-old Irish Parliament altogether by proposing the Act for the Union of Great Britain and Ireland. He reasoned that union would give Britain control over Ireland and release additional Irish resources for the war effort. To establish union, the Irish Parliament had to vote its own demise. England employed every form of 18th century persuasion to secure this vote. Pitt made a sincere promise to obtain Catholic emancipation. It was estimated that each vote in the Irish Parliament for the union cost the Crown 4,000 guineas.

Despite considerable opposition in Ireland, the Act of Union was passed by both the Parliaments of Britain and Ireland. George III signed the "United Kingdom of Great Britain and Ireland Act" in August of 1800 to become effective on January 1, 1801. Immediately after the Act passed, Pitt began to work on his promised Catholic emancipation bill. He felt that with the support of the cabinet he would be able to enlist the King's approval. But the King refused to break his coronation oath to uphold the Anglican Church. Suffering from this defeat, Pitt resigned on February 5, 1801 after eighteen years as Prime Minister, but for only three years.

The passage of the Act of Union and the failure of Catholic enfranchisement only aggravated the differences between Ireland and Britain and led to more than a century of continued vicious oppression.

# 47 On Peace, By Mr. Fox

Bodleian Library: The Curzon Collection, b. 21 (91) — Roud V21649

*Tune: Young Spencer the Rover; Broadside, 1844-56*

Wel - come sweet peace blood thirs-ty war be gone

Too long thy mi-se-ries Bri-tons have sus-tained.

Too long se-vere dis - tress by thee brought on,

Has with des-po-tic sway in Eng - land reigned.

Welcome sweet peace blood thirsty war be gone,
Too long thy miseries Britons have sustained.
Too long, severe distress by thee brought on,
Has with despotic sway in England reigned.

Be-gone fell monster heaven born peace appears
With the emblem of sweet concord in her hand.
O her gentle presence every bosom cheers
And speaks felicity throughout the land.

Now broils and dreadful conflicts will subside.
Now human blood no longer will be shed.
No longer through accurst tyranic pride
Will shocking tales of thousands slain be read

Now seaman will the briny main forego
No longer war their comforts will dismay
The sweets of languid life again they'll know
And perfect happiness with friends enjoy.

Now will the soldier's toils be at an end
Within his cot again he will find repose
Again he'll see each long deserted friend
And taste the bliss that rural life bestows.

Now commerce will again hold up her head,
And unmolested rove from shore to shore
Now plenty will her sweets profusely spread,
And hungers piteous cries be heard no more.

Now all the industrious will employment find,
Drooping mechanics will again be blest
Genius long grieved to mirth will be inclined
And poor mans wants completely be redressed.

Now agriculture will be seen to thrive
The fallow soil will fertile soon be made
Nature around will seemingly revive,
And bounty be in every scene displayed.

Now rustics will resume their wonted glee
The aged peasant will his song renew
The village maids again will joyous be,
And children will their alley sports pursue.

Now hills and valleys smiling will appear
The tinkling sheep bell pleasingly will sound
The shepherds pipe again will charm the ear,
And flocks delighted gambol o'er the ground.

Now universal happiness will reign
The sorrows of the poor will quickly cease
Long separated friends will meet again,
And each will hail the blest return of peace.

Entered at stationers Hall & Published according to act of Parliament,
November 16th 1801 by G Fox, No 13, Charlton Street, Fitzroy Square.

Published in mid-November 1801, this ballad celebrates the expectation of peace presented in the formal preliminaries to the Treaty of Amiens, signed in London on October 1. It is naively optimistic about the return of universal happiness and prosperity. It closes its eyes to the state of inflation and high unemployment. Seeing an end to the devastating carnage of war could have been reason enough to celebrate. The war in the Caribbean alone was horrendous: in eight years between the outbreak of war and the peace of Amiens the British army had sent 89,000 officers and men to the Caribbean, and lost 70 per cent of them. The total losses for army, navy and transport crews were believed to be near 100,000.

The song's optimistic view of the return to peace ignores the impact of the Monarch's insistence on continuing exclusion of Catholics and dissenters from Parliament. As important as Britain's embracing the end of hostilities should have been government spies' reports of increasing militancy of the United Briton's movements in the north of England. Activities in northern cities had initially centered on strongly worded petitions for price controls and calls for minimum wages during the expanding recession, but the government had summarily dismissed such petitions, and now it appeared that insurrection was likely. A wing of those remaining in the London Corresponding Society also became more revolutionary and merged with the militant United Britons.

The short-lived Peace of Amiens was signed at the Amiens Hotel de Ville on March 25, 1802. Representing Britain at Amiens was Lord Cornwallis of Yorktown and Dublin Castle fame. Napoleon's brother, Joseph, represented France. Thus began a short and fragile cessation of hostilities.

London celebrates Peace

## 48 Old Middlesex, Burdett, and Freedom For Ever!

Bodleian: Harding Collection B22 (229) – Roud V40789

*Tune: The Miller of Dee; Village Opera, 1729*

FREE sons of old Mid - dle-sex, ral - ly once more,

And your fran - chise main - tain in the rights of e - lec - tion;

We'll tri - umph a - gain, as we tri - umphed be - fore,

And the tools of the court meet our man - ful re - jec - tion,

Some new men - di-cant slave May our suf - frage crave,

Shall such re-pre - sent us in se - nate? NO, NE - VER

For a - gain, with one voice, We'll u - nite, by our choice,

Old MID - DLE-SEX, BUR - DETT, AND FREE-DOM for - e - ver!

FREE sons of old Middlesex, rally once more,
And your franchise maintain in the rights of election;
We'll triumph again, as we triumphed before,
And the tools of the court meet our manful rejection,
Some new mendicant slave
May our suffrages crave,
Shall such represent us in senate?—NO, NEVER!
For again, with one voice,
We'll unite, by our choice,
Old MIDDLESEX, BURDETT, AND FREEDOM forever!

For the Traders in Justice, in Chains and Bastilles,
Again the vile tools of corruption may struggle,
And Bow Street its thief catchers, scamps, alguazils,
Combine to maintain the political juggle.
Shall such a vile crew,
Boys dictate to you,
The candidate fit for election?—NO, NEVER!
Then again with one voice,
We'll unite by our choice,
Old MIDDLESEX, BURDETT, AND FREEDOM forever!

The mountebank Doctor of Downing-street chose
To dose you before with his pills of corruption;
And Pitt and Dundas, with immaculate Rose,
May again hope to dupe you without interruption.
Some pigmy they'll get,
Some treasury pet,
Their vassal—but shall we elect him?—NO, NEVER!
For again with one voice,
We'll unite by our choice,
Old MIDDLESEX, BURDETT, AND FREEDOM forever!

No Treasury mandate we'll ever obey,
That marks to our choice some political gander;
The Freedom of Middlesex we'll never lay
At the feet of a needy, expectant, court pander.
Staunch BURDETT we know,
Corruption's fell foe;
Shall he ever betray or deceive us?—NO, NEVER!
Then again with one voice,
We'll unite by our choice,
Old MIDDLESEX, BURDETT, AND FREEDOM forever!

Avaunt!—trading justices!—vile alguazils!
Ye vermin infesting our free constitution:
Biscuit contractors, ye lords of Bastilles,
Seek elsewhere reward for your base prostitution.
Corruption and bribe
May compensate your tribe,
But shall they our suffrages purchase?—NO, NEVER!
Again with one voice,
We'll unite by our choice,
Old MIDDLESEX, BURDETT, AND FREEDOM forever!

Unite, sons of Freedom, to Brentford away,
Elections Free Banners shall there be unfurl'd;
To BRITAIN's true CHAMPION we there shall display
A test of our zeal that shall challenge the world.
The friend of man's right,
Of Freedom the light,
Shall Middlesex FREEMEN abandon?—NO, NEVER!
For again with one voice
We'll unite by our choice,
Old MIDDLESEX, BURDETT, AND FREEDOM forever!

Printed by C. Mercier and Co. Northumberland-court, Strand — Copies may
be had by applying at the Ben Jerusalem's Head Great Wild Street

This 1802 campaign song supported MP Francis Burdett, a rising star of political reform. He campaigned for the same seat that John Wilkes fought to retain 34 years earlier. The 1802 election was the first for the new United Kingdom of Britain and Ireland. Burdett won one of two seats for Knights of the Shire of Middlesex. Brentford (in verse 6) was then the county seat of Middlesex, site of its election hustings. The air suggested in the manuscript, "Success to the Duchess Wherever she Goes," could not be found.

As an independent, Burdett opposed suspension of habeas corpus and other attempts to suppress individual freedoms. He championed prison reform, which made him incredibly popular with the working class. (Dinwiddy: 1980, 17) He was highly aware of the disgraceful treatment of prisoners in Coldbath Field Prison, commonly referred to in Middlesex as "the Bastille."

Years earlier, Edward Marcus Despard, whose distinguished military service included important positions in the West Indies and on the Spanish Main, had been held at Coldbath without charges. Returning to Britain and awaiting reassignment, he was erroneously rounded up and incarcerated on April 18, 1798—along with others throughout England, Scotland, and Wales—under the 1794 Suspension of the Habeas Corpus Act. The round-up came just weeks before the 1798 Irish Rebellion. With extensive lobbying by his African wife, Catherine, and the support of Burdett, Despard was finally released three years later without ever being charged with a crime.

Due to the authorities' paranoia, Despard was arrested again on November 16, 1802 while attending a meeting of forty workingmen in the Oakley Arms tavern. This time he was charged with sedition and sentenced to be hanged, drawn, and quartered. Despard's old friend Horatio Nelson spoke in Despard's behalf, but the sentence was only reduced to one of hanging and decapitation after death. Lord Nelson also solicited a pension for Despard's wife. (Pocock: 2002, 87) MP Sir Francis Burdett gave Mrs. Despard some money and paid her way to visit her family in Ireland.

# 49 Bold Robert Emmet

O Lochlainn Colm, Irish Street Ballads (1960): 172 – Roud 3066

*Tune: The Wandering Harper; Crosby's Irish Musical Repository, 1808*

The struggle is over, the boys are defeated,
Old Ireland's surrounded with sadness and gloom,
We were defeated and shamefully treated,
And I, Robert Emmet awaiting my doom.
Hung, drawn and quartered, sure that was my sentence,
But soon I will show them no coward am I,
My crime is the love of the land I was born in,
A hero I lived and a hero I'll die.

CHORUS
Bold Robert Emmet. the darling of Erin,
Bold Robert Emmet will die with a smile,
Farewell companions both loyal and daring,
I'll lay down my life for the Emerald Isle.

The barque lay at anchor awaiting to bring me
Over the billows to the land of the free;
But I must see my sweetheart for I know she will cheer me,
And with her I will sail far over the sea.
But I was arrested and cast into prison,
Tried as a traitor, a rebel, a spy;
But no one can call me a knave or a coward,
A hero I lived and a hero I'll die.

Hark! the bell's tolling, I well know its meaning,
My poor heart tells me it is my death knell;
In come the clergy, the warder is leading,
I have no friends here to bid me farewell.
Goodbye, old Ireland, my parents and sweetheart,
Companions in arms to forget you must try;
I am proud of the honour, it was only my duty—
A hero I lived and a hero I'll die.

Struggles for reform continued throughout the British Isles during the Peace of Amiens, though it seemed clear that French support for reform efforts was most unlikely. Nevertheless, in 1802 Robert Emmet went to Brussels as a representative of the remaining United Irishmen, and to visit his brother, who had recently been released from Fort George Prison in Scotland. Thomas Emmet had been arrested a few days before the 1798 Irish rebellion and been confined in Fort George Prison with other United Irishmen. At this point France was encouraging Ireland to time its uprising as a diversion from France's pending invasion of Britain. Under Emmet enough optimism remained to try one more time.

The Irish uprising of 1803 was doomed before it began: in July, a supply of ingeniously conceived weapons employing explosives was accidentally detonated at one of the United Irishmen's weapons depots on Patrick Street, seventeen days before the uprising was planned to begin. When the uprising started on July 23, its plans were skewed, resulting in a complete disaster, including the demise of the United Irishmen.

Emmet escaped, but was finally arrested on August 25, found guilty of high treason on September 19, and hanged, drawn, and quartered on September 20. His eloquence elevated him as a hero patriot, and his execution made him a martyr of the Irish cause. The sweetheart referred to in the song is Sarah Curran, daughter of the noted lawyer John Curran, who had defended Wolfe Tone and other United Irishmen in 1798. Sarah later married a British army officer who fought in the Peninsular War. Robert Emmet's brother, Thomas Addis Emmet, who was released during the brief Treaty of Amiens, immigrated to the United States where he became a successful lawyer.

"The failure of Robert Emmet's Rebellion broke the backbone of the [United Irish] Society in Ireland; and the United Irish leaders on the Continent never again managed to put new heart into united affairs at home." (Weber: 1997, 177)

**ROBERT EMMET, ESQ.**
EXECUTED SEPTEMBER 20th, 1803,
**IN THOMAS STREET,**
**DUBLIN,**
FOR HIGH TREASON,
*IN THE 22nd YEAR OF HIS AGE.*
Robinson, Typ.

## 50   The Ploughman's Ditty

Bodleian: Curzon b. (130) — Roud V12282

Tune: He That Has the Best Wife; Sailor's Opera, 1745

BE - CAUSE I'm but poor   And slen - der's my store,

That I've no - thing to lose   is the cry,   Sir, ___

Let who will de - clare it   I vow I can't bear it.

I give all such pra - ters the lye,   Sir.

I give all such pra - ters the lye,   Sir. ___

Being an answer to that foolish question
**"What have the poor to lose?"**

BECAUSE I'm but poor, And slender's my store,
That I've nothing to lose is the cry, Sir;
Let who will declare it, I vow I can't bear it,
I give all such praters the lye, Sir.

Tho' my house is but small, Yet to have none at all
Would sure be a greater distress, Sir;
Shall my garden so sweet, And my orchard so neat,
Be the prize of a foreign oppressor?

On Saturday night, 'Tis still my delight,
With my wages to run home the faster;
But, if Frenchmen rule here, I may look far and near,
For I never shall find a pay-master.

I've a dear little wife, Whom I love as my life,
To lose her I should not much like, Sir;
And 'twould make me run wild, To see my sweet child
With its head on the point of a pike, Sir.

I've my Church, too, to save, And will go to my grave,
In defense of a church that's the best, Sir;
I've my King too, God bless him! Let no man oppress him,
For none has he ever oppressed, Sir.

British laws for my guard, My cottage is barred,
'Tis safe in the light or the dark, Sir;
If the squire should oppress, I get instant redress,
My orchard's as safe as his park, Sir.

My cot is my throne, What I have is my own,
And what is my own I will keep, Sir;
Should Boney come now, 'Tis true, I may plough,
But I'm sure that I never should reap, Sir.

Now do but reflect, What I have to protect,
Then doubt if to fight I should choose, Sir;
King, Church, Babes, and wife, Laws, Liberty, Life;
Now tell me I've nothing to lose, Sir.

Then I'll beat my ploughshare, To a sword or a spear,
And rush on these desperate men, Sir;
Like a lion I'll fight, That my spear now so bright,
May soon turn to a ploughshare again, Sir.

The Peace of Amiens began to dissolve; it became clear that Napoleon was building a huge force and planning to invade Britain. Most British people did not want to resume war, and those in power resorted to issuing broadside ballads to rally support. This one was written by Hannah More, a moralizing playwright and poet who, with her sisters, also ran schools. Her work with the Society for the Abolition of Slavery and the anti-slavery sentiments expressed in her famous "Slavery, A Poem" (1788) did not, however, translate into concern for British working poor. She did not favor other reforms; she praised Edmund Burke, and her pamphlet *Village Politics* was written to counter the spreading influence of Paine's *Rights of Man*.

"My plan of instruction is extremely simple and limited. They learn, on weekdays, such coarse works as may fit them for servants. I allow of no writing for the poor. My object is not to make fanatics, but to train up the lower classes in habits of industry and piety." (Young/Ashton: 1956, 239)

If this song had any play at all among the intended recipients of its wisdom, surely it was because of its inherent humor. One doubts that "if the squire should oppress, I get instant redress" would get much agreement from oppressed agricultural workers.

## 51 Nelson's Death and Victory

Bodleian Library: Firth Collection c.12(39) – Roud 522

*Tune: Death of Nelson; Richard Grainger, 1972*

Ye sons of Britain in chorus join and sing:
Great and joyful news is come to our royal king.
An engagement we have had by sea
With France and Spain our enemy,
And we've gained the glorious victory
Again, my brave boys.

On the twenty-first of October at the rising of the sun
We formed the line for action, at twelve o'clock begun.
Brave Nelson to his men did say:
"The Lord will prosper us today.
Give them a broadside, fire away,
My brave British tars."

Broadside to broadside our cannon balls did fly,
And small shot like hailstones on the deck did lie.
Their masts and rigging we shot away;
Besides, some thousand on that day,
Were killed and wounded in the fray,
On both sides, brave boys.

Heaven reward Lord Nelson and protect his men.
Nineteen of the combined fleet was sunk and taken then;
The *Achille* blew up amongst them all,
Which made the French for mercy call.
Nelson was slain by a musket ball,
Mourn, England, mourn.

Many a brave commander in tears he shook his head,
But yet their grief was no relief for Nelson he was dead.
It was a fatal musket ball
Which caused our hero for to fall.
He cried, Fight on, God bless you all,
My brave British tars.

Huzza! valiant seamen, for we have gained the day,
Tho' you've lost a bold commander who on the deck does lay:
With joy we've gained the victory,
Before me death I now do see.
I die in peace, bless God, said he,
The victory is won.

Let's hope this glorious battle will bring a peace
That our trade in England may flourish and increase,
And our ships from port to port go free,
As before let us with them agree,
May this turn the heart of our enemy,
Huzza! my brave boys.

Many versions of this patriotic song exist; this may be one of the oldest. The tune was adapted by Richard Grainger in modern times. Some broadsides mistakenly put the battle in August; others say that Nelson was killed by a cannon ball. There may have been more broadside ballads written about the Death of Nelson (October 21, 1805) than on any other subject, except for perhaps the death of Napoleon or that of Queen Caroline.

A French marksman in the rigging of the *Redoubtable* hit and mortally wounded Nelson, who died three hours later, after learning that the British had won the battle. "Lord Nelson's corpse was floating head-down in a large barrel of brandy lashed upright on the main deck of the *Victory* as she wallowed under tow, towards Gibraltar." (Pocock: 2003, 208) The *Victory* had major damage requiring repairs before it could sail back to Britain. It is said that sailors on the *Victory* managed, with the help of a drill and straw, to sip from that barrel. Thus the shanty line: "a drop of Nelson's blood wouldn't do us any harm." (Hugill: 1861, 151)

The ballad refers to the explosion on the *Achilles*, a French battleship of 74 guns. It is interesting to note that Admiral Hood captured a vessel of the same name and capacity at the Battle of the Glorious First of June in 1794. That (now British) warship and its French replacement of the same size and name were both at the battle of Trafalgar. (von Pivca: 1980, 95)

Returned to London, the body of Nelson was carried to Saint Paul's Cathedral, but it required great pressure on officials to allow the men of the *Victory* to march in the procession. As Nelson lay in state at Saint Paul's, his first mourner was Caroline, estranged wife of George IV, the Prince of Wales, who had a private visitation. The thousands of people who jostled to file past the coffin alarmed the authorities who feared a riot.

The victory at Trafalgar did not assure immediate peace, but a grateful nation mourned the loss of a true hero and felt relief from the threat of invasion. Nelson's courage and determination gave Britain the will to continue the war against Napoleon.

Lord Nelson's funeral

## 52 The Voice of Africa

Bodleian Library: Johnson Ballads 1952 – Roud V30283

*Tune: Caledonian Hunt's Delight; Gow's Reels, 1788*

Ye Bri - tons, a - rouse! Now the mor - ning is gleam - ing

The sun - beams of Peace shed their ray on your isle;

Your ban - ners un - ferl'd, o'er the world have been stream - ing,

Dis - pla - cing Am - bi - tion's foul tints by their smile:

To whom shall poor A - fri - ca, lost and ne - glect - ed,

Ap - peal for her rights, or un - fold her sad care;

A - ban - doned by you, she, a - las! Un - pro - tect - ed,

Re - signs e - very home and ex - pires in des - pair!

"Ye Britons, arouse! Now the morning is gleaming:
"The sun beams of Peace shed their ray on your isle;
"Your banners unferl'd, o'er the world have been streaming,
"Displacing Ambition's foul tints by their smile:
"To whom shall poor Africa, lost and neglected,
"Appeal for her rights, or unfold her sad care;
"Abandon'd by you, she, alas! Unprotected,
"Resigns every hope, and expires in despair!

"Ah! Where now those prospects, so false and deceiving,
"Those hopes that elated each African's breast?
"Those dreams of wild fancy, we, fondly believing
"Thought Africa's sons soon like *men* shall be blest:
"And why did your country thus mock and deceive us,
"Why aught did we know but the base galling chain?
"Why sip'd we of Freedom?—and then, worse to grieve us,
"Consign us to Slavery's dire thralldom again!

"O Britain! Thou chiefest of isles in the ocean,
"Where Freedom and Wealth, with the Graces now dwell!
"To thee sable Africa pays her devotion:
"O Heaven of the Earth, pity Africa's hell!
"Ye friends of the friendless—ye foes to Oppression,
"With you sad Affliction's complaint may avail;
"No tyrant sways o'er us his rod of Depression,
"Should Britain espouse the poor African's tale.

"Shall France, your dependents for all you have granted,
"Deny unto us what themselves would enjoy?
"In their favour'd land you have Freedom implanted,—
"Shall they your decisions affect to destroy?
"No- Britons arouse! Now awake to your calling!
"In our land, too, you planted fair Liberty's tree!
"By France that fair plant of your hands, lo! Is falling;
"O haste to our succour!—Set Africa free."

O Africa, cease! All thy wrongs we have ponder'd
Though long we ill-treated thy sons on their shore;
Like demons, not men, we thy treasures have plunder'd
And worse!!!—These foul infamies brand us no more!
As Men now we view you;—as Brethren, though sable;
Your kindred, now prov'd, we shall never disown;
And should ingrate France our best efforts disable,
Your cause, our Jehovah shall plead as his own!

N.B. The above Lines were written at the moment when Petitions were issuing from all
   parts of the nation to the Houses of Parliament, praying for their influence towards
   the full and final abolition of that Sanguinary and infernal traffic which yet disgraces
   civilized Europe, and which, to our eternal shame and infamy, once had the sanction
   of Great Britain itself.

Newcastle: Printed by Mackenzie and Dent.
By Thomas Horn
(Extracted from the 'Tyne Mercury' of the 12th of July, 1814.)

This ballad reflects the power of public opinion over Parliament even during wartime. It celebrates the success after long struggle to enact the Abolition of Slave Trade Act of 1807, ending the traffic that had taken more than three million captive Africans onto British ships for the middle passage. Signed into law on March 25, the act had taken two decades of hard work to be adopted, but it would be another thirty years before slavery was fully abolished in Great Britain and its colonies.

By 1808, a token British West African Squadron of two vessels was deployed for a trial journey to determine what was needed to implement the new law. The two ships were small, slow and incapable of preventing a multimillion-dollar trade. (Thomas: 1997, 575) This effort proved necessary since Britain ultimately seized approximately 1,600 slave ships and freed 150,000 Africans who were aboard them.

Petitioning Parliament

## 53 Burdett Our Leading Star

Sir Frederick Madden's Collection of Broadside Ballads, 03/2186 – Roud V38648

*Tune: A Begging We Will Go; Joshua Jackson, 1798*

Oh, brave Burdett! thy country's friend,
Britannia's darling son,
Blessings will long thy name attend,
Thou virtuous patriot bold.
Oh! may'st thou drive Corruption far;
Be thou, Burdett, our leading star.

Our constitution and our laws,
For these he nobly stood;
The legacy our fathers left,
And purchas'd with their blood—
And shall we basely them resign?
Forbid it, ye powers divine.

His name the upright will revere,
His cause is pure and just,
His country's laws to him are dear,
He ne'er betray'd his trust.
Oh! may'st thou drive Corruption far;
Be thou, Burdett, our leading star.

What though within the Tower walls
His foes have him confin'd,
His noble spirit is unaw'd,
Pure and upright his mind.
The wicked flee when none pursue;
But thou, Burdett, art firm and true.

Long may'st thou live thy country's pride,
To see her rights restor'd.
Her foes with shame their faces hide,
And peace to reign once more.
Then shall Corruption stand afar,
Bright Equity our ruling star.

This song of the continuing support for Francis Burdett was written in 1810 while he was imprisoned in the Tower of London for speaking in Parliament against the confinement of the Chair of the London Corresponding Society, John Gale Jones. Burdett's transgression was increased when his testimony was illegally printed in William Cobbett's *Weekly Register*.

At the time, Burdett was serving as MP from Westminster and was at the height of his popularity. The level of hero worship for Burdett exceeded that of John Wilkes in his heyday. According to Dorothy George, "Burdett was subject to concentrated pictorial eulogy in political caricatures throughout this period." (George, D: 1959, 125–6)

The attempts to arrest Burdett triggered a massive outpouring from supporters. When he initially resisted arrest, numbers of people swelled into the street; the government, fearing a return of the Gordon Riots of thirty years earlier, brought out all soldiers within miles of London. Eventually, soldiers broke into his home and took him to the Tower.

When the issue of sedition was again put to a vote in Parliament, Burdett was released. "He then disappointed the crowds that gathered to celebrate his discharge by avoiding the carriage and going home by boat on the Thames."(Turner: 2000, 134)

At the time that this song was being sung on the street, Jones, Burdett, and Cobbett were all three in separate prisons. Jones and Burdett were held for a few months, but Cobbett remained imprisoned for two years. Some have speculated that this unfairly prolonged sentence provoked the ultimate radicalizing of Cobbett. His imprisonment might have strengthened his radical opinions, but long before 1810 Cobbett had been adamant in his disdain for the mistreatment of British soldiers on the Continent, so much so that government jumped at this chance to put him away for this minor offense.

## 54 General Ludd's Triumph

Roy Palmer, *A Touch On the Times* (1974): 286

Tune: The Miller of Dee; Village Opera, 1729

No more chant your old rhymes about bold Robin Hood
His feats I do little admire.
I'll sing the achievements of General Ludd,
Now the hero of Nottinghamshire.
Brave Ludd was to measures of violence unused
Till his sufferings became so severe,
That at last to defend his own interest he roused,
And for the great fight did prepare.

The guilty may fear but no vengeance he aims
At the honest man's life or estate;
His wrath is entirely confined to wide frames
And to those that old prices abate.
Those engines of mischief were sentenced to die
By unanimous vote of the trade,
And Ludd who can all opposition defy
Was the grand executioner made.

And when in the work he destruction employs,
Himself to no method confines;
By fire and by water he gets them destroyed,
For the elements aid his designs.
Whether guarded by soldiers along the highway,
Or closely secured in a room,
He shivers them up by night and by day
And nothing can soften their doom.

He may censure great Ludd's disrespect for the law,
Who ne'er for a moment reflects
That foul imposition alone was the cause
Which produced these unhappy effects
Let the haughty the humble no longer oppress,
Then shall Ludd sheathe his conquering sword;
His grievances instantly meet with redress,
Then peace shall be quickly restored.

Let the wise and the great lend their aid and advice
Nor e'er their assistance withdraw,
Till full-fashioned work at the old-fashioned price
Is established by custom and law.
Then the trade when this arduous contest is o'er
Shall raise in full splendour its head;
And colting and cutting and squaring no more
Shall deprive honest workmen of bread

Roy Palmer identified the source of this important ballad as a manuscript in the Home Office papers, presumably thanks to an informer who set it up as evidence. (Palmer: 1974, 288) As the song says, workers were not used to taking violent actions, but their sufferings became so severe that they needed to defend their own interests. Parliament had passed Combination Acts in 1799 and 1800 that made trade unionism and collective bargaining illegal; it was against the law for workers to join together to seek redress of wages and working conditions. This restriction and the continental blockade greatly affected workers in the weaving industry. Mill owners were hiring non-apprenticed workers at low wages to weave large pieces of cloth on the wide frame machines. The resulting fabric was flawed and the merchandise made from it was shoddy and fell to pieces. Parliament, frightened and vicious, passed a Bill making frame-breaking (already punishable by fourteen years' transportation) a capital offence. (Cole & Postgate: 1961, 185)

In early 1811 workers in Nottinghamshire who were affected by these changes began to secretly organize to smash frame machines. Their tool of choice was the Enoch sledgehammer; Enoch Taylor of Marsden, Yorkshire also made the pot metal of which the weaving frames were made. '*Enoch did make them, Enoch shall break them.'* In November of 1811 the smash-ers started leaving messages—handwritten notes that attributed the de-struction to the direction of a General Ned Ludd, an imagined character who became legendary. Parliament, including most of its Whigs, support-ed the law to make frame-breaking a capital offense. Several spoke in the house of Parliament in support of the workers. Lord Byron delivered a fervent address in their favor in the house of Lords.

Large numbers of troops were dispersed to the industrial areas, yet ma-chine breaking spread throughout most other northern industrial areas and continued through 1813. Turner says, "Crucial to the outbursts was an ideology of redress, premised on the notion that workers had to change state and society because their governors, and employers had failed them." (Turner: 2000, 132)

Luddites Wielding Enoch

## 55 Hunting a Loaf

Bodleian Library: Firth Collection, c 16(9) – Roud V39318

*Tune: Kitty Magee; John and William Neals, 1724*

Good people I pray, now hear what I say,
And pray do not call it sedition;
For these great men of late they have cracked my poor pate:
I'm wounded, in a woeful condition.

CHORUS
And sing fal lal the diddle i do,
Sing fal the diddle i do,
Sing fal the lal day.

For in Derby it's true and in Nottingham too,
Poor men to the jail they've been taking;
They say that Ned Lud, as I understood,
A thousand wide frames have been breaking.

Now is it not bad there's no work to be had,
The poor to be starved in their station;
And if they do steal they're straight sent to jail,
And they're hanged by the laws of the nation?

Since this time last year I've been very queer,
And I've had a sad national cross;
I've been up and down from town unto town,
With a shilling to buy a big loaf.

The first that I met was Sir Francis Burdett,
He told me he'd been in the Tower;
I told him my mind a big loaf was to find,
He said, "You must ask them in power."

Then I thought it was time to speak to the Prime,
Master Perceval would take my part;
But a Liverpool man soon ended the plan:
With a pistol he shot through his heart.

Then I thought he'd a chance on a rope for to dance,
Some people would think very pretty;
But he lost all his tun, through the country he'd run,
And he found it in fair London city.

Now ending my song I'll sit down with my friend,
And I'll drink a good health to the poor;
With a glass of good ale, I have told you my tale,
And I'll look for a big loaf no more.

This broadside ballad appears on a sheet with another ballad, "Boney's Disappointment," which mentions the defeat of the French Army in Russia. They were likely both written in 1813 during the height of the battle with General Ludd. This song mentions Sir Francis Burdett's incarceration in the Tower of London in 1810. It also refers to the assassination of Prime Minister Spencer Perceval in 1812 in the lobby of the House of Parliament by John Bellingham, a business man who had been unable to obtain redress for losses he incurred in trade with Russia. The word got out in the streets in the potteries when "a man came running down the street, leaping into the air, waving his hat round his head, and shouting with frantic joy, Perceval is shot hurrah! Perceval is shot hurrah!" (Thompson: 1966, 571)

By 1810 those who still had work were on short pay, and the unemployed from manufacturing numbered in the thousands. Starting in Nottingham, the Ludd movement soon spread to Derbyshire. Large frames in the steam-powered textile mills were smashed by the mythical General Ludd, who among other things was calling for fair wages and better working conditions. Parliament was quick to respond to mill owners' concerns, but not to those of workers. Troops were sent to guard factories and a law was soon passed making smashing machines a hanging offense. Prior to March 1812 when the capital felony machine-breaking law went into effect, ten

Luddites had been arrested and seven were sent to Australia. The Cheshire commission assigned fourteen death sentences, and two of these prisoners were actually executed. In Yorkshire, six men were given seven years' transportation for administering illegal oaths. Seventeen others were hanged and one transported for life. (Cole, Postgate: 1938, 188) Eventually, it took more troops deployed in the north of England than those who were fighting under Wellington on the Iberian Peninsula to put down the Luddite movement.

Fourteen Luddites Convicted to Death

## 56 Bonaparte's Farewell to Paris

Bodleian Library: Johnson Ballads fol. 282 – Roud V44094

*Tune: Miss Forbes Farewell to Banff; John Miller, 1799*

Fare - well to__ Pa - ris__ love - ly scene! Fare -
well my__ friends and a - dieu! My Ar - my__ has me
much de - ceived, Whom I al - ways thought were true.
The frowns of__ fate on me have fall - len And
Scep - ter__ dwin-dled to de - cay; To__ El - ba__ now I__
steer my course, A - mongst the__ Mar - ble and cold clay.

Farewell to Paris lovely scene!
Farewell my friends a sad adieu!
My Army has me much deceived,
Whom I always thought were true.

The frowns of fate on me have fall'n
And Scepter dwindled to decay;
To Elba now I steer my course,
Amongst the Marble and cold clay.

And O ye bonny banks of Seine!
Your purling streams I bid adieu;
May Frenchmen ever happy be,
And ne'er revive year Ninety-two.

I fought your battles far from hence,
But why do I remind such things;
Man was surely made to mourn,
A symbol of the fate of kings.

I do not mourn my sad downfall,
I wish that rightly understood;
But O alas! When I think on
The curs'd crime of ingratitude!

I'll blame not either friends or foes,
Even when exiled afar;
But mathematically sum up
The pro's and con's of raging war.

It is well known I have a wife,
Like other Princes ev'n two;
A lovely Son, my darling boy,
A King; but like his Father now!

But still he is as dear to me,
All honest men they will assert;
Altho' he's not the Romish King,
He's still the Son of Bonaparte.

Amongst the mistakes that e'er I made
The greatest one I made in life,
Instead of fighting in Russia's snows,
'Tis there I should have got a wife.

Good bye John Bull my steady Lad,
Again poor Bonny you've a brief;
I've often threaten'd to come o'er
To taste your English Ale and Beef.

G Summers, Printer, Sunderland

This is an early version of the well-known popular pro-Napoleon song "Napoleon's Farewell to Paris." In addition to No. 61 (below) there have been many versions of this song throughout the years, but only two are titled "Bonaparte's Farewell to Paris." It was hard to find, since it is impossible to read on the Bodleian Library's Broadsides online. It became accessible by submitting an enquiry to the library who mailed a clear image. This song was written before the Battle of Waterloo.

On April 12, 1814 the allies completed the documents for Napoleon's dethronement. That night, Napoleon took the vial of poison he always carried around his neck. But the poison was too old, so he survived. In two days he had recovered enough to write to his former wife Josephine,

> "I have heaped benefits on thousands of wretches. But what have they done for me in return at the end? They have betrayed me, yes

all of them, except the good Eugene so worthy of you and me...
Good bye my dear Josephine, resign yourself as I have had to do,
and never forget him who never has forgotten you and never will."
(Shom: 1997, 702)

This broadside, like the letter quoted above, reflects Napoleon's bitter
feelings during his fall from power and pending exile to the island of Elba.
Both refer to the support Napoleon had received from his stepson Eugene
Beauharnais, son of Josephine and her first husband, General Beauharnais,
who was guillotined in 1794. The song mentions hope that the 1792 reign
of terror does not return. It also tells that many believed Bonaparte wanted
to come and live in Britain. This is the first of many British pro-Napoleonic
ballads. In this case it shows sympathy with Britain's longtime adversary,
who was now losing the power that might have been used to liberate the
people from the oppression of Britain's aristocratic oligarchy.

Napoleon at Fontainebleau, March 31, 1814

## **57** John Bull in a Rage at the Corn Laws
Bodleian Library: Harding Collection, B 17(146b) – Roud V16847

*Tune: Down in Yon Forest; traditional, 15th C.*

Lit - tle    Bo - ney  done    o - ver,    hos - ti - li - ties  o'er,

And Kings, Prin - ces  and  Em - per - or's   placed as   be - fore,

John - ny    Bull  thought  from    his     cares  a    re - lease,

And to    taste  the  sweet joys    of    this    glo - ri - ous peace.

Little Boney done over, hostilities o'er,
And Kings, Princes, and Emperor's placed as before,
Johnny Bull thought from his cares a release,
And to taste the sweet joys of this glorious peace.

Ah, ah he exclaimed, and bright sparkled his eyes,
As his finger he rubbed and looked wondrous wise.
All along through the war I thought how it would be,
And how well all these powers at last would agree.

Now we've settled the hash of that Corsican chief,
We shall all stuff plumb pudding and gobble roast beef,
And the growth of all climates that lie at our feet,
And our only concern be in future to eat.

While John was indulging this raptures thought,
In the midst of his transports the paper was brought,
In the which 'twas declar'd that for reason most weighty,
Wheaten corn should in future ne'er fetch less than 80.

Down, down went the table erect stood his hair,
His jaws were wide open his eyes wildly stare,
Why the scoundrels he cried, think that I'm such an oaf,
As to give sixteen pence for an eight penny loaf.

Mr. Bull be pacific, said Grindwell the squire,
Who inclos'd all the commons in every shire,
"Oh a curse on your nonsense get out of my house,
I don't care for enclosure three skips of a louse."

But remember says Grindwell "the duty on port,
And my daughters must finger the piano fort,"
I remember, quoth John when you farmers drank ale,
And your daughters could finger a dirty cows tail.

When strong porter was sold us for three pence a quart,
And a good quartern loaf was sold for a groat,
When our butter was sweet and our bacon was sound,
And a prime leg of mutton fetch'd four pence a pound.

So be off master Grindwell and draw in your horn,
You'd best not interfere with the price of the corn,
But let Englishmen see with the blessings of peace
Trade and commerce both flourish, and plenty increase.

Printed and sold by J. Pitts,
14 Great St. Andrew Street, Seven Dials

Surely workers would find recompense after two decades of war, high food costs, loss of their ancient commons, and deaths of many breadwinners. But then Parliament enacted the horrible Corn Laws.

This song sympathizes with John Bull, the common Englishman, conversing with "Grindwell," landowner and prosperous farmer. Johnny anticipates that peacetime will improve his situation. But during the war years, thanks to the general Enclosure Law enacted in 1801, Grindwell had been enclosing common lands. As corn prices increased, his newly acquired lands became more profitable, and it is Grindwell who is enjoying a better quality of life.

The Corn Laws were not designed to save a tottering sector of the economy, but rather to preserve the abnormally high profits of the Napoleonic war-years, and to safeguard farmers from the consequences of their wartime euphoria, when farms had changed hands at the fanciest prices, and loans and mortgages had been accepted on impossible terms. (Hobsbawm: 1999, 175)

Landed gentry, who controlled Parliament, feared that continental corn would cut their revenues. They could either lower farmers' rents to reduce production costs, or curb imports to maintain high prices. Their choice was easy. The 1815 Corn Law, first of several over three decades, benefitted landowners but not producers and consumers, and was devastating to working and manufacturing classes. Food riots broke out, and armed troops had to defend the Houses of Parliament against angry crowds.

Chapter 6

# SUPPRESSION: 1815–1819

*'Rise like Lions after slumber in unvanquishable number—*
*Shake your chains to earth like dew*
*Which in sleep had fallen on you—*
*Ye are many — they are few.'*
— Shelley, *The Mask of Anarchy* (1819)

Following the Napoleonic wars, working class discontent was manifest throughout all of Britain. Realizing the enduring needs for decent housing, safe water, better working conditions, lower food prices, fair pay, lower taxes, equal justice, and the right to vote, the large working class knew that it had gained nothing from twenty-two years of war. Many felt that they could have been better off if Napoleon had won, which might have ended their unbearable lives controlled by Britain's aristocracy. Knowing how the dethroned French emperor continued to impact the lives of Britons, songwriters retold and embellished the ongoing saga to advance efforts for reform.

On March 1, 1815, less than a year after his banishment, Napoleon escaped his exile in Elba and landed at Golfe-Juan on the south coast of France. He was greeted with jubilation everywhere he went. Marshal Ney was sent to arrest Napoleon; instead, he and his men joined Napoleon's triumphant march to Paris. Within one hundred days Napoleon reassembled his army to march against the Duke of Wellington and the Prussian General Blucher at the Battle of Waterloo in Belgium. He hoped to strike a decisive blow before the Russians and Austrians could join the allies. But in the Battle of Waterloo, on June 18, 1815, the French suffered massive losses and Napoleon was defeated. He ultimately surrendered at Rochefort to Captain Maitland, of the man-of-war *Bellerophon*, and was taken to Plymouth, where thousands boarded small boats to view him pacing the deck of the *Bellerophon* at anchor in the harbor. He was then taken to

Portsmouth to sail onboard the *Northumberland* to his final imprisonment on the tiny remote south Atlantic island of Saint Helena. Wellington, joined by his victorious allies, triumphantly paraded in London, but the euphoria of the Waterloo victory was soon replaced by the desperation of the working people. Adding to the despair of the workers, the largest volcanic eruption known on the planet during the past 10,000 years occurred with the 1815 eruption of Mount Tambora in Indonesia. This disaster caused famine by reducing crop yields internationally the following year, known as "the year without a summer."

Unemployment spread everywhere. Farm produce prices fell, and farmers who had acquired property during the war began to default on their mortgages. Wages were cut, and those who had work were on short time. The income tax which had raised funds from people of means during the war was eliminated, leaving the poor to bear the brunt of the national debt by paying taxes on consumer goods basic to survival. To shore up the falling prices of wheat, a new Corn Law was passed by Lord Liverpool's government in 1815, which prevented the import of wheat until the domestic price exceeded £4 a quarter ton. Although it was claimed to be a way to maintain production in Britain, the law was known to bail out the landed gentry, who continued to control Parliament. War had distorted the economy, and farming, industry, and business had to adjust to new conditions. (Turner: 2000, 138) These hard times were exacerbated by the addition of demobilized soldiers and sailors to the ranks of the unemployed.

Seizing opportunity, parliamentary reform advocates stepped up their efforts. Major John Cartwright organized Hampden Clubs, first in London and then across industrial areas of England, where workers joined with intellectuals to stimulate parliamentary reform. On an impressive schedule, Henry Hunt spoke at rallies throughout major industrial areas. The stamp tax on newspapers was raised in 1815 to fourpence, a price impossible for the working man to pay. William Cobbett circumvented the stamp tax by selling his *Weekly Political Register* in an unfolded, unstamped edition for two pence. The first edition of the *Register* in its new format, published on November 3, 1816, was the starting point of Cobbett's great career as a working class leader. It was a huge success, achieving circulation of more than 40,000. Groups met to read aloud Cobbett's prose on the people's perspective, as had the supporters of Paine before.

The old radical Thomas Spence had died in 1814, but it was after his death that adherents to Spencean beliefs engaged in a more radical fight for reform. On November 15, 1816, members of the "Society of Spencean Philanthropists" participated in a meeting at Spa Fields (Islington) to adopt a petition calling for redress of grievances and for parliamentary reform. Henry "Orator" Hunt addressed the meeting of 10,000 people and attempted to deliver the petition, adopted by the assembly, to the regent Prince George, but the petition was not accepted. On December 2, another meeting was held at Spa Fields to consider the Regent's response to the petition from the previous meeting; it was estimated that 20,000 people attended. Prior to the appearance of Orator Hunt the crowd was whipped up by Spenceans including Arthur Thistlewood and John, the son of Dr. James Watson. Several had split off from Spa Fields and started to wreak havoc, but they were met by troops. Those arrested were later released after it was revealed that their agitation had been provoked by government agent John Castle.

The Spa Fields of December 2 inaugurated the mass platform; while the revolutionary party fell into the Government's secret spy trap, Hunt established a new structure of open, popular, constitutional, radical endeavour. From this point on, radicalism was synonymous with mass meetings, mass Petitions, and the program of universal suffrage, annual parliaments and the ballot—a program for which all could strive. (Belchem: 1985, 64)

In 1817, two futile uprisings resulted from the work of another infamous government agent provocateur, William Oliver. Oliver traveled to many industrial villages, encouraging uprisings to correspond with an alleged revolution to take place in London. The first uprising occurred in March, when several hundred starving factory workers in Manchester attempted to carry their petition for food and reform to the Regent. This was called the "Blanketeer's March," since each man was to carry a blanket and his basic needs. The Lancashire men were to march peacefully with their petitions upon London, holding meetings and gathering support on the way. (Thompson EP: 1966, 649) Even before the marchers left St. Peter's Field in Manchester, several hundred were arrested. Soon most of the other marchers were arrested by dragoons, and only one marcher arrived in London to present the petition. The second incident, also provoked by Oliver, started on June 9 in Derbyshire and became known as the "Pentrich Rising." A relatively small number of stockingers, quarrymen, ironworkers, and laborers from the villages of Pentrich, South Wingfield, and Ripley marched on Nottingham with a few guns, pikes, bludgeons, and scythes. They were met by dragoons who rounded up 85 men for trial in Derby. Twenty-three were tried for high treason by a special commission, three were hanged, three were transported for fourteen years each and fourteen for life.

Home Secretary Viscount Sidmouth used these government-provoked activities, and another incident where protesters set upon the Regent, to once again suspend habeas corpus, and he obtained the Tory government's approval of the "Two Gagging Acts of 1817." One gagging law banned meetings of over fifty people. The other called for magistrates to arrest anyone suspected of spreading seditious libel. The government imagined that it had a clear mandate to pass legislation that would curb reforms that threatened the status quo.

In the autumn of 1817 grief arose from the death in childbirth of Princess Charlotte, who was the only child of the future King George IV and his estranged wife Caroline. Charlotte had been second in line to the throne. Her early death, and that of her child, totally altered the line of succession.

Princess Caroline, meanwhile, no longer carried the status of a future Queen Mother. Politically speaking she was deprived of her future, and in the public mind, a victim of fate. (Robins 2006: 55)

Conditions improved slightly in 1818, but not in the industrial areas where ongoing issues including back pay, rising costs, and decreased work persisted. The Government began to look for ways to test the new Gagging Acts and the Combination Acts. During the summer of 1819 Viscount Sidmouth learned of plans for a major reform meeting to be held in Manchester. Seeing this as the opportunity to strengthen the government's position, he dispatched troops to prevent the meeting from becoming effective. The meeting took place on August 16, 1819 at St. Peter's Field. The local committee had asked Henry Hunt, Major Cartwright, and publisher Richard Carlisle to be the featured speakers. Because of his advanced age and poor health, Major Cartwright declined the invitation. By late morning the huge and peaceful crowd of men, women, and children, estimated to be over 50,000, was observed by a group of magistrates who strategically watched the happenings from the safety of chambers overlooking the field. When Hunt arrived and began to speak, the magistrates ordered him arrested by the Manchester and Salford Yeomanry. The Yeomen, having spent the morning at a local public house, happily accepted the job of charging on horseback into the crowd, wildly swinging their sabers. For a short time, the crowd bravely held off the Yeomen, but was soon overwhelmed when the 15th Hussars joined the chaotic fray. Within minutes all of the dignitaries at the speaker's platform were arrested, with the exception of Carlisle, who somehow escaped to London where he published an account of the event. James Wroe, a founder and representative of the *Manchester Observer*, attended the meeting and is believed to be the one who coined its name "The Peterloo Massacre." Both Wroe and Carlisle were later jailed for publishing their stories. Eleven people were killed, and over 400 men and women were seriously injured. Charging violation of both gagging laws, the government arranged trials and convictions in York for the leaders of the meeting, which resulted in Henry Hunt being sentenced to 30 months in jail, while others received one-year sentences. (Marlow 1970: 193)

LIBERTY *SUPPENDED!* with the *Bulwark of the Constitution!*

## 58 Battle of Waterloo

Bodleian Library: The Firth Collection, c 17(304) – Roud 5824

*Tune: The Nut Girl; Broadside, 1819-44*

'Twas on the eight-teenth day of June Na-po-leon did ad-vance,

The choi-cest troops that he could raise with-in the bounds of France;

Their glit-tering ea-gles shone a-round, and proud-ly looked the foes,

But Bri-tain's li-on tore their wings at the plains of Wa-ter-loo.

With Wel-ling-ton we'll go, __ go, with Wel-ling-ton we'll go,

For Wel-ling-ton com-mand-ed us __ on the plains of Wa-ter-loo;

'Twas on the 18th day of June Napoleon did advance,
The choicest troops that he could raise within the bounds of France;
Their glittering eagles shone around, and proudly look'd the foes,
But Britain's lion tore their wings at the plains of Waterloo.
  With Wellington we'll go go, with Wellington we'll go,
  For Wellington commanded us on the plains of Waterloo;

The fight did last from ten o'clock until the dawn of day,
While blood and limbs and cannon balls in thick profusion lay.
Their Cuirassieurs did quickly charge our squares to overthrew.
But Britains firm, undaunted stood, on the plains of Waterloo.

The number of the French that at Waterloo was slain,
Was near sixty thousand, all laid upon the plain;
Near forty thousand fell upon that fatal day,
Of our brave British heroes who their prowess did display.

It's now the dreadful night comes on, how dismal is the plain,
When the Prussians with the English join'd above ten thousand slain,
Brave Wellington and Blucher bold, most nobly drove their foes,
And Buonaparte's imperial crown was taken at Waterloo.

We followed up the rear till the middle of the night,
We gave them three cheers as they were on their flight,
Says Bonny, damn those Englishmen they do bear such a name,
They beat me here at Waterloo, at Portugal and Spain.

Now peace be to their honoured souls who fell that glorious day,
May the plough ne'er raise their bones, not cut the sacred clay;
But let the place remain a waste, a terror to the foe,
And when trembling Frenchmen pass that way, they'll think of Waterloo.

Many broadside ballads were written about the Battle of Waterloo but none can adequately portray the horror of the field of battle. After two days of slaughter, France left 25,000 dead and wounded and 220 cannon on the now silent battlefield of Waterloo and a total of 64,602 men during the entire Belgian campaign. The Allies suffered 62,818 casualties. (Schom: 1997, 760) Ditches were filled with the dead, and huge piles of corpses lay where entire regiments were cut down. Equally horrible were the thousands of living and dying wounded, many of whom lay for more than three days on the field of carnage where Belgian peasants came forth to rob the bodies and in some cases put an end to the victim's misery. After dark on the night of the dreadful battle, survivors had to spend the night listening to the moans and cries of the dying and breathing the smell of the dead.

Though this ballad lauds the English troops as the victors, less than one third of the 68,000 men commanded by Wellington were British. His force was mainly Dutch and Hanoverian. It was the late arrival of 30,000 Prussians that spread terror and disorder and caused the French to flee the battlefield.

After the Battle

## 59 Napoleon Buonaparte's Exile To St. Helena

Bodleian Library: The Firth Collection, c 16(93) – Roud V1174

*Tune: Sweet William's Farewell to Black Eyed Susan; Leveridge, 1730*

In Roch - ford dock the fleet lay moored, the
stream - ers wa - vered in the wind When Na - po - leon Bo - na - parte
came on board, Saying "where shall I some re - fuge find:
Tell me ye jo - vial sai - lors, tell me true
If to old Eng - land, if to old Eng - land
I shall sail with you"

In Rochford dock the fleet lay moored,
The streamers wavered in the wind,
When Napoleon Bonaparte came on board.
Saying, "where shall I some refuge find:
Tell me ye jovial sailors, tell me true,
If to Old England, I shall sail with you."

Then Captain Maitland thus did say:
"Yes, to Old England you shall go with me."
Soon as Napoleon these words did hear,
He bowed, he sighed, & hung his head,
Saying, "my wife, my kingdom, & my glory's lost,
And I'm an exile on the ocean tossed."

The seamen who high upon the yards,
Rock'd by the billows to and fro,
Soon as Napoleon's voice they heard,

Like lightning they flew down below;
All rushed on deck to see this mighty man,
Who oft'times threaten'd to invade our native land.

The boatswain gave the dreadful word,
The ships with opening bosoms spread.
No longer must they stay on shore,
He sighed, he hung his head:
As the shores of France retired from his view,
Adieu, adieu, he cri'd, ungrateful France, adieu.

Believe no more what the Frenchmen say,
They doubt within their wavering minds:
They told me if I with them would stay,
Firm in their cause I should them find:
Past experience tells me that they are untrue,
And I for ever bid them all adieu.

J. Pannell, Printer, 24, Byrom St. Liverpool

After the Battle of Waterloo, Napoleon was not ready to abdicate and left the battle field with some remaining soldiers for Paris. By June 29, Blucher's army arrived at his doorstep and the Provisional Government was anxious to negotiate with them. Ultimately arrangements were made for Bonaparte and his family to proceed to the port of Rochfort and board a frigate going to the new world. The port was under blockade by the British Battleship *Bellerophon* requiring that passage be permitted by its Captain Maitland.

Arriving in Rochefort July 3, the group boarded the French Frigate *La Saale* which was under orders to sail within two days after Napoleon was on board. The plan was to sail to Boston or Philadelphia. Napoleon's brother, Joseph, proposed to go on the *Bellerophon* instead, but Napoleon would have none of it. Of course Maitland denied Napoleon a passport.

A little after six o'clock in the morning of Saturday July 15, 1815, Napoleon was piped aboard the *Bellerophon*, receiving full honors and escorted to the captain's own cabins, which he had vacated for his special guest. As the sails were unfurled and they put to sea, Napoleon watched the shores of his empire slowly fade from sight. Joseph sailed in another ship for the United States. (Schom: 1997, 765)

## 60 Isle of St. Helena

National Library of Scotland: Chapbooks Printed in Scotland. L.C.2877(35) – Roud V853

Tune: The Isle of St Helena; James Watt of Paisley, 1817

Now Bo-ney he's a-wa' from his war-ring and fight-ing,
He's gone to a place That he ne'er can de-light in,
may sit now and tell of the scenes that he's seen a'
While for-lorn he doth mourn On the Isle of St. He-le-na.

Now Boney he's awa' From his warring and fighting,
He's gone to a place That he ne'er can delight in,
He may sit now and tell of the scenes that he's seen a',
While forlorn he doth mourn On the Isle of St. Helena.

No more at St. Clouds He'll appears in great splendor.
Nor go forth with his crowds, Like the great Alexander
He may sigh to the wind, By the great mount Diana
With his eyes o'er the waves, That surrounds St. Helena.

Now Lousiana weeps For her husband departed,
She dreams while she sleeps, And awakes broken hearted
Not a friend to condole, Even those that might they winna,
And she mourns while she thinks On the Isle of St. Helena.

The rude rushing waves As our shores round us washing,
And the great billows heaves, As the wild rocks a dashing.
He may look upon the moon, And think on Lousiana,
With his heart full of woe, On the Isle of St Helena.

Now ye that have great wealth, Beware of ambition;
For some decree of fate May change your condition,
Be ye stedfast in time, For what 's to come ye Kenna,
May be your race may end At the Isle of St. Helena.

J Catnatch, Printer

This early pro-Napoleon song originated in Scotland and, according to Peter Wood, the author was James Watt from Paisley, and the earliest version in print is a broadside by Fraser of Stirling from 1817. (Wood: 2015, 115) This version from the National Library of Scotland dated 1817 is the first song in a chapbook of five songs dated 1817, labeled "printed by Fraser of Stirling." Later editions of this song are printed as broadside ballads, and end with a verse on the death of Napoleon such as,

"O you Parliaments of Law and your Holy Alliance
To your prisoner of war, you may now bid defiance.
For your base intrigues and your baser misdemeanors
Have caused him to die on the Isle of St. Helena."

Over the years this song has been slightly altered and reprinted many times in Britain and the United States. According to Gale Huntington it appeared in the Log Book of the American whaleboat *Galaxy* in 1827 under the title "Bonaparte on St. Helena." (Huntington, G: 1964, 205)

Napoleon at St. Helena

## **61**  The White Cliffs of Albion

Bodleian Library: The Harding Collection, B 11(4159)

*Tune: Wandering Girl; Broadside, 1817-28*

On the white cliffs of   Al-bion, as   mu-sing I   stood. Sur - vey-ing the

waves of the rough swell-ing flood,   I   saw from the sur-face a   fe-male a -

rise   And with wings like   an   ea - gle she   moun-ted   the skies.

On the white cliffs of Albion, as musing I stood,
Surveying the waves of the rough swelling flood,
I saw from the surface a female arise
And with wings like an eagle she mounted the skies.

Her figure was comely and noble her mien,
I looked and knew it was Liberty's Queen;
With sword in her hand she shouts as she flies,
Ye Rulers of Britain be prudent and wise

For this island I chose, long before you had birth,
For the seat of my empire, the freest on earth;
And tho' you have forged them no chains shall she wear,
Nor e'er be enslaved whilst a sword I can bear.

So saying she brandished her sword in the skies,
And aloud to the sons of Britannia she cries,
O will you endevour your freedom to gain,
Or basely submit to the ignoble chain.

We will not submit was soon echoed around,
By millions of people who stood on the ground;
When Burdett and Cartwright stood in the van,
Saying we will live to be free or die to a man.

But deign gentle goddess, the way to impart,
To crush the fell monster that preys on the heart
Of that noble structure now gone to decay,
Which once was the glory and pride of the day.

With looks all complaisance, and smiling said she,
The charter I gave you, was Britons be free.
And though that corruption its beauties has torn,
'Twill blossom again after timely reform.

Reform it, Reform it, they shouted aloud,
And the breath from their voices soon formed a cloud
In which she departed and gave them a nod,
Saying the wish of the people's the will of a God.

During the infamous year of 1816, unemployment reached new heights, affecting most working people. In this song "Liberty's Queen" returns to Britain's shores to motivate her troubled people, just as she had visited sailors during the Strike at Spithead. She mentions Major Cartwright, now aged 73, who is back to lead the van with the new standard bearer, Francis Burdett. "Liberty's Queen" knows that their good hands are needed to help move all forward. Most radicals wished for a range of political, social and economic changes, but they placed parliamentary reform at the top of their agenda. (Turner: 2000, 138)

The feelings expressed in this song reflect the motivation behind two meetings in late 1816. A small group of former Spence followers organized a meeting on Spa Fields in Islington for November 15 that drew a much larger crowd than could have been expected. Major Cartwright and William Cobbett had decided not to speak at this event because of the radical and potentially volatile nature of Arthur Thistlewood, the leader, and other Spencean organizers. The highly respected orator Henry Hunt agreed to step up and speak, but because of the size of the crowd he spoke from the second story window of a public house, to a crowd of over 10,000. Hunt spoke in opposition to the Corn Laws, high taxes, high prices, borough mongers, and of the need for parliamentary reform. He also counseled restraint from violent confrontation. The outcome of this peaceful meeting was that Hunt and Burdett were selected to deliver a petition to the Prince Regent calling for parliamentary reform, including universal (male) suffrage, annual general elections, and the secret ballot. Burdett opted out of carrying the petition, so Hunt tried, unsuccessfully, to place the petition in the hands of the Regent himself. (Halevy 1961: 17) After the meeting Hunt and several Spenceans met back at his hotel to celebrate the success of the event. During the course of the evening, John Castle, one of the leaders, made this toast, "May the last of Kings be strangled with the guts of the last Priest." (Thompson: 1966, 634)

The second gathering, on December 2, was even larger than the November meeting. Whether by design or fate, this second meeting resulted in disaster. Hunt arrived late, and several Spence disciples who had organized the meeting had already left the field with a crowd of disbanded sailors. The crowd became agitated, and magistrates had the police disperse the meeting. Before the day was over, unruly crowds spread throughout London. The chemistry resembled conditions during the Gordon Riots. Dr. James Watson, Arthur Thistlewood, Thomas Preston, and John Hooper were arrested and charged with high treason. Watson was the first to be tried, just as sensational revelations appeared in the *Leeds Mercury* about Oliver and the Government spy system. (Belchem: 1985, 76) He was acquitted when the Government's principle witness, the provocateur John Castle, was proved to be employed by the government. Charges were then dropped against the other defendants.

Britannia

## 62 Bonaparte's Farewell to Paris

Bodleian Library: The Harding Collection, B 26 (71) — Roud 1626

*Tune: Napoleon's Farewell to Paris; Tommy Flynn, 1980*

Fare - well you splen - did ci - ta - del, so tower-ing, grand and charm-ing,

Fare - well you splen - did pa - la - ces, you peers and court - ly dames

Fare - well you lof - ty moun-tains of va - lor's no - ble dar - ing

Court - ed eve - ry morn - ing by Sol's re - ful - gent beams

All joined with bright Au - ro - ra ad - vanc - ing from the or - ient

The ra - diant light a - dorn - ing with pure re - ful - gent light.

Com - mand - ing Cyn - this to re - tire Where the glass win-dow flame like fire.

Which the great u - ni - verse ad - mire With bril - lian - cy so gleamed

Farewell you splendid citadel so towering, grand and charming,
Farewell you splendid palaces, you peers and courtly dames
Farewell you lofty mountains of valor's noble daring
Courted every morning by Sol's refulgent beams
All joined with bright Aurora advancing from the orient
The radiant light adorning with pure refulgent light.
   Commanding Cynthis to retire
   Where the glass window flame like fire.
   Which the great universe admire
   With brilliancy so gleamed

While Flora's spreading fragrance the fertile plains decorates,
Enamelled with flow'ry banks and clear purling streams
The lofty capital of France, metropolis called Paris,
The trees are neat and various where multitudes advance
Rich citizens in muffs and farms with veils step out in order
But now the allied army I fear will make them dance.
   Alas! my golden Eagles rent
   My steeds etherneal from me sent;
   My treasure confiscated,
   No friend to bemoan

Some say it was my first downfall to PART my C. Josephine
And take the German's DAUGHTER which wounded me sore
THE FEMALE TRAIN I do not blame. The never did me defame
They saw my sword in BATTLE flame and did me adore;
Others say I FELT THE ROD, for meddling THE Church of God
And MELTING golden images; THOUSANDS away I bore.
   But I lament it was the case,
   That I deserved God's dire disgrace
   But if he gave me time and place
   I would them back restore

I'm Napoleon Bonaparte the conqueror of nations
I banished German legions and drove kings from their throne
I trampled Dukes and Earls and splendid congregations
But now I am transported to saint Helena's shore
Like Hannibal I crossed the Alps the burning sands and clifts
Over Russian hills in snow and frost I still the laurel wore
   Now in a desert Isle anoyed by rats
   Without good Christians or good cats
   To tread those wild forlorn pats,
   I never trod before.

My golden eagles were pulled down by the allied army
My forces disordered no longer stood the field
their reinforcement came too soon on the 18th day of June
On the vast plains of Waterloo which caused me to yield
thou not in the allied yoke with fire and sword made them smoke
And on the plain stood like oak with sword and brilliant shield
   Now I am rejected near the Zone,
   Without my consort or son Bone
   I'd rather fall by a cannon ball
   With honour and renown.

Far to the south of Africa near the Atlantic Ocean
to view the wild commotion and flowing of the tide
Banished from my royal crown of imperial promotion
from the French throne of glory to see the billows glide
three days I conquered on the plain Liberty's cause to maintain
thousands there I had left slain and covered in their gore
   I did not fly without revenge
   Nor from the allied army cringe:
   But now my sword is sheathed
   And all France for me deplore

Printed at HALY'S, 59, South Main St., Cork

This broadside could be thought of as the sequel to No. 56, but instead of the destination of Elba, it is now St Helena, the small island in the middle of the South Atlantic. This song bids goodbye to Paris again, and could have been printed as early as 1816, when its printer, James Haly, was in business at 59 South Main, Cork, Ireland. If so, this version of the ballad precedes all the other ones. Those titled "Napoleon's Farewell to Paris" appear to be later and more advanced versions that were printed all over Britain for several decades. The words and the style of this one appear very Irish and no other versions are entirely the same as this one. Several tunes have been associated with this song, but the tune that Jim Mageean of Tynside learned from Tommy Flyn suits this song best.

Dr. Barry Edward O'Meara, an Irishman, served as a Royal Navy surgeon on board the *Bellerophon* which transported Napoleon to Britain after his post-Waterloo abdication. Bonaparte enjoyed his company enough to request that O'Meara serve as his personal physician on St Helena. From there, O'Meara sent periodic reports to his friend at the Admiralty complaining of misconduct and mistreatment of Bonaparte by Sir Hudson Lowe, Governor of St Helena. Learning of these reports, Lowe suspected O'Meara of plotting Napoleon's escape. Lowe had him recalled to Britain in August, 1818. O'Meara's book *Napoleon in Exile, or A Voice from St. Helena* (1822) was highly popular.

## 63  Song on the Death of Her Royal Highness The Princess Charlotte

Bodleian Library: The Harding Collection, B 16(274d) – Roud V19619

*Tune: Rosebud in June; The Merry Musician, 1716*

Our Princess is gone cries every tongue in the nation.
And all the amusements at Claremont are o'er;
The partner bewails thee with grief and vexation
Crying, Charlotte, "Oh! Charlotte," Our love is no more.

Our hope is exhausted, expecting to hail thee,
As a bright star of heaven on our old English shore.
Thy partner survives thee no comforts assuage him
But the hope of soon meeting, to part never more.

Thy parent who bore thee what must be her oppression;
When she hears the sad tale of disaster and woe;
She will drop like a willow with the greatest affliction
For the loss of her offspring, that Charlotte's no more.

May heaven who claimed thee for happier realms,
Yield consolation to your parents once more
And may him that's in anguish now think of the pleasures
Crying, Charlotte, "Oh! Charlotte," Our love is no more.

Princess Charlotte, the only legitimate child of the heir to the throne of Britain, died in childbirth. She was the only daughter of the future King George IV and Princess Caroline of Brunswick. Born in 1796, she grew up in a hostile environment characterized by constant battles between her parents, who separated when she was young. Her father retained custody of his daughter and did everything possible to prevent Charlotte from having contact with her mother. At age 17, Charlotte broke her engagement to Prince William of Orange, and in May of 1816 married Prince Leopold of Saxe-Coburg. Several hours after delivering a stillborn male, she hemorrhaged and died on November 5, 1817. "Prince Leopold was stricken with unbearable grief. He forbade anyone from touching Charlotte's belongings insisting that her bonnet and cloak remain on the chair in the hallway and that her watch not be moved from the mantelpiece." (Robins: 2007, 52)

Many were holding their breath that something might keep Regent George from assuming the throne when his deranged father died, and the one saving grace had been Charlotte. Though Charlotte was not allowed to spend much time with her mother, Caroline remained close enough to influence her views on the virtues of the Whig party, and its members were anxious to maintain that influence. "They were merely casting round for any stone to throw at the Regent, anything with which to discredit The Tory Ministers." (Fraser: 1996, 225) With Charlotte's demise, her unmarried Uncle William became second heir to the throne. The expectations for Whigs dimmed, as this jovial un-regal former sailor and father of an illegitimate family was unlikely to favor a Whig government.

Princess Charlotte

# 64 Answer to the Threats of Corruption

*The Black Dwarf* (1817), 1:750

Tune: Adieu Sweet Lovely Nancy; Broadside, 1796–1853

The toc-sin sounds, and free-dom's foes A-gain as-sert their im-pi-ous po-wer; De-fend the guilt by which they rose, And like vin-dic-tive de-mons lour. Yet can their frowns ap-pall the brave? What ter-rors has the gloo-my grave To him who fights for free-dom, To him who fights for free-dom.

The tocsin sounds, and freedom's foes
Again assert their impious power;
Defend the guilt by which they rose,
And like vindictive demons lour.
Yet can their frowns appall the brave?
What terrors has the gloomy grave
To him who fights for freedom(?).

Though wide the sanguine stream be spread,
And seas of patriot blood be split,
To save a venal statesman's head,
Or wash away a monster's guilt
Fearless will stand or fall the brave: —
Write, write but on the hero's grave
He died, he died for freedom.

Should their fell vengeance sweep the land,
And every son of freedom fall —
And tyrant rage but stay its hand
When desolation buries all;
Sweetly will sleep the patriot brave: —
While the chained slave that treads his grave
Envies a death for freedom.

This tribute to the executed Pentrich rebels was written by Thomas Wooler, editor of the weekly satirical pamphlet *The Black Dwarf*. Circulation of non-stamped newspapers and satirical journals like *The Black Dwarf*, written for working class people, well exceeded that of more traditional periodicals in those days. But publishing was a risky business, as William Cobbett knew. It would only be a short time before he was sentenced back to prison. Instead he traveled secretly to Liverpool and sailed for the United States on March 27, 1817. (Cole: 1924, 217)

Government operatives encouraged workers to get involved in hopeless demonstrations and insurrections. The so-called Pentrich Rising was a clandestine demonstration engineered by government agent provocateur William Oliver. The tiny village of Pentrich, located some twenty miles from Nottingham, had a population of around 200. Oliver tricked the villagers into demonstrating, giving the government the opportunity to enforce bills which had been passed: suspension of habeas corpus in March, 1817; limits on the size of meetings; penalties for expressing treasonable thoughts; and other restrictions collectively called the "gagging acts." These new laws worked well in the highly visible trials of the workers from the area of Pentrich. Some seventeen were transported to Australia, and three of the leaders were hanged; due to the kind heart of the Regent, they were not drawn and quartered, only beheaded.

After Spa Fields in 1816, Cartwright concentrated on establishing Hampden clubs in Middleton, Oldham, Manchester, Rochdale, Ashton-under-Lyme, and Stockport. All of these clubs were infiltrated by government spies, who repeated the same pattern time and time again: provoke illegal activities, then arrest those who participate. Examples were the Blanketeers March of 1817, Pentrich Rising of June 1817, Peterloo Massacre of August 1819, and the Cato Street Conspiracy of February 1820. (Cox: 2004, 56)

## 65 A New Song on the Great Lock-Out and Strike Of The Lancashire Factory Operatives

Bodleian Library: The Firth Collection. c.26(229) – Roud V4706

*Tune: The Miller of Dee; Village Opera, 1729*

Good people give attention and Listen to my song
Some facts to you I'll mention and will not keep you long
In Ashton, Oldham, and Staleybridge, the operatives are on strike
We hope they'll stick together boys and one and all unite.

> CHORUS
> Then pull yourselves together boys,
> United we'll be strong
> And if we pull together, boys
> The strike it can't last long

The Strippers and the Grinder's also struck, it is the truth I tell
Some people say they have raised Old Nick, Brimstone and Sulphur
  as well.
The Miners now are on the strike, we hope they'll win the day,
And show the masters that they can, if they only get fair play.

I hope you'll all take my advice, And don't get drunk and cross,
Or they will lock you up my boys, and make you pay the costs,
And all you men who beat your wives, Just take them by the wizen,
You can't afford to kick them now, Since clogs and boots have risen.

Now if you should in trouble get and brought before the Court,
The lawyers they will raise the fee, Your case for to support.
And should your wife fall in the straw, The Doctors are no gabbies,
They have lately raised the midwife fee, So that's a rise in Babys

So to conclude and make an end, and finish up my song,
We hope that you will win the day, And that before it's long,
I hope the masters they'll agree to give the men their due,
And then they'll go to work again, Like Briton's bold and true

> Then pull yourselves together boys,
> United we'll be strong
> And if we pull together, boys
> The strike it can't last long

This song was written during the strike that started in Lancashire in July of 1818, when cotton manufacturers reneged on their commitment to restore two-year-old wage cuts to spinners. Workers had accepted the cuts during a reduction of the price for spun yarn during harder times, with the guarantee that wages would be restored when the price had recovered, but the manufacturers broke that promise. The spinners responded by striking. The strike was sufficiently grave to attract the notice of the London Press. (Halévy: 1961, 57)

It appeared that Lancashire was on the verge of a general strike when weavers and miners joined them, but two months later the spinners accepted manufacturers' terms and the entire action ended. This and other strikes were broken, partly because hunger forced the strikers back to work but also by the arrest and conviction of their leaders on the charges of combination and conspiracy. (Cole, Postgate: 1961, 225)

## 66 The Tradesmen's Complaint

Sir Frederick Madden's Collection of Broadside Ballads, 11/7468 – Roud 1206

*Tune: Roast Beef of Old England; James Aird, 1731*

Draw near bro-ther trades-men, lis-ten to __ my song,

Tell me if you can where our trade is all gone,

For long I have tra-veled but I can get none,

Oh! the dead times in Old Eng-land, In Eng-land what ve-ry bad times.

Draw near brother tradesmen, listen to my song,
Tell me if you can where our trade is all gone,
For long I have traveled but I can get none,
Oh! the dead times in Old England,
In England what very bad times.

If you go to a shop and ask for a job,
The answer is no with a shake of the nob,
'Tis enough to make a man turn to and rob
Oh! the dead times of Old England, &c.

There's many a tradesman you'll see in the street,
Walks from morning to evening employment to seek,
'Till he has scarcely any shoes to his feet.
Oh! the dead times &c,

There are sailors and soldiers returned from the wars,
Who bravely have fought in their country's cause,
To come home to be starved better staid where they was,
Oh! the dead time &c,

Provisions is pretty cheap it is true,
But if you have no money there's none for you,
What is a poor man with a family to do,
Oh! the dead times &c,

So now conclude and finish my song,
Let's hope these dead times they will not last long,
That we may have reason to alter our tone, and sing of
Oh! the good times in Old England,
In England what very good times.

Mate, C., No. 9 Market Place, Dover.

The economy for much of the country began to improve by 1818 in man-ufacturing areas, as pointed out in this song, but the boom was short-lived. By the middle of 1819, depression was as deep as it had been two or three years before. (Cole, Postgate: 1961, 225)

By now the general unrest throughout Lancashire, Derby, and other manufacturing districts was ripe for organizing by the advocates of reform. Other ballads at this time compared the conditions of the British working-man to those of slaves in America. Considering that housing and food were provided to slaves and not to the British workingman, a case was made for the slave being better off. No wonder the working man was considered a wage slave.

Satanic Mills

## 67 The Meeting at Peterloo
Bodleian Library: The Johnson Collection, 2673 – Roud V17536

Tune: The Nut Girl; Broadside, 1819-44

Come lend an ear of pi-ty while I my tale do tell,

It hap-pened at___ Man-ches-ter a place that's known right well,

For to ad-dress our wants and woes re-form-ers took their way,

A law-ful meet-ing being called up-on a cer-tain day.

CHORUS

With Hen-ry hunt we'll go___ With Hen-ry hunt we'll go,

We'll mount the cap of li-ber-ty in spite of Na-dine Joe.

Come lend an ear of pity while I my tale do tell,
It happened at Manchester a place that's known right well,
For to address our wants and woes reformers took their way,
A lawful meeting being called upon a certain day.*

On the sixteenth day of August Eighteen Hundred and Nineteen,
There many thousand people on every road were seen,
From Stockport, Oldham, Ashton and other places too,
It was the largest meeting reformers ever knew.

Brave Hunt he was appointed that day to take the chair,
At one o'clock he did arrive our shouts did rend the air,
Some females fair in white and green near the hustings stood,
And little did we expect to see such scenes of blood.

Scarcely had Hunt begun to speak three cheers was all the cry,
What to shout we scarcely knew but still we did comply,
He saw the enemies, be firm said he my friends,
But little did we expect what would be the end.

Our enemies so cruel regardless of our woes,
They did agree to force us from the plain of Peterloo,
But if that we had been prepared or any cause for fear,
The regulars might have cleared the ground, and they stood in the rear.

Then to the fatal ground they went and thousands tumbled down,
And many harmless females lay there bleeding on the ground,
No time for flight was given us still every road we fled,
But heaps on heaps were trampled down some wounded and some dead.

Brave Hunt was arrested and several others too,
Then marched to the New Bailey, believe me it is true,
Numbers were wounded and many there were slain,
Which makes the friends of those dear souls so loudly to complain.

O God look down upon us for thou art just and true,
And those that can no mercy show thy vengeance is their due;
Now quit this hateful mournful scene and look forward with this hope,
That every murderer in this land may swing upon a rope.

But soon reform shall spread around for sand the tide won't stay.
May all the filth in our land right soon be washed away,
And may sweet harmony from hence in this our land be found,
May we be blessed with plenty in all the country round.

*This broadside is frequently sung today with the chorus:
  *With Henry hunt we'll go, With Henry hunt we'll go,*
  *We'll mount the cap of liberty, in spite of Nadine Joe*

The slaughter at St Peter's Field in Manchester on August 16, 1819 was, for a brief time, the turning point in public sentiment for the move for reform. This song represents the view adopted by most as word spread of the carnage.

Deputy constable Joseph Nadin (Nadine Joe) wielded immense corrupting power in Manchester. With virtually unlimited powers of arrest, and holding corruptible power in a dozen other ways, Nadine was a force to be reckoned with. For twenty years he was said to be the *real* ruler of Manchester.

Henry Hunt was escorted to the stage by a squadron of women dressed in white. Estimates of the size of the crowd as in all such meetings vary considerably depending on the leanings of the observer, but Hunt estimated the crowd at 180,000 to 200,000. *The Manchester Observer* estimated the crowd at 153,000, but most settled on the number of 60,000. "An astonishing figure it was too, being six per cent of the total population of Lancashire. Of the people in the South-east area of the county, upon which the meeting drew, about 1 in 2 were present." (Marlow: 1970, 25)

Then, who knows why, a stampede started. The yeomanry began to charge in earnest at the helpless crowd, which fled in panic. Eleven were killed and many hundreds were injured, some by saber cuts and some by being trampled underfoot by the horses of the yeomanry or by the fleeing crowd. Two women and a child were left among the dead. (Cole Postgate: 1961, 226)

E. P. Thompson recounts how Samuel Bamford left Manchester on that disastrous day searching anxiously for his wife on the road along which hundreds were streaming in disarray to the upland districts. Having caught up with a great number of the Middleton and Rochdale contingents, he remembers: "I rejoined my comrades, and forming about a thousand of them into file, we set off to the sound of fife and drum, with our only banner waving, and in the form we re-entered the town of Middleton." (Thompson: 1966: 710)

Peterloo

Chapter 7
# GAGGED: 1819–1830

*I asked the fiend, for whom these rites were meant?*
*"These graves," quoth he, "when life's brief oil is spent,*
*When the dark night comes, and they're sinking bed wards,*
*I mean for Castles, Oliver, and Edwards."*
— Charles Lamb, "The Three Graves"

This era started in newsworthy tumult. Greatly distressed by the Peterloo Massacre, working people faced more assaults designed by the Tory government to obstruct their pursuit of Parliamentary reform. As if the two Gagging Acts of 1817 weren't enough, the notorious Six Acts were passed on December 30, 1819, confirming the government's intent to suppress all forms of public effort to influence national policies. To assure the effectiveness of these drastic new measures, informers and provocateurs continued to infiltrate organizations thought to favor altering the electoral process of Britain, to provoke actions that could be used to justify the passage of the new Six Acts. Adding to the turmoil around these new Gagging Acts were the death of the mad King George III; the assumption of the throne by his hated son George IV; the death of Napoleon Bonaparte on St Helena; and the death of the adored Queen Caroline. Beneath the official news covered by the mainstream press were the popular opinions about these events, and the ongoing undercurrents of hardship and reform recorded in the alternative press and in broadside ballads.

The notorious Six Gagging Acts to rein in working class action were:

*Training Prevention Act*—Training or drilling with weapons became subject to arrest and transportation.

*Seizure of Arms Act*—Private property could be searched, weapons seized, and their owners arrested.

*Misdemeanors Act*—Processes were expedited for the punishment for violations.

*Seditious Meetings Act*—Permission was required for public meetings of more than 50 people.

*Blasphemous and Seditious Libels Act*—Penalties for such crimes increased to fourteen years' transportation.

*Newspaper and Stamp Duties Act*—Increased taxes were levied for publishing opinion and not news.

By the end of 1819 all the Acts were law, hampering further efforts toward political reform.

Despite passage of the Six Acts, some saw the need for violent action. There followed in the next few months three major confrontations between workers and the government. They were the Cato Street Conspiracy in London on February 23, 1820, the West Riding of Yorkshire Revolt starting on April 1, and the Scottish Insurrection of early April. All involved poorly armed workers, the military, and the intervention of government provocateurs, resulting in hangings, imprisonment, and transportation of large numbers of people. Government-paid provocateurs who were thought to have organized these traps included John Castle, George Edwards, and Alex Richmond. It is now clear that, regardless of desire and need, neither the conditions nor the leadership for a successful insurrection existed at this time. (Morton: 1979, 367)

On November 20, 1819, Tom Paine returned posthumously to the country of his birth. William Cobbett had exhumed his bones in New Rochelle, New York, and returned with them to England. Evading the Newspaper and Stamp Duties Act, the unstamped radical press continued to enjoy sales exceeding those of the mainstream press, and new publications were regularly starting up in major cities, but Cobbett decided to comply with the Newspaper and Stamp Duties Act by paying all fees, and found no shortage of news to present in his *Weekly Political Register*. (Thompson: 1966, 674) In 1820, he ran for a seat in Parliament.

In January, 1820 the blind and insane George III died, and his son George IV, who had been effectively ruling as Regent since 1811, officially inherited the throne. This prompted George's estranged and exiled wife Caroline to return from the continent to claim her crown. Nothing at the time equaled the immense public excitement over the story of Queen Caroline. "Propagandists created an image of a wronged woman bravely standing up to the wicked king and corrupt ministers who had attacked the people's liberties." (Turner: 2000, 165) Her popularity stemmed from the universal dislike of the new Monarch. But she was denied her crown and, the year after her return, she suddenly fell ill and died. Judging by the number of broadside ballads on the saga of Caroline's death and her rejection by the power elite, her plight was long and deeply felt by hard-pressed tradesmen and workers.

Napoleon died three months before Caroline, on Saturday, May 5, 1821. In his July 14 edition of the *Weekly Political Register*, Cobbett said he had received a request from an able writer who, on good authority, wanted him to print the real facts concerning Napoleon's death. The able writer was most likely Dr. Barry O'Meara, former physician to Napoleon while on St Helena, who had long warned that Napoleon was being poisoned. In 1822 O'Meara published *Napoleon in Exile, or A Voice from St Helena*, which was widely sold, and started an extra wave of English sympathy for Napoleon. A large number of elegant pro-Napoleon ballads continued to be produced in Ireland, Scotland, England, and the United States throughout the 19th century. The sentiments of the ballads echo those expressed in ballads written in tribute to Queen Caroline.

Members of Parliament interested in Reform continued their attempts to pass reform acts throughout this decade. In 1821, MP John George Lambton, who was called "Radical Jack," submitted a strong Parliamentary Reform Bill that was soundly rejected. In 1822, Earl Russell's motion to transfer seats from under-populated boroughs to unrepresented cities was defeated 269 to 164. During the first four months of 1830, the ultra-Tory Blandford's Parliamentary Reform Bill was defeated 160–57; Russell's bill to give direct representation to Birmingham, Leeds, and Manchester was defeated 188–140; Daniel O'Connell's bill for universal manhood suffrage, secret ballot, and triennial parliaments was defeated 319–13; and finally, Russell's proposal to take away 60 seats from smallest boroughs and transfer them to biggest towns and counties was defeated 213–117.

Farm labor both in Ireland and the southeast of England continued to suffer from low wages, underemployment, and high food costs. Adding to the rural worker's plight were the continuing enclosures of public lands and the ever-oppressive poaching laws. The plight of agricultural workers led to several incidents of burning hay rigs as early as 1822. At the same time, the agricultural workers of Ireland were greatly afflicted by a serious decline in the much relied upon potato crop. In June of 1822 it is believed that more than 100,000 died from starvation in Ireland. The famine reached catastrophic proportions in the 1840s.

In 1823, Irish politician Daniel O'Connell formed the Catholic Association to fight for Catholic emancipation, repeal of the Union with Britain, land reform, an end to tithes, and democratic suffrage. Members of the Association paid a penny each month, which eventually amounted to as much as £1,000 a week to support the Association's causes. (Kee: 1976, 182) Although as a Catholic he was ineligible to serve in Parliament, O'Connell was overwhelmingly elected to represent County Clare in 1828. (Irish "two-pound" Catholic householders were eligible to vote but could not hold public office.) Fearing the consequences of refusal to seat O'Connell, Wellington's Tory government in April 1829 was compelled to pass the Catholic Emancipation Act. (Cole & Postgate: 1938, 248) The Tory Governments enacted additional needed regulations including:

Reducing the number of crimes subject to capital punishment, 1823

Ending combination acts that had prevented workers from forming
trade unions, 1824

Establishing the municipal police force, 1828

Eliminating the Test Act which enfranchised Protestant dissenters, 1828

An economic downturn in 1826 that returned to levels experienced immediately after the Napoleonic War led to real depression by 1828, contrib-
uting to public unrest. Major strikes and lockouts in the garment industry
resulted in workers losing wages for as long as six months during 1828–9.
John Doherty was a labor leader and organizer of the Grand Union of
Operative Cotton Spinners throughout Britain. At a meeting on the Isle of
Wight in December 1829, he emerged with an agreement on a National
strike pay of 10s. To keep the pot boiling, Henry Hunt formed a new
Radical Reform Association in 1829, and Cobbett visited northern industrial cities in 1830, speaking on the need for reform.

Cobbett carrying the bones of Paine

# 68 Gagging or The Worst Robbers of All

Sir Frederick Madden's Collection of Broadside Ballads: 8/5215

Tune: Derry Down; ballad tune, pre-1700

In the Days of our fathers, when matters of state
Were freely discussed without rancor or hate,
A question arose, whom with truth we might call,
Midst rogues of all kinds, the worst robbers of all.

The *Footpad* who gags the poor devils he robs,
Does no more than *great men* when engaged in *black jobs*;
But, in fact, though *such gagging* we horrid do call,
We cannot count him the worst robber of all.

Said a grave-looking elder, I'll soon let you see,
And certain I am you'll not differ from me;
The *Baker* who poisons, a villain we call,
But yet he is not the worst robber of all.

The *Doctor* who robs you of health with his fee,
While out of my dotage shall ne'er physic me;
With pain when he tampers, a rogue you may call,
But still we've not found the worst robber of all.

In the *Lawyer's chicane*, when he urges to sue,
You all the world over a rascal may view;
But though with strict justice a knave you may call,
The issue won't prove the worst robber of all.

The *Brewer*, the Merchant, with sugar of lead,
Your bowels may ruin, and madden your head;
'Tis true, these most justly you villains may call,
But of *rogues, they* are not the worst robbers of all.

The *Seducer*, when innocence falls in his way,
Has to answer for her whom his arts lead astray;
A villain detested we ever should call,
But yet we've to seek the worst robbers of all.

The *Detracter*, more base, still exceeds him in crime,
For in cold-blooded darkness he chooses his time;
Though in evil most fatal his practices fall,
Even he we can't say's the worst robber of all.

But abhorrence, you cry, of new language has need,
To paint him who merits this stigma, *indeed*;
Indignation will burst for its utt'rance to call,
Delinquents so vile,—the worst robbers of all.

They're the slaves who pervert the best claims of the T—e,
Who by gagging the nation would rule all alone,
Who would *rob a whole People of Freedom*, we call,
And execrate—sure, the WORST ROBBERS OF ALL!

Published by John Fairburn, 2, Broadway, Ludgate-Hill
Price Twopence
Marchant, Printer, Ingram Court, London

Recognizing the level of apprehension that these severe decrees provoked, it is surprising that this broadside included the name and address of both the publisher and printer. Perhaps it was a form of civil disobedience.

The meeting at Peterloo was planned to be the springboard to make Parliament transform the United Kingdom into a people's democracy. Instead, the Peterloo Massacre was used to justify cutting back civil rights by enacting the Six Gagging Acts, building on the two earlier Gagging Acts of 1817. Passed on December 30, 1819, the six new Gagging Acts further restricted freedoms by renouncing ancient rights to meet, express opinions, or own weapons, and they expanded what constituted seditious and blasphemous libel. Additionally, the combined acts instituted new punishments for violation of these draconian laws, including transportation for seven years, and shortening the time between indictment and trial. (Chase: 2013, 45)

A FREEBORN ENGLISHMAN,
*the Admiration of the World; the Envy of Surrounding Nations;*
*&c &c.*

## 69 The Coventry March

Bodleian Library: G. A. Warw b.2(783) — Roud V38874

*Tune: Scots Wha Hae*

Ye who Cob-bett's doc-trine wed Ye who Har-ry Hunt has led

Bet-ter ye were all sick in bed Than join such trea-che-ry.

Sit at home sir's snug and warm, Wise-ly shun the com-ing Storm

A-way with Ra-di-cal Re-form Tis naught but Fool-e-ry

Ye who Cobbett's doctrine wed
Ye who Harry Hunt has led—
Better ye were all sick in bed
Than join such treachery.

Sit at home sirs snug and warm,
Wisely shun the coming Storm
Away with Radical Reform
Tis naught but Foolery.

Why across the Atlantic Main,
Comes the old knave back again,
Bringing the rotten bones of Paine?
Base effrontery.

The rogue but wants to steal your pence
He'll pay you back in impudence;
His patriotism is mere pretense,
To 'scape from poverty

Then save your cash, my friends I pray
From Coventry he'll sneak away,
And Botany's appropriate bay,
Soon no doubt he'll see.

Happy the day for Britain's Isle,
When Hunt and Cobbett quit our soil,
With impious Howe and mad Carlisle
The dregs of Blasphemy.

Turner Printer

"The Coventry March" is an anti-Cobbett election hit piece written when he first sought election to Parliament in 1820. This election was required by the death of George III and the ascension of George IV. It is a shame that this disparaging song was set to the beautiful melody that Burns used for "Scots Wha Hae."

Unaware of the pending invocation of the new Gagging Acts, and carrying the bones of Tom Paine, William Cobbett arrived back in Liverpool on November 20, 1819, returning from the United States where he had sought sanctuary from prosecution under the English Gagging Laws of 1817. He intended to make amends for the disparaging remarks he had made about Paine's character and philosophy in earlier issues of his *Weekly Political Register* by carrying Paine's bones to England, "there to enshrine them in a mausoleum worthy of the great services which the great author of *The Rights of Man* had done to mankind." (Cole: 1924, 235)

Cobbett described his almost two-year escape to America:

> When I retreated to America, it was not to secure myself from personal suffering so much as to be able to finish, in spite of gags, dungeons, and halters, the great work of exposing the horrid system, by the means of which this country has been brought to its present most miserable and degraded state; and I am glad to perceive, that you are of opinion that I have succeeded in putting the finishing hand to that exposure. (Cobbett: 1819, 402)

The story behind this Coventry election illustrates the poor state of the British electoral system at the time, and how, without secret ballot, elections could be manipulated. Cobbett was running against two prominent incumbent Whigs, Peter Moore and Edward Ellice, for one of two Coventry seats in Parliament. From a husting set up at a place called Cross Cheaping, the candidates addressed the crowd before eligible voters walked to their candidate's booth and voted by signing their name. Coventry had a long history of wild battles at the hustings, and the election of 1820 was no exception. Cobbett told of his supporters having their coats ripped up behind, and under Ellice's instigation some ruffians attempted to beat him up. The result of this election was: Ellice, 1,474 votes; Moore, 1,442 votes; and Cobbett, 517 votes. Ellice ran again in 1826, and lost by over 3,000 votes.

Plagued with debts, Cobbett faced the dilemma of complying with the new Gagging Law (Six Acts) or facing the consequences. He ultimately gave in and started to pay the "tax on knowledge" and to charge sixpence for his *Weekly Political Register*. This greatly reduced his readership and was a loss to those most in need of the information he disseminated.

## 70 Dark Bonnymuir

National Library of Scotland, Digital Gallery, Word on the Street — Roud V26972

*Tune: Afton Water; Alexander Hume, 1850*

As eve - ning dashed on the west - ern o-cean,
Ca - le - do - nia stood perched on the waves of the Clyde;
Her arms wide ex - ten-ded she raised with de - vo - tion,
'My poor bleed - ing coun-try' she ve - he-ment - ly cried.
A - rise up my coun - try and hail re - for - ma-tion;
A - rise and de - mand now the rights of __ our __ na - tion.
Be - hold your op - press - ors shall meet the de - so - la - tion;
That marked the brave vic-tims at Dark Bon - ny - muir.

As evening dashed on the western ocean,
Caledonia stood perched on the waves of the Clyde;
Her arms wide extended she raised with devotion,
'My poor bleeding country' she vehemently cried,
Arise up my country and hail reformation;
Arise and demand now the rights of our nation.
Behold your oppressors shall meet the desolation;
That marked the brave victims at dark Bonnymuir,

On the 5th of April, eighteen hundred and twenty,
The great Baird & Hardie did march from their homes;
To guard their freedom, homes, rights, peace and plenty,
But tyranny conquered and gave them a tomb.

Like traitors they died on the 8th of September;
In the cold silent grave they were consigned to slumber,
But heaven will avenge them let tyrants remember;
And raise up new heroes on Dark Bonnymuir,

Though freedom has bled on the field sorely wounded,
Shall liberty perish and die in its bloom?
Shall tyranny triumph though freedom has grounded?
The arms of the hero's that lie ill in the tomb,
But freedom shall rise to the greatest perfection,
Avenging her wrongs with hard words of correction;
When on my country with filial affection,
I sigh for the martyrs of Dark Bonnymuir.

How long shall tyrants usurp over freedom?
How long shall we groan in their vile servile chains?
Arise up my children & sink them like Sodom.
E'er sad desolation reigns over the plains;
O, muse on the day when great Wallace was rearing,
The broadsword of Scotland, when tyrants were fearing;
At the sound of the trumpet were thousands appearing,
To die, or to conquer on Dark Bonnymuir.

Those dear sons of freedom prosperity shall never,
Forget Baird and Hardie, who would them disown;
In the breast of the country their memory shall ever,
Be a monument more lasting than sculptured stone;
Remembrance shall dwell on their tragical story,
*That will be told in song, verse and story forever, **
But heaven shall reward them with bright shining glory,
In regions far distant from Dark Bonnymuir.

But why should I pass that great patriot Wilson.
Who died by oppressive and arbitrary laws;
He left his dear Straven, with a band of brave hero's,
Resolved to have justice, or die for the cause
But alas! He was taken while fate seemed to waver;
All bloody his head they did cruelly sever.
But the heart of the country shall reverence for ever;
The fate of great Wilson and Dark Bonnymuir

No longer the enemies of justice and freedom,
Shall make the sons of Scotia, in poverty to mourn;
Our noble patriotic Reformers shall make them
O, how shall we make them a grateful return?

Mechanics shall prosper, and commerce shall flourish,
The horn of plenty our country shall nourish,
When the tyrant and all despots shall perish,
With prosecuted freedom on Dark Bonnymuir.

\* missing line reconstructed by the author

Despite the Six Acts, radical reformers were provoked to risk three notably aggressive actions in early 1820. They were the Cato Street Conspiracy, involving London members of the Spencean Philanthropists; the Scottish Insurrection in Scotland, ending with its Battle of Bonnymuir; and The Yorkshire West Riding Revolt, that took place over a wide area for twelve days in April. The Cato Street Rebellion was a sting operation put together by a government provocateur, George Edwards, who had planted a sham newspaper notice saying that the Prime Minister and his entire cabinet would dine at a certain home on a certain evening, February 23rd. The radicals' plan for a stunning slaughter of the entire group was easily thwarted.

This Scottish ballad is about a minor incident toward the end of a relatively obscure insurrection. Much like other insurrections of that time, it was provoked by government provocateurs, but the ballad praises the bravery shown by the heroes who risked their lives in the cause of Scottish freedom. The Scottish Radical War started with a false proclamation that was posted widely across five counties in southeastern Scotland. Addressed to "Inhabitants of Great Britain and Ireland," it announced formation of a provisional government that would enable the secession of Scotland from the United Kingdom. In Glasgow it was soon realized that the fake proclamation referred to the Magna Carta and the Bill of Rights, rather than to Scotland's Declaration of Arbroath, and must have been written by an Englishman. Much of the misdirection that occurred in the Radical War was directed by then Home Secretary Sidmouth's spies, including "John King who called himself a weaver but did not apparently follow any particular calling and always seemed to be in funds, who emerged as the chief of these agents." (Berresford Ellis, Mac A'Ghobhainn: 1989, 138)

Based on the posted notice, almost all the laboring population in southeastern Scotland abandoned their work on Monday, April 3. Over the next few days, military forces were brought out and uprising leaders, including James Wilson, were taken into custody. One of the last actions in this "Radical War" was the "Battle of Bonnymuir" that took place on April 5 near Bonnybridge, where a small band of poorly armed workers were marching to join an alleged larger contingent. They were stopped by soldiers, and eighteen were arrested and taken to Sterling Castle along with their leaders: weaver Andrew Hardy, and Peninsular War veteran John Baird, who are cited in this song. (Chase: 2013, 119) A concurrent uprising in the West Riding of Yorkshire followed a similar set of happenings where marchers believed that they would be supporting their Scottish neighbors.

Of the thirteen tried for participation in the Cato Street Conspiracy, five were hanged and beheaded and six were transported for life. Of the participants in the Radical War, three were hanged and beheaded, and twenty were transported for life. Of the twenty-six arrested in the West Riding of Yorkshire, fourteen were transported for life, and twelve served jail sentences. The eight people who were beheaded were the first to be beheaded in England since Colonel Despard on February 21, 1803, and the last ever to be beheaded in the United Kingdom.

Yorkshire Revolt, Cato Street Rebellion, Scottish Insurrection

## 71 The New Bunch of Loughero

Sir Frederick Madden's Collection of Broadside Ballads: 12/8410 – Roud V43649

Tune: Bonny Bunch of Roses; Joyce, 1830

By the Da-nube as I walked ___ One eve-ning in the month of June

Where the warb-ling fea-thered song - sters Their cheer-ful notes did sweet-ly tune.

I heard a love-ly fair one, Who seemed to be in grief and woe;

Those words she was re - peat - ing: I have lost my Bunch of Lough-e - ro ___

By the Danube as I walked One evening in the month of June,
Where the warbling feathered songsters Their cheerful notes did
    sweetly tune,
I heard a lovely fair one, Who seemed to be in grief and woe;
Those words she was repeating: I have lost my Bunch of Loughero.

Oh then had I the indies, Likewise the Peruvian store,
I'd give them to be landed, This day on St Helena's store;
With tears and kind entreaties I would invoke my bitter foe,
To give me in my arms My Bonny Bunch of Loughero.

When the powerful allied Army Surrounded my imperial throne,
Dejected and sequestered I afterwards was left alone.
Likewise, my cruel father Assisted in the overthrow,
Which leaves me here bewailing My Bonny Bunch of Loughero.

Through Egypt and through Syria He marched with honour and renown,
Twice Italy he conquered, Made Germany three times stoop down,
Until that fatal hour That he did go to Waterloo,
Which ended the proceedings Of my Bonny Bunch of Loughero.

Then a lovely youth stepped forward And took this lady by the hand,
Saying madam, do have patience, Till I am able to take command,
I'll raise a powerful army, And through tremendous dangers go,
If providence assists me, I will restore your Bunch of Loughero.

If fortune does not slight me, I will make St Helena shake;
I know my lovely countrymen Will not young Bonaparte forsake;
Should I once see my father Arise against the imperious foe,
With spirit and resolution, I would assist your Loughero

I'm told that Telemuchus To find his father once did roam,
With determin'd resolution To gain the point or ne'er come home:
The emblem of true virtue Conducted him through all his woe,
And perhaps she will be my guardian, Till I restore your Loughero.

She took him in her arms, Between joy and hope did smile,
Saying, O my lovely child, Abandon all such slavery and toil;
Ulysses did return When no man else could bend a bow,
And the case may be similar With my Bonny Bunch of Loughero.

When first I saw the great Bonaparte, I went on my bended knee
To beg my father's life of him He granted it most courteously.
The secrets of our story Are now to tedious to know,
So I'll live like chased Penelope, Still hoping for my Loughero

HALY, Printer, Hanover St., Cork

In this song "Loughero," the Irish name for rushes, appears to symbolize Napoleon Bonaparte and his legacy. It was printed by the prolific Irish printer, J. Haly, who operated during this time on Hanover Street in Cork. This Irish song seems to be the source of the most popular and most widely known British pro-Napoleon song, "Bonny Bunch of Roses O" as printed in *The New Penguin Book of English Folk Songs*. (Roud, Bishop: 2012, 8) The words appear to have been written before the death of Napoleon in 1821 and certainly before the death of his son, Francois Joseph-Charles Bonaparte in 1832. Notes for "Bonny Bunch of Roses O" in *The New Penguin Book of English Folk Songs* offer several candidates for the first printer or composer, but none are Irish.

Napoleon had not seen his son, young Napoleon, since 1814, when the boy was only three years old. Will and Ariel Durant note that Napoleon wrote in "Advice to My Son" shortly before his death in the spring of 1821: "May my son make everything blossom that I have sown! May he develop all the elements of prosperity which lie hidden in French soil!" (Durant: 1975, 768)

Since Napoleon Bonaparte's exile to Elba, young Napoleon had lived in Vienna and was known as the Duke of Reichstadt. "He remained in Austria, where he became something of a political pawn. …The young Duke nicknamed 'LAiglon,' 'the eaglet' showed a liking for military affairs as he grew, but was never allowed to correspond with his father, or was in robust health." (Haythornthwaite: 1998, 236–7)

## 72 The Knight-errant or The Distressed Queen

Bodleian Library: Johnson Ballads fol. 128 – Roud V6790

Tune: *Fall of the Leaf; Broadside, pre-1834*

When the Queen was de-tained on the Ga-li-cian shore, For want of a ves-sel to bring her safe o'er, And when in great need of pro-tec-tion she stood She found a knight-er-rant in Al-der-man wood.

When the Queen was detained on the Galician shore,
For want of a vessel to bring her safe o'er,
And when in great need of protection, she stood
She found a knight-errant in Alderman Wood.

He put her on board and without more delay,
The winds and the waves quickly bore her away
To the white cliffs of Dover, where myriads stood
To welcome the Queen and Alderman Wood.

From city to city she moved along
Midst ringing of bells and the shouts of the throng,
Who applauded her spirit and said it was good
Too nobly confide in Alderman Wood

Like some ancient heroine, she gracefully led,
The thousand on foot and the long cavalcade
Up Parliament Street by the royal abode
While on her left hand sat Alderman Wood.

All ranks and degrees did her majesty greet,
As she slowly moved on to South Audley Street
For nothing was heard from the vast multitude
But God bless the Queen and brave Alderman Wood.

The spirit of chivalry which long has been gone
And ceased to descend from the father to son,
That Spirit so noble so generous so good,
Is revived in the soul of Alderman Wood.

Alderman Matthew Wood and other radicals championed Caroline, mother of Princess Charlotte who had been second heir to the throne after her father, George IV. During Charlotte's life, it had been advantageous for radicals to support Caroline, anticipating the demise of both George III and the loathed George IV. With Charlotte's early death and the long decline of George III, there remained a high level of popular support fostered by the radicals for Queen Caroline. Her return to England in June 1820 was a good way to rub raw the sores of discontent over passage of the Six Acts and the distaste for George IV.

George IV had married his cousin Caroline of Brunswick in 1795, but they had lived together for less than a year. The King's long list of indiscretions, including his earlier clandestine marriage to the Catholic widow, Mrs. Fitzherbert, was common knowledge. In 1806, while Regent, he had attempted to divorce Caroline, and insisted that her name be omitted from the liturgy of the Church of England. (Robins: 2006, 97) Following the death of George III, not willing to settle for anything less than Coronation and recognition as Queen, Caroline returned to England on June 3, 1820, after living a highly publicized bohemian life on the Continent since 1814.

Wood, a radical Member of Parliament and former Mayor of London, met Queen Caroline in France and escorted her via Dover to London. "En route, she was greeted by adoring crowds. At the small market town of Sittingbourne, the clergy, though forbidden from mentioning her name in the church liturgy, stood by the road and blessed her as she passed." (Fraser: 1996, 367)

Caroline of Brunswick

# 73 The Queen
## or the Birth, Rise, and Progress of The Green Bag!!!

Bodleian Library: Johnson Ballads fol.294 – Roud V10267

Tune: The Legacy; Thomas Moore, 1808

A King it appears, who lived sixty odd years
Was determined his Queen to Divorce sir.
But that could not be, as you plainly may see
For she'd led the life of a saint sir,
However not daunted, his noodle he haunted
Till his majesty pitch'd on a plan sir,
To traduce our dear Queen, thro' agent's unseen
And vice chancellor Leach, was the man Sir.

Away then he went, and to Milan was bent
To act a most dastardly part Sir,
Which he did complete, and hastened to greet
His Employers, with gladness of heart Sir,
No sooner retur'd, than the Ministers burn'd
To know the success of their Plot Sir,
With wide-open eyes, they examined the prize
And they returned thanks to the knight Sir.

And now to proceed with the greatest of speed
A cabinet Council was called Sir,
To Debate on the plan, and the way to begin
So agreeably were they employed Sir,
The question was solv'd, and at length 'twas resolv'd
That while she remain'd contented Sir,
That nothing should be done, but if she came home
A green bag, should be presented Sir.

Our Royal Queen came, which did them so inflame
That the very same day was brought down sir,
A green Bag with Seals, and attach'd to its heels
A Royal Message from the Crown Sir,
Upon which it was mov'd, with hopes of being prov'd
That the Papers the Bag contained Sir,
Should referred be, to a Secret Committee
For them to report, as they found Sir.

A short time after, being all for their Master
The Committee made their report Sir,
And thought that the Queen, was too guilty to screen
Although they had tried her to Bribe Sir,
A bill was brought in, by these fine men of sin
Our gracious Queen to degrade Sir,
But we hope it won't pass, which should it alas
Why Englishmen, you must support Her.

King George IV wanted to divorce Caroline but had to prove her infidelities to do so. The sealed "green bag" of this song allegedly contained evidence revealing the Queen's many indiscretions while living abroad. Under the king's orders, the House of Lords formed a secret committee to review the bag's contents. The committee called on July 4, 1820 for a bill of Pains and Penalties to be introduced to the House of Lords. If passed, the bill would deprive the Queen of her royal title and dissolve the marriage.

Henry Brougham, a liberal Whig Member of Parliament and prominent lawyer, represented the Queen at Westminster, while Cobbett and most of the radical press persisted with articles supporting Caroline.

After four months of deliberations the Peers eventually passed the measure on November 6, but only by nine votes. Passage by such a small majority in the Lords meant certain defeat in the House of Commons, and the matter was withdrawn, after being tabled for six months. "The results of the trial touched off celebrations throughout the country. The outcome was at least a notable triumph for public opinion and strengthened the Whigs' ongoing battle for parliamentary reform." (Dinwiddy: 1986, 38)

## 74 A New Song on Lambton's Motion for Reform

The Bell/White 2 collection at Newcastle University

Tune: Weel May the Keel Row; McClean Collection, 1772

When this Nation is ruled by a set of base knaves,
Who've extinguished our Rights and would have us be slaves,
*A Chip off the old Block* is still left off that tree,
Which flourished in Albion when Britons were free.

CHORUS
Lambton and Liberty!—Priests without Politics!
Lambton and Liberty! Lambton huzza!

O in history the Lambton's for ages have stood,
Fam'd for Independence—of old and tried blood;
Unbiased, un-pension'd, their virtues so rare,
Has descended to Lambton, the pride of the Wear.

To his flowing speeches ye people attend,
He stands forth a protector, your Rights to defend;
Nor longer he says, can we *weather the storm,*
Unless they attend to his plan of Reform.

Each attack on our Freedom doth always oppose,
And "Corruption he bravely does twitch by the nose,"
With gratitude glowing our bosoms appear,
Long, long, shall the deeds reign of Lambton of Wear.

In him the oppressor shall ne'er find a friend,
The Oppressed One who always their wrongs will defend,
Fame's records resplendent his name shall adorn,
And his virtues be cherish'd by ages unborn.

Those exalted men who've supported his cause,
Our praise do inspire, … our warmest applause;
Still, still in our isle reigns that spirit held dear,
That spirit that animates Lambton of Wear.

Grey, Cartwright, Burdett, and Hobhouse do stand
In the cause of Reform, a patriotic band,
Coke Wilson and Whitbread, their efforts do join,
With Wood, the staunch friend of Queen Caroline.

With many more worthies, the pride of our land,
O may they a speedy Reform soon command,
With such zealous friends we may hope it is near,
And success crown the efforts of Lambton of Wear!

May our Coal Trade and Commerce unboundedly thrive
And the blessings of Peace, all its Bounties revive;
So now to the end of my song I draw near,
Success to Reform, and the trade of the Wear.

In early 1821 Lord John Russell proposed that the rotten borough of Grampound in Cornwall be disenfranchised for gross corruption and that its two parliamentary seats be transferred to Leeds. It was realized in discussion that the Leeds constituency included a large number of working class electors, so the seats were transferred instead to county seats in Yorkshire. Passage of the Grampound Bill encouraged John George Lambton to propose a bill to shorten Parliament terms to three years; to enfranchise all copyholders, leaseholders, resident householders, and payers of direct taxes; and to revise constituency boundaries in England and Wales. On April 17, 1821 Lambton moved for a committee to consider the state of representation, intending to submit his bill for consideration, but the proposal was easily defeated. (Turner: 2000, 174) Clearly Parliament did not hold similar views to the working people at this time.

Lambton, known as "Radical Jack," was the son-in-law of Earl Charles Grey. He became Baron of Durham in 1830 and the first Earl of Durham in 1833. Grey incorporated many of Lambton's ideas into the Reform Bill of 1832 and called upon the new Baron to lead the fight for its passage.

## **75** Verses On the Death of Queen Caroline

Bodleian Library: The Harding Collection, B 25(337) — Roud V41734

*Tune: Three Merry Men of Kent; The Jovial Crew, 1731*

Weep Bri-tons weep and shed a tear, For now your vir-tuous Queen is dead,

Her trou-bles they are end - ed here, And now her soul to hea-v'n is fled,

Her hard-ships long she did en-dure, But now her trou-bles and sor-rows are o'er

She's gone to wear a crown of glo - ry, To dwell up-on the heaven-ly shore.

CHORUS

Weep Bri-tons weep and shed a tear, For Ca - ro - line your Queen is no more.

She is gone to wear a crown of glo - ry, to dwell up-on the hea-ven-ly shore.

Weep Britons weep and shed a tear,
For now your virtuous Queen is dead
Her troubles they are ended here,
And now her soul to heav'n is fled,
Her hardships long she did endure,
But now her troubles and sorrows are o'er,
She is gone to wear a crown of glory,
To dwell upon the heavenly shore.

CHORUS
Weep Britons weep and shed a tear,
For Caroline your Queen is no more,
She is gone to wear a crown of glory,
To dwell upon the heavenly shore.

When from her tender child was parted,
It griev'd her sorely to the heart,
Cruel men to be so hard hearted,
To force her to travel in foreign parts,

And then vile men was put in motion,
To follow after her as spies,
Just for to watch her ways and notions,
And bring a green bag full of lies.

She traveled the earth half over,
And visited the Holy Land,
She crossed the banks of Jordan's River
Where Joshua ordered the waters to stand,
Likewise, she visited the sepulcher,
Where our blessed Lord and Savior lay,
But now she has gone to endless glory,
All for to sing his praise always.

She was deny'd a crown on earth
But now a crown in heaven she wears,
With tens of thousands standing round her,
Welcoming her with their heavenly cheer,
Farewell Caroline thou brightest genius,
Once thou was old England's pride,
But now thou art gone to endless glory,
With heavenly angel's side by side.

Barred from coronation, the Queen suffered a quick decline in health, until she died on August 7, 1821 of symptoms similar to those of Napoleon, only one month after learning of his death. No autopsy was performed, but her death was attributed to inflammation caused by intestinal blockage. Although she had wanted to be buried at Windsor with her daughter, the Government quickly made plans to transport her body to Brunswick for burial. Her catafalque, guarded by soldiers, was to leave London via an obscure route to avoid crowds. But the procession, setting out early in the morning, found the roads had been blocked with enormous crowds. "The Life Guards attempted to forge a way through despite a heavy downpour of bricks and stones, along with driving rain.... In the end the Chief Metropolitan Magistrate... surrendered to the will of the crowd and allowed Caroline's body to be taken to the city." (Robbins: 2006, 317) The disenfranchised people's sentiment on the affair is well summed up by Flora Fraser:

> Excluded from Parliament by the net of patronage and interest, many saw her cause as mirroring their own. In their eyes, she was an injured queen, wife and mother, and a weak woman who needed their help to fight against a tyrant king, as they fought against a tyrant government. The Queen was to be a symbol of their own oppression, and a tool with which to dig at the Government. (Fraser: 1996, 366)

As for the working class uproar over the unruly Queen Caroline, Professor Elié Halévy writes: "the British public now gave another proof of its ingrained devotion to monarchy even in its attack upon George IV, by dropping the cause of manhood suffrage to display its sympathy with a persecuted Queen. The Radical agitators found themselves relegated to the background." (Halévy: 1961, 103)

Funeral Procession of Queen Caroline

## 76 Catholic Rent

Mulcahy & Fitzgibbon, *The Voice of the People* (1982) – Roud V8352

Tune: The Cottage Maid; Larry Dillon, early 1800s

You genuine muse divine your aid to me incline,
While I announce a happy visitation.
The Lord has decreed, our clergy should proceed,
and Gather in this innocent taxation.
'Tis a virtuous Plan not formed to trepan,
but to redress once More the sons of Erin.
Our rights for to reclaim for our sons of fame,
O'Connell may above be your station.

Our foes were fully bent this for to prevent.
Still they tremble at our pious institution.
In Union we consent to pay this Christian rent,
In compliance with our King and constitution,
Our island is distressed by penal laws oppressed,
And our children are drove to desolation.
Our clergy can't withstand our saintly land,
As we find in Divine Revelation.

When proud Lucifer fell and he was cast into Hell,
Through licentious inclinations,
And legions won his wit as we read in holy writ,
Which caused me to renounce divine ordination,
To the sign of the nags Head reform'd pagans fled;
With Ridly, Cranmer, Cox and Parrer,
The demon's soon decreed, our clergy for to weed,
Nothing since was seen but cruel slaughter.

Old Erin's sons awake your clergy's council take,
Be obedient to the laws of the nation,
In Union, we consent to pay this Christian Rent,
As an avenue to Emancipation.
'Twill put oppression down and those who on us frown,
And restore to us ancient Melicians, priest hunters we'll subdue,
Our rights again renew,
O'Connell you are the pride of our nation.

The demand for Catholic emancipation has a long history in Ireland. This ballad tells of winning over the priesthood in Ireland to promote Catholic emancipation throughout Britain. The third verse refers to the days of the Reformation: Bishop Ridley, an Oxford martyr under the rule of Queen Mary, was burned at the stake in 1554; Archbishop Cranmer, author of the Book of Common Prayer, died at the stake in 1556; Bishop Cox fled to the continent during the time of the burnings, returned when Elizabeth came to the throne, and worked under Archbishop William Parker. This song implies that those involved in producing the Catholic rent are mythological descendants of the Milesians who were believed to be from Spain.

Ireland's Catholic Association organized by Daniel O'Connell in 1823 was one of the most effective democratic political movements of the 19th century. As a Dublin lawyer, O'Connell had observed the abuses of British law in the courts of Ireland. His ultimate objective was to obtain repeal of the Union of Britain and Ireland. It was necessary to first obtain Catholic emancipation, and to do so a large fund was established by asking priests to collect one penny from each celebrant each month. This was very effective, gathering as much as £1,000 each week. These funds were used to assist renters who had been evicted by their landlords for voting for emancipation candidates, and to fund campaigns for Protestant candidates who promised to work for Catholic emancipation. Other movements in the struggle for reform subsequently adopted this so-called "Catholic Rent" tactic.

By 1825, the organization was so successful that the government made it illegal. O'Connell got around this by changing its name to the New Catholic Association. That same year, the House of Commons passed a Catholic emancipation act authored by Francis Burdett, but the House of Lords rejected it. (Turner: 2000, 189)

O'Connell proposing the formation of the Catholic Association

## 77 O'Connell's new Song on Emancipation

Mulcahy & Fitzgibbon, *The Voice of the People* (1982)

Tune: Bendemeer's Streem; Thomas Moore, 1817

I'm Daniel O'Connell, the mighty Agitator,
Descended from Gadhael, of a regal grand line,
In the annals of fame my ancestors were traced of,
From the earliest period to the present time.
For 28 years I have fought most courageous,
Tho' surrounded by enemies, I never yet retreated,
Without the loss of a man I have gain'd Emancipation,
And added fresh laurels to Erin go Bragh.

I have roll'd up a mill-stone against a steep mountain,
By the assistance of O'Gorman Mahon, and Sheil,
Back'd by John Lawless of the Order of Liberators,
And the praiseworthy champion brave Thomas Steel.
When we had it at the pinnacle we were sure of being victorious,
We had 7 million Catholics to roll it down head foremost
Going to the City of London we heaved it on before us
It being the conditions of Erin go Bragh.

We roll'd it up to the Parliament House in clover,
Where we met our old friend the noble Anglesey,
Says Wellington to O'Connell, you are welcome over,
My brave second Moses, your country shall be free,
I have known the Irish to be firm and true,
They fought most courageous at the battle of Waterloo
And upon the continent their foes they did subdue,
And soon let them know they were from Erin go Bragh.

After the Bill was read and laid on the table,
There was a majority of one hundred and four,
Each liberal Member his talents display'd most able,
The like in the Senate was never heard before.
May peace and plenty flow on our native isle,
And cause our distressed workmen again for to smile,
May trade and industry be promoted likewise,
To cheer up the sons of Erin go Bragh.

Now we're emancipated, God bless his gracious Majesty,
He may sit in pomp and dignity in peace on his throne
No jealousy in future, nor any animosity,
By the true members of the holy Church of Rome;
As Dan, our noble advocate, boldly pleads in Parliament
From his country's services no bribe can him draw,
The valiant sons of Granua will loudly give, with one consent,
Three cheers for O'Connell and Erin go Bragh.

O'Connell seized the chance to press for Catholic emancipation when he successfully contested the County of Clare Parliamentary seat in 1828. As a Catholic, O'Connell could legally stand for election but could not be seated unless he renounced the Roman Catholic religion. He did not intend to renounce, thus triggering a political crisis with the backing from his large devoted following in Ireland. Wellington feared that failure to seat O'Connell could touch off another insurrection in Ireland. With pressure from Robert Peel and Lord Anglesey he was able to convince the House of Lords and the Regent to pass the Catholic Emancipation Act in 1829. "In the following year, against the squabbling and divided Tories, the Whigs under Lord Grey came to power; and the country knew that Parliamentary Reform would be pressed forth at last." (Cole & Postgate: 1938, 248)

The emancipation victory wasn't as sweet as first thought. The act had small print which, although allowing Catholics to serve in most offices, limited voting to ten-pound householders (who own or rent property costing more than ten pounds a year). This meant that the majority two-pound householders who supported the Catholic Association were now disenfranchised. O'Connell had won his victory but had alienated the peasant base of his support.

The second verse cites men who assisted O'Connell in this effort. O'Gorman-Mahon was initially a strong force in O'Connell's campaign, but he eventually became one of O'Connell's severest critics. He became a soldier of fortune, fighting in armies throughout the world. Richard Lalor Sheil was a fantastic spokesperson for Catholic emancipation, and was a playwright who would become a radical Member of Parliament. John Lawless was editor of many important Irish publications and a former member of the United Irishmen. O'Connell called him "mad Lawless" after he broke with him.

Daniel O'Connell

## 78 The Handloom Weavers Lament

John Harland, *Ballads and Songs of Lancashire* (1865): 259

*Tune: Ye Parliament of England; Huntington, 1964*

You gen - tle - men and trades - men as you ride a - bout at will

Look down on these poor peo - ple it's e - nough to make you crill

Look down on these poor peo-ple as you ride up and down

And if there is a God a - bove he'll pull your pride right down

CHORUS You ty - rants of Eng - land your race will soon be run,

You will be brought in - to ac - count for what you've sore - ly done.

You gentlemen and tradesmen as you ride about at will
Look down on these poor people it's enough to make you crill
Look down on these poor people as you ride up and down
And if there is a God above he'll pull your pride right down

    You tyrants of England your race will soon be run,
    You will be brought into account for what you've sorely done.

You've pulled down our wages so shamefully to tell,
You go into the market and you say you cannot sell,
And when that we do ask you when these bad times will mend,
You quickly give an answer when the wars are at an end.

When we look upon our children, it grieves our hearts full sore,
Their clothes are all in rags and they cannot get no more.
With little in their bellies they to their work must go,
While you're so dressed as Manxy like a monkey in a show.

You go to church on Sunday and I know its naught but pride
How can there be religion when humanity's swept aside?
If there is a place in heaven as there is in the exchange,
Our poor souls must not come near there; like lost sheep they must range.

With the choicest of strong dainties your tables overspread,
With good ale and strong brandy, you make your faces red,
You invite a set of visitors, it is your chief delight,
To put your heads together for to make our faces white.

You say that Bonaparty has been the spoil of all,
And that us poor folks should pray for his downfall.
But Bonaparte is dead and gone and it is plainly shown
That we've got bigger tyrants here in Boneys of our own.

And so my friends and to conclude and for to make an end,
Let us form a plan that these bad times will end.
So give us our old prices as we have had before,
And we live in happiness and rub out the old score.

Roy Palmer suggests that this song was written around 1805, about the time of "Joan O Grinfeldt." (Palmer: 1988, 100) Since, however, all of the available versions include reference to the death of Bonaparte in the next to last verse, it was probably written in the disturbed 1820s. It tells a convincing tale of working class resentment at the gap between the rich and the poor. Coupled with severe economic recession in 1828, these resentments blossomed into full-scale demonstrations and emerging union activity. This song tells of the need for parliamentary reform and reflects on the loss of the promise of change that Napoleon's victory would have brought.

Ten years after Peterloo, the un-enfranchised workers of Manchester were still burdened by low wages, long hours, dreadful working conditions, and continuing price inflation. Child labor was the norm. Women worked long hours. Industrialists were making great fortunes while the workers starved. These hard times fueled the organization of new radical bodies to agitate for political and economic reform. The National Union of the Working Classes held meetings to discuss the ideals of Tom Paine and Robert Owen. These beginnings eventually merged into the Birmingham Political Union led by Thomas Attwood.

Chapter 8
# UNION: 1830–1836

*I'd be a Reformer destroying the power*
*Of those who would barter an Englishman's right;*
*To accomplish the project, I'd strive every hour,*
*It should be my prayer both by day and by night.* (Song No. 84)

The stunning emergence in 1830 of "Political Unions" and the demise of the despised George IV finally opened the way to achieving Britain's first Political Reform Bill. By the beginning of 1830 the need for political reform became more acute, but as long as George IV ruled, the chances of making it happen were remote. The continuing economic recession meant extreme hardships escalated for all workers in Britain. Unemployment remained rampant in the manufacturing industry, and then it spread to agricultural workers, who quickly developed "a political and class consciousness that rivaled that of the weaver, the miner and the cabinet maker." (Dyck: 1992, 75) Swing Riots arose in the southeast of England with burning of hay rigs but progressed to smashing of the newly developed steam-fired thrashing machines by late summer of 1830, and evolved into the tragedy of the Tolpuddle Martyrs from Dorsetshire in 1834.

Founded by former banker Thomas Attwood, the Birmingham Political Union was modeled after Daniel O'Connell's highly successful Irish Catholic Association, which had, against all odds, achieved Catholic emancipation in 1829. This Birmingham union, unlike most other groups, was composed of both middle class and working class men dedicated to achieving political representation for the second largest city in Britain. They sought to expand voter eligibility, remove property requirements, secure pay for Members of Parliament, and shorten the length of parliaments. The first meeting of this political union was in January 1830; it was reported that over 10,000 were in attendance. The success of the Birmingham Political Union encouraged similar groups to form in other major cities throughout Britain. In the following year, under the leadership of Place and Burdett, these bodies joined into a National Political Union, which came to represent the main body of reform opinion outside of Parliament. (Cole, Postgate: 1971, 249) The sheer number of people attending political unions throughout Britain added to the urgency for Parliamentary action in addressing their concerns.

In the winter and spring of 1830, three separate reform bills were submitted by Daniel O'Connell, John Russell, and the ultra-Tory great-grandfather of Winston Churchill, George Spencer-Churchill, Marquis of Blandford. Weak support in Parliament resulted in the defeat of all three. Then on June 26, 1830, King George IV died, clearing the way for real reform. He was succeeded by William IV, who, in spite of his many shortcomings, could not begin to be despised as much as his brother George IV. William did have some friends, but according to the press, "He was a weak common place, sort of a person who suffered from feebleness of purpose, and littleness of mind." (Pearce; Stearn: 1994, 105)

The number of members in Parliament supporting reform legislation increased slightly with the September 14, 1830 election required by the ascension of William IV to the throne. The Tories, however, maintained a slim majority and the prime minister, the Duke of Wellington, made it clear that he would not support political reform. With the rising tide of National Political Union support for reform, Wellington resigned as Prime Minister. He claimed he was doing so to prevent Brougham, who was becoming one of the chief reform spokesmen in Parliament, from submitting and passing a Progressive Reform Bill. The King then asked the reform-minded Whig, Earl Grey, to form a new government. On November 22, 1830 Grey made his opening speech as Prime Minister. He said that his Government would be introducing a measure of reform with the King's approval. (Woodbridge: 1970, 33) Lord Russell was asked to lead a committee to draft the bill, which he forwarded in March of 1831. The bill removed most "rotten boroughs" and added representation to larger cities, but was weak, as it didn't include a secret ballot, nor enable many working men to become voters. When brought to a vote it cleared the second reading by only one vote. Realizing the futility of expecting this bill to pass in both houses after such a slim majority, Grey dissolved Parliament and called for a new election. The results of this June 1, 1831 virtual plebiscite on reform gave the Whigs a substantial majority. The reform caucus in Parliament had previously increased with the election of "Orator" Henry Hunt, of Peterloo fame, at a by-election for Preston earlier in the year. (Belchem: 1985, 220) The new majority moved the Russell bill rapidly through the House of Commons, but it was predictably defeated on October 8, 1831 by the House of Lords.

Overwhelming public, social, and economic unrest resulted from the House of Lord's defeat of the Reform Bill. Major demonstrations and riots raged in Derby, Birmingham, Bristol, and Leeds through the remainder of 1831. Bristol protestors broke into and destroyed its famous Mansion House. The Bristol jail and Bishop's Palace were set on fire. Over two days, troops killed twelve and arrested 100 people. Thirty-one were condemned to death, but only five were actually executed. It was estimated that as many as 400 people died in this violence. Most people believed that similar unrest would erupt in London unless Parliament hastened to reform the voting system. After much deliberation Parliament wrote, passed, and sent a third version of the Reform Bill to the House of Lords. On May 7, 1832 the House of Lords vetoed the bill again. The days after this defeat were known as the "Days of May," and were believed by many to be the final trigger that would start a national revolution.

William's Queen Adelaide feared sharing the fate of Marie Antoinette and went into hiding in the royal pavilion at Brighton. Even so, William IV was unwilling to commit to appointing more pro-reform peers to the House of Lords in order to pass a reform bill, so Earl Grey tendered his resignation. William then invited Wellington to form a new government. But Wellington was unable to form a government, so Grey stayed on to see the battle through. Under heavy pressure from Parliament, from the newly amalgamated National Political Union, and especially from Earl Grey, the King was forced to take some action. Only when William threatened to increase the number of members of the House of Lords, to tip the majority to support reform, did the Lords finally approve a version of the Reform Bill—officially titled the "Representation of the People Act"—on June 7, 1832.

After this prolonged, treacherous struggle, the watered-down Act that emerged fell far short of the reforms espoused by Wilkes, Paine, Cartwright, Hunt, and the others who had dedicated their lives to the cause. Because the bill did not provide for universal suffrage, Henry Hunt refused to vote for it. It did not establish "one person, one vote," or secure the secret ballot. It did not sufficiently reduce the remaining number of pensions and sinecures awarded to the powerful. It did not provide pay for elected members of Parliament, nor establish uniform-sized electorates, and it did not reduce the number of years between elections. It did provide 143 new Parliamentary seats that were assigned to urban areas, and the number of eligible electors was increased to an unprecedented 7% of men. It eliminated 56 old boroughs entirely and created twenty new one-member boroughs. It leveled the qualifications for voters to rent payers of ten pounds or more per year, which resulted in fewer people eligible to vote in several areas. This was true in Preston, where the electorate had previously enjoyed universal suffrage. The new electorate in Preston, after passage of the Reform Bill, did not return Henry Hunt to Parliament. Any hope that working class people would see improvement in their desperate situation still appeared lost. Although this Reform Bill was not what was needed, perhaps it was all that the nation's deeply divided class system deserved.

The election held soon after passage of the Reform Bill resulted in the election of William Cobbett to MP, but, sadly, he died in 1835. He didn't see passage of the important bill of 1836 that reduced the newspaper tax from four pence to a penny. The new reform Parliament also finally abolished slavery throughout the British Empire and put some limits on working hours for women and children in textile factories.

In early 1834, fearing continuing labor unrest, the Whig Government chose to make an example of a tiny Agricultural Workers Union in the village of Tolpuddle in Dorsetshire. Its six members were rushed to trial on the grounds that they had violated an old law used against the Naval Strikes of 1798 (see Chapter 4). All six were convicted of administering an illegal oath and sentenced to be transported to Australia for seven years. Their cause was taken up by a number of consolidated trade unions throughout the country and resulted in demonstrations by tens of thousands. The "Tolpuddle Martyrs" were eventually pardoned and returned to Britain, where today they are still seen as symbols of solidarity.

On the night of October 16, 1834, to the delight of the masses, all of the Parliament buildings at Westminster burned to the ground. People lined the banks of the Thames or sat in boats to watch the breathtaking sight. The public credited "Captain Swing's brigade" for its good work. The government investigation, however, concluded that the fire was caused by careless staff people who burned old tally sticks in a furnace that overheated and ignited ancient wood paneling.

As the shortcomings of the reform bill began to sink in, the government passed the hated Poor Law Amendment Act of 1834. The act eliminated the relief system that had existed from the time of Queen Elizabeth and, in its place, substituted a draconian system of workhouses that separated the sexes and separated children from their parents. Poor people needing relief were forced to wear uniforms that identified them as paupers and to do heavy, demeaning labor. This new law fanned the flames of discontent, inspiring many new broadside ballads on the "starvation act."

William IV died in 1837. His reign ended with a frenzy of railway building, a step into modernity, and with passage of the much-needed Metropolitan Reform Act that required local officials to be elected and to be held accountable for expenditures.

Suppression of Bristol Protest over Reform Defeat

## 79 Present Times or Eight Shillings a Week

Bodleian Library: The Harding Collection, B 11(3144) — Roud V1255

*Tune: Fathom the Bowl; S. Baring-Gould, 1794*

Come all you bold Britons where're you may be,
I pray give attention and listen unto me,
There once was good times but They're now gone by complete,
For a poor man lives now on eight shillings a week.

Such times in old England there never was seen,
As the present ones now, but much better have been.
A poor mans condemned and considered a thief,
And compelled to work hard on eight shillings a week.

Our venerable fathers remember the year,
When a man earned three shillings a day and his beer,
He then could live well, keep his family neat,
But now he must work for "Eight Shillings a week".

The nobs of old England of shameful renown
Are striving to crush a poor man to the ground,
They'll beat down their wages and starve them complete,
And compel them to work hard for "Eight Shillings a week".

A poor man to labour (believe me it's so)
To maintain his family is willing to go
Either hedging or ditching, to plough or to reap,
But how does he live on "Eight Shillings a week".

In the reign of old George, as you all understand,
Then there was contentment throughout the whole land.
Each poor man could live and get plenty to eat,
But now he must pine on eight shillings a week.

So now to conclude and to finish my song,
May the "Times" be much better before it is long,
May every labourer be able to keep
His children and wife on "Twelve Shillings a week".

This ballad only scratches the surface of the agricultural laborer's plight that led to what were called the Swing Riots. "It began in East Kent, where landowners might expect to find the following menacing message left overnight: Revenge for thee is on the wing from thy determined Captain Swing." (Fraser: 2013, 14)

Laborers were plagued by low wages and major losses in the quality of their lives. With the advent of steam-powered thrashing machines, farm workers lost their winter employment of thrashing corn in barns. Enclosures continued of the traditional commons that were once available to all. Desperately hungry workers were transported for poaching landlords' animals, including rabbits that destroyed workers' own food crops grown on their own small plots of land or on the rapidly diminishing commons. Echoing the Luddite Movement two decades earlier, the first thrashing machine was destroyed at Lower Hardres, near Canterbury in East Kent, on August 28, 1830.

"Small sparks which would have produced little except a few burned ricks or broken machines, turned into a conflagration when fanned by the double wind of another winter like the last, and the ongoing political tumult. What began at Orpington and Hardres ended in the jails of England and the convict settlements of Australia." (Hobsbawn/Rude: 1975, 91) Over the next four years, protest and agitation for better treatment was caused by desperation of hunger-driven families.

The insurgency spread rapidly from East Kent through Sussex into most agricultural areas of Britain. The mythical spokesperson "Captain Swing" proved to be as good a leader for farm laborers as General Ludd had been for factory workers. Captain Swing signed the notes of laborers' cautions delivered to farmers. Some farmers gave in to Swing's demands, but large landowners often got military assistance to quell discontent.

As in the past, and heedless of the cause, Government responded in an aggressive and provocative way. The toll was heavy: 1,976 people were arrested and tried; 800 were acquitted, 644 served time in jail, 252 were sentenced to death, 19 were hanged, and the remainder were deported to Australia, along with 208 originally sentenced to deportation, bringing the total deported to 581. (Hobsbawm/Rude: 1975, 309)

## 80 To The Electors of Great Britain Reform Song

Sir Frederick Madden's Collection of Broadside Ballads, 11/7535 – Roud V5911

*Tune: Scots Wha Hae*

Now's the day and now's the hour! Free-dom is our na-tion's dower,

Put we forth a na-tion's power Strug-gling to be free!

Raise your front, the foe to daunt! Bide no more the snare, the taunt!

Peal to High-est hea-ven the chant, "Law and Li-ber-ty!"

Now's the day and now's the hour!
Freedom is our nation's dower,
Put we forth a nations power,
Struggling to be free!
Raise your front, the foe to daunt!
Bide no more the snare, the taunt!
Peal to Highest heaven the chant,
"Law and Liberty!"

Gather like the muttering storm!
Wake your thunders for reform!
Bear not like the trodden worm,
Scorn and Mockery!
Waking from their guilty trance,
Shrink the foes as storms advance,
Scathed beneath a nations glance,—
Where's their bravery?

Waves on waves compose the main;
Mountains rise by grain on grain;
Men and empires might sustain,
Knit in Unity!
Who shall check the ocean tide?
Who overthrow the mountain's pride?
Who a nations strength deride,
Spurning slavery?

Hearts in mutual faith secure,
Hands from spoil and treachery pure,
Tongues that meaner oaths abjure,
These shall make us free!
Bend the knee and bare the brow!
God our guide will hear us now!
Peal to highest heaven the vow,—
"Law and Liberty."

Price Printer Portsmouth

It is easy to picture this song being raised at the first meeting of the Birmingham Political Union meeting on January 25, 1830. Borrowing tactics from O'Connell's Catholic Association, Thomas Attwood, a former banker, began plans to found this organization in 1829. In addition to working to obtain representation for Birmingham, its early objectives included:

Shorter-term Parliaments to enable more participation of the electorate

Elimination of property qualifications for MPs, enabling non-property owners to serve

Payment of MPs so that working people could serve

The vote for all men who pay local or national taxes, either directly or indirectly

Political Unions functioning in areas throughout Britain effectively helped strengthen the resolve of those prepared to work for passage of a true Political Reform Bill. The Birmingham Political Union grew rapidly and was soon joined by 100 political unions that were formed throughout the nation between 1829 and 1832. Dues paying members numbered between 15,000 and 18,000, and political union sponsored rallies attracted well over 200,000 at nationwide locations. (LoPatin: 1999, 12)

## 81 Briton's Pilot The Patriot King

Sir Frederick Madden's Collection of Broadside Ballads, 11/7565

Tune: The Drummer & The Cook; Broadside, 1850–55

Come Britons all from far and near and listen to my song,
You'll find it not offensive, Or anything that's wrong;
It's of our noble King, the father of his people,
He'll stick as close to them, As the church is to the steeple.

Then Britons Raise your voice, And of King William sing
The lover of his country, when had we such a King.

King William we are told, will do good for great and small;
By lowering of taxation, it will benefit us all;
He's a King of noble worth, And a patriot most true,
A seaman bold and brave, And He'll live and die true blue.

The orders of our King, will shortly play the deuce,
With placemen and all sinecures, far there will be reduced;
The day at last is o'er, of their ill-gotten gains,
Like borough mongers they have got, Their labour for their pains.

When the house he did dissolve, His valour he did show,
Says he, I'm King of England, and that they soon shall know;
For splendour I don't care, But then I'll quick approach,
So Russell, Gray, and Althorpe, Go fetch a hackney-coach.

Now for to make an end, May William happy be,
And with his consort Adelaide, Reign in posterity.
May trade and commerce flourish, In England's happy isle,
And the artisan and farmer, have ever cause to smile.

Then Britons once and all in chorus loudly sing
God bless the day William was born, And Adelaide his Queen.

This is one of many broadside ballads lauding the rule of William IV and his alleged willingness to help see the Reform Bill passed. William was no doubt flattered by the praise in this and other songs. His rule was a welcome change after the tyranny of his brother George IV. Perhaps his years in the Navy had opened his mind to a broader electorate. For most, William was a relief.

The parliamentary election of September 14, 1830 that followed the ascension of William IV on June 26 delivered a slight Tory majority, which enabled Wellington to tenuously remain as prime minister. But soon after the election Wellington resigned, making a speech in which he pledged with respect to political reform that as long as he held any station in the government of the country, he would always feel it his duty to resist such measures when proposed by others. (Fraser: 2013, 42) The resulting sequence of events returned Earl Grey to form a new government, and he in turn asked Lord Russell to draft a new Reform Bill, which barely passed through Commons and was likely to fail in Lords.

When Prime Minister Grey was unsuccessful in passing a real Reform Bill, he asked King William to declare another election. The king agreed, and with a new election the Whigs obtained a substantial majority. Grey's government wasted no time after the election to steer this second version of the Reform Bill through the new Whig majority House of Commons. Initial reading, the cumbersome Cabinet process, the second and the third readings were completed in only 113 days. The revised Reform Bill was approved in the Commons on September 22, 1831 by 345 to 231.

With such an overwhelmingly positive vote it was now hoped that the King would follow through with his earlier threat to appoint enough pro-reform members to the House of Lords to secure passage of the Bill. All reformers now believed that at last they would achieve what they had fought for, for so long. But two weeks later, the House of Lords would defeat the bill.

## 82 The Mitred Majority

W. F. Patton, *Political Expression Through Song and Verse* (thesis), 1983, University of Belfast, 387

Tune: Tyburn Tree; Beggar's Opera, 1728

Oh! Did you e'er hear of the mi - tred Peer, Who sits in his
The sheep that are shorn, and the hay and the corn That fall from the

lord - ly stall?____ The priest that doth Hook with his pas-to-ral
far - mer's scythe,____ The land that he digs, his___ poul-try and

crook What-e'er in his reach may fall_____
pigs__ The par-son will have__ the tithe._____

CHORUS

Then sings this priest, this mi - tred priest, Who doth sit___ in

high de - gree;_____ With hey for his crook, and ho for his

crook The mi-tered ma - jor - i - ty._____

Oh! Did you e'er hear of the mitred Peer,
Who sits in his lordly stall?
The priest that doth Hook with his pastoral crook
Whate'er in his reach may fall—
The sheep that are shorn, and the hay and the corn
That fall from the farmer's scythe,
The land that he digs, his poultry and pigs—
The parson will have the tithe.

Then sings this priest—this mitred priest,
Who doth sit in high degree;
With hey for his crook, and ho for his crook—
The mitered majority.

As the story is told, the priests of old
Did live on beggar's alms;
Barefoot they did trip with their staff and scrip.
With stomachs that had no qualms.

But our modern priest is first at a feast,
And never a feast will lose;
In a coach doth he ride with a dainty pride,
For walking would soil his shoes.

> Then sings this priest—this gentleman priest,
> Who doth sit in high degree;
> With hey for his crook, and ho for his crook—
> The mitred majority

The gifts of the earth were as nothing worth,
They sought but their masters love;
T'was their humble way to preach and to pray
But to one great Lord above;
But who will avow that our priesthood now
Have spirits not so devine?
To a mitred Peer, there are sacred here
One Hundred and ninety-nine.

> Then sings the Peers—the mitred Peers
> Who do sit in high degree;
> With hey for his crook, and ho for his crook—
> The mitred majority.

After an all-night deliberation ending at 5AM in the morning of October 8, 1831, the House of Lords defeated the Reform Bill with 199 votes to 158, losing by 41 votes. 108 of 112 peers with titles created before 1790 voted for the bill; it was defeated by the relatively new creations of Pitt and his Tory successors. (Woodbridge: 1970, 54) Huge numbers of reform supporters had staunchly attended meetings and rallies during the negotiations of the House of Lords. The unstamped and the non-conservative press kept reporting on the struggles to pass the bill. Groups on the streets taunted the Peers involved in the deliberations. Then bells began to solemnly toll as the word spread throughout the country. The *Sun* newspapers telling of the vote of the House of Lords were edged in black, stores were shut, and a merchant found a sign posted outside his store reading "199 against 22,000,000."

This song, documented by William F. Patton, ridicules the role played in this defeat by the bishops, who by their station were voting members of the House of Lords. The bill lost by only 41 votes, and 21 bishops were known to have voted against it; hence the bill would have passed if they had voted for what the people wanted. The song also alludes to resentments over the oppressive tithe system of the Church of England. This blame on the church carried over to the next Guy Fawkes Day (November 5), when Anglican Bishops' miters took the place of Guy Fawkes' black hat crowning the stuffed figures on the bonfires. (Fraser: 2013, 173)

**83** The Nottingham Tragedy!!! Lines to Their Memory
Nottinghamshire archives

Tune: See Amid the Winter's Snow; John Goss, 1871

Hark! The trumps are mournful sounding
Wafting souls to realms above,
Where there's naught but bliss abounding.
Glorying too for Jusu's love.

The reckless fate of these poor creatures,
Fills town with sad dismay,
For Nottingham, with its bright features,
Could not check that dreadful day.

To see the prime of youth now wither,
'Midst relations, friends so dear,
It makes one's blood almost to shiver,
Who could stop the burning tear.

Hearson, Beck, and Armstrong boldly
Met their fates beneath the tree.
Villains swore against them coldly,
And their doom we all shall see.

Unstamped news and broadsides kept people up to date. When the House of Lords rejected the long awaited Reform Bill in early October 1831, this was the last straw. Recent disturbances involving agricultural workers had resulted in nineteen hangings and 441 transportations. Industrial uprisings in Merthyr Tydfil in early June, 1831 resulted in even more casualties than at Peterloo — over twenty demonstrators had been shot and killed, five were transported, and it is believed that 100 were wounded by soldiers. Some say this was the first demonstration where the red flag was used.

People gathered in the streets to show their dissatisfaction. By the evening of October 8, London homes of leaders opposed to reform were damaged, including that of Wellington. That night in Derby, a reform opposer's home was attacked, and the next day its prison was stormed in an attempt to release those arrested the night before. On October 10 the Duke of Newcastle's Nottingham castle was sacked and burned. On October 19 at Sherborne and October 21 in Yeovil, homes of reform opposers were damaged. On October 29 a major rebellion took place in Bristol, sacking the Bishop's Palace and the Mansion House where the hated judge, Sir Charles Wetherell, sought shelter. Its new prison was greatly damaged, all its prisoners released, and unpopular citizens' homes and shops were looted and burned.

This commemorative broadside was sold at the time when three participants in the Nottingham Riots were publicly hanged. Like other songs, it sympathizes with those convicted rather than those who were affected. It is no wonder that masses of spectators attending such executions were sobbing. The broadside included this frank statement:

> The cause of the execution of these unfortunate men must be fresh in the recollection of all persons of every class throughout the British Dominions; and it must, also be equally apparent to the country that the cause of these disturbances both at Derby, Nottingham, and Bristol, was the rejection of the Reform Bill, by the house of Lords, That such excesses should have been committed is equally to be deplored as the cause from which they sprung, but a half employed multitude, with starvation before them seldom know the bounds to restrict their feelings and indignation. (Nottinghamshire archives)

## The Nottingham Tragedy ! ! !

Three Protesters Hung in Nottingham

## 84 I'd Be A Reformer

Sir Frederick Madden's Collection of Broadside Ballads, 11/7614

*Tune: I'd Be a Butterfly; Thomas Haines Bailey, 1797-1839*

I'd be a Re - form - er de - stroy - ing the po - wer

Of those who would bar - ter an Eng - lish - man's right,

To ac - com - plish the pro - ject, I'd strive eve - ry hour,

It should be my pra - yer both by day and by night;

O where can the slave be, that would not de - sire,

to see his na - tive land both hap - py and free,

If he still e - xists let the vil - lain re - tire,

Des - pised by his coun - try the das - tard should be.

CHORUS: I'd be a Re - form - er de - stroy - ing the po - wer

Of those who would bar - ter an Eng - lish - man's right.

I'd be a Reformer destroying the power
Of those who would barter an Englishman's right;
To accomplish the project, I'd strive every hour,
It should be my prayer both by day and by night;

O where can the slave be, that would not desire,
To see his native land both happy and free,
If he still exists let the villain retire,
Despised by his country the dastard should be.

    I'd be a Reformer destroying the power
    Of those who would barter an Englishman's right;

Round the standard of freedom, we'll rally once more,
Let the old rotten tree be felled to the ground,
Corruption forever, her efforts give o'er,
To his King every Briton should faithful be found.
From their nests the cormorant's disgracefully driven,
A refuge may seek in what country they can,
The tree of corruption by the lightning riven,
For Reform let Britons stand up to a man.

All Britons united shall level the power
Of those on our vitals who so long have fed,
No longer our country the cormorants devour,
Then Britons push forward King William's your head.
My countrymen rally, corruption gives way,
The base borough-mongering system must yield;
Three times three give to noble Russell and Grey,
And under the standard we'll all take the field.

Based on the popular song "I'd Rather be a Butterfly" by romantic writer Thomas Bayley, this colorful song acknowledges the depth of the peoples' enduring commitment to achieving parliamentary reform. Determination for reform continued, regardless of the disgust with the government's inability to pass the needed measure.

During the tumult following the Reform Bill's rejection by the Lords, the King prorogued Parliament, ending the session on October 20, 1831 to enable a cooling-off period. Rumors that political unions were preparing for armed revolution added to the paranoia of the elite. Grey and his government of elitist ministers took advantage of this time to obtain a Royal Proclamation on November 22 outlawing political unions. William IV was easily persuaded to do this, in order to stay in the good graces of his consort. (Fraser: 2013, 176) By January 15, 1832, "ministers had for what it was worth, a royal promise to create enough peers to pass the Bill." (Pearce: 2003, 227) When Parliament reconvened December 6, 1831, it wasted no time to produce a third version of the Reform Bill, little different from its predecessors; it did not reduce the total number of members of the House of Commons, and the changes that reflected the recent national census were adopted. At 1AM on March 23, the third reading passed in the House of Commons. Three days later, the Bill was formally presented for the endorsement of a packed House of Lords. (Fraser: 2013, 209)

## **85** The Gathering of the Unions

William Jones, *John Cassell's Illustrated History of England*, Volume 7 (1890)

Tune: Gathering of the Unions; Eliza Flower, 1832

Lo! We ans-wer! see We come! Quick at Free-dom's ho-ly call;

We come! we come! we come! we come! To do the glo-rious work of all;

And hark! We raise from sea to sea Our sa-cred watch-word Li-ber-ty!

And hark! We raise from sea to sea Our sa-cred watch-word Li-ber-ty!

"Lo! We answer! see We come!
Quick at Freedom's holy call;
We come! we come! we come! we come!
To do the glorious work of all;
And hark! We raise from sea to sea
Our sacred watchword Liberty!

"God is our Guide! from field, from wave,
From Plough, from anvil, and from loom,
We come, our country's rights to save,
And speak a tyrant faction's doom:
And hark! We raise from sea to sea
The sacred watchword Liberty!

"God is our Guide! no swords we draw,
We kindle not war's battle fires;
By union, justice, reason, law,
We claim the birthright of our sires;
We raise the watchword, Liberty,
We will, we will, we will be free!

Some think this song was composed by George Loveless, who is said to have composed it in 1834 on a scrap of paper and discarded it as he was led from his nonsensical February 1834 trial in Dorset. However, Loveless must have heard it at a previous rally since it had been printed as early as 1832, and the printer said it was "well known." The lyrics are by Harriet Martineau, one of the great political figures of the age. The music is by

Eliza Flower, the most notable female English composer of the period and its chief political composer.

This song was sung at a gathering of political unions led by the Birmingham Political Union on Newhall Hill near Birmingham on May 7, 1832. The gathering is believed to have been the largest political rally held in Britain to that date. 200,000 people are known to have attended, though some believe there were 400,000. This jovial and gigantic gathering was to celebrate passage of the third version of the Reform Bill by the House of Commons and to influence the House of Lords, where it was still being debated after clearing the second reading. As Thomas Attwood spoke to the gigantic crowd, the Warwick and Bromsgrove Unions arrived in a distant part of the field and were greeted with deafening shouts of applause. Attwood proposed that in order to greet their distant friends, "The Gathering of the Unions" should be sung, which was accordingly done by the whole assembly. (Jones: 1890, 757) This song aroused the mighty crowd, enabling people to envision fulfillment of their long struggle. Sadly, however, toward the end of the rally, a note forwarded to Attwood informed him that the Lords had voted in committee to wreck the third version of the Reform Bill by postponing the clauses to disenfranchise rotten boroughs, thus killing the chances of the Bill's passage.

The Gathering of the Unions on New Hall Hill, Birmingham

## 86 Resignation Of His Majesty's Ministers

Bodleian Library: Harding Collection, B 14(323) – Roud V26423

*Tune: Oh Dear, What Can the Matter Be; James Aird, 1796*

Oh dear, what row o-ver the na-tion, Two years and a half trades
been in stag-na-tion The peo-ple a-las are born
down with tax-a-tion And the mi-nis-ters have all re-signed.
The Re-form Bill is dead I will tell you no sto-ries
Mas-sa cred and thrown out by the van-quish-ing To-ries, And the
peo-ple do say that old___ No-sey will go-vern old Bil-ly a-gain.

Oh, dear what row there's all over the nation,
Two years and a half trades been in stagnation,
The people alas are born down with taxation
And the ministers have all resigned.
The Reform Bill is dead I will tell you no stories
Massacred and thrown out by the v__ Tories, *[vanquishing?]*
And the people do say that old Nosey
Will govern old Billy again.

You all must allow it's a shocking disaster,
On the mouth of the bill to clap a large plaster
The Tories has beat both servant and master,
And poor Billy is conquer'd, alas,
Come Britons arouse, be firm and united,
Pray don't let your hopes for a moment be blighted.
Perhaps the poor Bill is only near sighted,
And once more they may open his eyes. O dear,

All over the town people hang down their heads,
And says one to the other the Reform Bill is dead,
Grey and Brougham resign'd yesterday it is said,
And King William accepted the same
The people lament and their eyes run with tears.
Crying why didn't Billy create all the Peers
Oh, never no more can we banish our fear,
If the Soldier takes office again, Oh, dear.

Such a sad piece of work there never was seen
And a row through the country there lately has been
If you like you may drink to the King and Queen,
What a fellow is B_____ B_____                    *[Billy Barlow]*
Some said our Queen fell down on her knees,
And said, Royal William my dear if you please
Turn a Tory like me learn to pocket all fees,
So she conquered old B___ B___.

The Wigs and the Tories are birds of a feather
People thought to the bill they would all stick like leather
If the devil should come, he will collar together
All the Tories and B__ B__
They have murdered Reform, made the people to rue
He was shot by the soldier, I vow it is true,
In a very short time he will see Waterloo,
When the d___ gets hold of his nose.              *[devil]*

Towards Windsor last night, a fine carriage did go,
And thousands of people did go to and fro,
Lawk a daisy, says one, there is old B__          *[Billy]*
With his breeches all smother'd in mud
On the windows and wall, it is true I declare
Till the Reform Bill is pass'd, there is no taxes paid here,
And if that is the case all the Tories will stare,
And go hungry will B__ B__

There was turmoil during the dreadful "Days of May" in 1832, as the country reeled in shock from the demise of the third version of the Reform Bill in the House of Lords, during its second reading. When London awoke on May 8, placards were still pasted on walls everywhere saying:

Seventh of May
Crisis Day

As members of the House of Lords, the entire cabinet had met the night before, after defeat of the Bill, and again at 11AM the next day. It was decided that Lords Grey and Brougham would journey to Windsor that day to deliver the minute on the resignation of the government. To everyone's surprise, on the following day Lord Grey informed the House of Lords that the King was graciously pleased to accept their resignation. The King turned to the Tories again to form a new Government, demanding that it was for the express purpose of passing the Reform Bill. The uncomfortable threat of yet another Wellington ("old Nosey") Government now became a reality.

Reflected in this song is the shift from praise to distaste for his majesty. It reverts to using the epithet "Billy Barlow," which the King was frequently called before his coronation. Billy Barlow was a popular comical actor of the time who was thought to resemble William IV.

People had believed that the King would appoint enough new Whig Lords to assure passage of this version of the Reform Bill. They now feared another stalemate by yet another Wellington administration. The song also implies that the Tory Queen, Adelaide of Saxe-Meiningen, thought by many to be infatuated with Wellington, was pushing William to rethink his allegiance to the Whigs and to pocket all bribes that were no doubt offered to those who might end the entire spat over reform.

The song reflects on how, when bound for Windsor, the King's coach was splattered with mud by provoked subjects, and it mentions the threat of a tax boycott. Revolution seemed imminent. On May 8 *The Times* wrote, "It is no time for conventional politics... Life and death are in the scale... There existed a state of Revolution to be terminated only by frank acceptance of the Bill."

William IV (center) balances between Earl Grey and the Duke of Wellington as John Bull tips the scale

# 87 A Word of Advice to Reformers of England

Bodleian Library: Johnson Ballads, 1073 – Roud V33132

*Tune: Lillibullero; Henry Purcell, 1689–90*

Re - for - mers re - joice for the day is your own,
And Bri - tons have prov'd that they'll ne - ver be slaves,

The loud voice of free - dom's been heard by the throne, _____
Nor e'er _____ put down by a par - cel of knaves; _____

The King has re - turned to his du - ty a - gain. And Pet - ti - coat

Go - vern-ment spurns with dis - dain. For - get and for - give, but be

re - so - lute still, And Free-men of Eng-land you shall have your Bill.

Reformers rejoice for the day is your own,
The loud voice of freedom's been heard by the throne,
And Britons have prov'd that they'll never be slaves,
Nor e'er put down by a parcel of knaves;
The King has returned to his duty again.
And Petticoat Government spurns with disdain.
Forget and forgive, but be resolute still,
And Freemen of England you shall have your Bill.

When the bridge of reform was first rear'd we had fears
The foundation was Sandy and faulty the Piers
We'd no fear the Workmen their trust would betray,
And the first Overseer in experience was GREY;
While resting secure with a Shock we awake,
The stones are Dividing, the Balustrades shake.
Distracted we call on the Master for aid,
Now all is Secure, though the Work was Delay'd

You've heard an old proverb, that all must admire
A child that once burnt, will forever dread fire,
Be Watchful and Firm (the allusion is plain,)
A Man Once Untrue, may deceive us again:
Our Friends are re-call'd, and the crisis is near,
But as the concession was granted through fear,

Rally around the bright standard of Liberty still,
And in spite of the Tories we will have the Bill.

Some told us the Whigs had deserted our cause,
And blam'd the brave men who deserve our applause,
Who've shown us our enemies strip'd of Disguise,
And torn down the veil that's long darken'd our eyes;
Huzza for Lords Althorp, Grey, Russell, and Brougham,
Confusion to every base foe to Reform,
Rally round the fair standard of liberty still,
And Freemen of England you shall have your Bill.

Quick, Printer, Bowling Green Lane, Clerkenwell;
and at 43, Fashion Street, Spitalfields

The looming spectre of another Wellington Tory government—one that would surely block reform—ended when Wellington conceded that he could not recruit enough people to form one. The song declares that now the strong foundation of Whig leadership will hold through the delivery of reform.

"Thus Monday 14, May, a week after the double Crisis Day, dawned with revolution in the air, calls for political action, posters everywhere, a run on the Banks commencing and no government as yet in place." (Fraser: 2013, 236) It must have been hard for Tories to make their way through the streets full of angry people, past the newly pasted signs that read:

TO STOP THE
DUKE
GO FOR
GOLD

The people yearned for passage of the Reform Bill, and without question opposed Wellington becoming prime minister. When Wellington failed to form a government, the King met with Grey and Brougham and clearly voiced his objections to stacking the House of Lords for the sake of the Reform Bill. It was at this point that ministers demanded the King's un-equivocal pledge for a large creation of peers, which he reluctantly gave on May 18. (Turner: 2000, 248) Grey announced that the Whig cabinet would stay in office and would forward the Reform Bill.

## 88 The Champion of Reform

Bodleian Library: Harding Collection. B 27(18) – Roud V8436

*Tune: Grenadier's March; John Playford, 1686*

Ye sons of Free-dom now give ear to what I have pen'd down,
The glo - rious news I let you hear has just ar - rived in town.
The Bills are past now, at length we've gained the day,
Brave Earl Grey has gained the day, And no - bly braved the storm:
Let bon - fires blaze, your voi - ces raise, three cheers for Earl Grey!
Through Bri - tain's Isle he shall be styled The Cham - pion of Re - form.

Ye sons of Freedom now give ear to what I have pen'd down,
The glorious news I let you hear has just arrived in town.
The Bills are past now, at length we've gained the day,
Let bonfires blaze, your voices raise, three cheers for Earl Grey!

Brave Earl Grey has gain'd the day,
And nobly braved the storm:
Through Britain's Isle he shall be styled
The Champion of Reform.

The fourth of June, that afternoon, the last debates began;
And lasted till next morning, and ended about one.
One hundred and six were for the Bill, oppose'd by twenty two,
So now at last the bills are past, what will the Tories do?

When London folk they heard the news that they had won the day,
The great metropolis did ring with cheers for Earl Grey.
It's in the city such a sight was never seen before.
Rockets did fly towards the sky, and small guns they did roar.

Now this brave champion of Reform, and likewise Mr. Hume,
O'Connell, Russell, Lord Althorp, and Lord Chancellor Brougham.
The names should all be all set in gold, on pure white marble stone.
Placed in the center of the globe to let their deeds be known.

For eighteen months the borough men to baffle us did try,
Even the German ladies had a finger in the PYE;
But those great worthies I have named, they fought it out quite cool.
A petticoat government, says they, the land shall never rule.

As for the German Ladies, Earl Grey he does declare,
With our national politics they shall not interfere.
In Britain's court, no longer now these madams will find room.
They may go hawk the country, crying—Who'll by a Broom.

It was only by commission the Bills were signed at last,
It makes no odds how they were sign'd, since we have got them past.
The Scotch and Irish Bills are now passed, you may rely,
Then let the three recorded be in the glorious month, July.

A free representation now we'll have in every town,
Against their will the Corn Bill and Taxes must come down;
The pensioners may go and seek some post in Botany Bay
And Bishops they will not be fit their journeymen to pay.

Working people all over the country celebrated passage of the Reform Bill
even though only one in six males would be able to vote. It was clear that
"the extra-parliamentary agitation of 1829–32 was the natural climax of
a half century of focused, if sporadic, agitation." (Evans: 2000, 21) Once
it was clear that the King was committed to authorizing the addition of as
many new Lords as needed to pass the bill, the Lords' dismantling amendment was dropped, and on June 4 the Lords passed the third reading of
the bill by 106 to 22. Realizing that appointments were inevitable in the
absence of passage, the Lords reluctantly gave their final approval of the
Third Parliamentary Reform Bill. Obviously most members abstained rather than vote for the bill.

As this broadside declares, the King chose not to sign the bill in person,
but sent the necessary Commission to give Royal Assent. On June 7, 1832
The Bill became the Reform Act (2 and 3 Will 4, c. 45). (Woodbridge: 1970,
65) It was not a perfect Bill, since it fell far short of the ideals expounded
by John Wilkes nearly seventy years before. It did not include universal
manhood suffrage, the secret ballot, annual elections, pay for elected members, or equal size electoral districts—as advocated by Major Cartwright
sixty years before. It did make some important changes. The number of
male voters increased by 57% from 516 to 813 thousand. Rotten districts
with only a handful of constituents were removed from Parliament. Thirty
boroughs that had fewer than 4,000 constituents were reduced to only one
representative each.

Though not the most enthusiastic advocate for reform, Earl Grey was one
of the few souls capable of getting even this mild measure past the political

obstacles of the time. "What but a sense of duty could have induced me to plunge into all the difficulties, not unforeseen of my present situation." (Fraser: 2013, 149) He clung to the reins through amazing turmoil over the many months that it took the House of Lords to give up a little bit of power and pass the law.

Remarkably, within six months of the Reform Bill's passage, an election was held to establish new representation. The bill set boundaries for 42 newly enfranchised boroughs, realigned 65 existing boroughs, and revised county representation nationwide. The election commenced on December 8 and ended with a decisive Whig victory on January 8, 1833.

Charles Grey, 2nd Earl Grey

## 89 Negro Slavery

Sir Frederick Madden's Collection of Broadside Ballads, 03/2567 — Roud V28107

*Tune: Aberystwyth; Joseph Parry, 1879*

Now's the time and now's the hour, To Parliament partitions pour,

Oh Britons pray exert your power, To set ___ the Negro free,

Who stood forth in time of ___ need, Who did so nobly for us plead,

Who wished the Negro slave was free, 'Twas Wilberforce 'twas he.

Now's the time and now's the hour,
To Parliament partitions pour,
Oh Britons pray exert your power,
To set the Negro free,
Who stood forth in time of need,
Who did so nobly for us plead,
Who wished the Negro slave was free,
'T'was Wilberforce 't'was he.

He knew the poor Negro suffered great,
Upon the rich planters estate,
And pitied their lamented fate,
And tried to set them free,
They labour hard in heat of day,
For course provisions and no pay,
Oh Britons to your King then Pray
That we may all be free

Am I not a man and brother,
And like you I have a mother,
But she's a slave like many other,
And sighs for liberty,
Then Britons pray take no delay
Remember soon will come the day,
Before your Lords and Commons lay,
Prayer against slavery.

Who for paltry glittering gold
Was from his parents stole and sold,
To planters rich who's blood is cold,
Poor Negro slave 'tis he,
Then rouse ye Britons struggle hard,
Petition all with one accord,
And heaven will be your just reward,
For feasting of the free.

The Printer Wholesale Reasonable Warehouse
6 Great St Andrew Street Deal.

The newly elected Parliament appeared to jump off to a good start in 1833, dealing with social issues that had been postponed from action for decades. However, closer scrutiny puts some of their motives into question.

This ballad advocates for passage of The Slavery Abolition Act, which became law August 28, 1833. The song has the ring of Thomas Fowell Buxton's "Society for the Mitigation and Gradual Abolition of Slavery." Buxton, an evangelical Christian, served as a Member of Parliament for Weymouth from 1818, until he was defeated in the election of 1837. After the retirement of William Wilberforce in 1825, Buxton became the main Parliament spokesperson for abolition. Wilberforce and Charles James Fox, with strong public support, had finally managed to obtain legislation in 1807 to prohibit slave trade throughout the British Empire, but ownership of slaves continued. The bill also was passed as a result of the Jamaican slave revolt of December 1831; partly because the Whig government was ready, after the Parliamentary Reform Bill of 1832, to turn its attention to something new, and partly because slave owner members of Parliament Sir Robert Peel and Gladstone's father were satisfied with the terms. (Thomas: 1997, 650)

It required four men to carry the enormous petition calling for the passage of The Slavery Abolition Act when it was presented to the newly seated Parliament by Buxton in 1833. The bill passed in the House of Parliament three days before the death of Wilberforce on July 29 and passed the House of Lords a month later.

Abolition was expensive. Slave owners were paid ridiculous amounts for loss of their "property," and former slaves were required to continue to work for their former masters as low-paid apprentices for seven years. One of the larger beneficiaries of the handouts was the Church of England, which was paid for 411 slaves at its Codrington plantation. Further sweetening of the pot arrangements were made to import indentured servants from Britain's Indian colonies, paid for by a tax on the former slaves' low wages.

## 90 John Bull and the Unions: Unity is Strength
Bodleian Library: Firth Collection. c. 16 (271) – Roud V41194

*Tune: I Met Her in The Garden; Johnny Patterson, 1840-89*

You he - roes all at - ten - tion give of e - very rank and sta - tion,

See what a piece of work there is all o - ver this great na - tion,

Be - cause the peo - ple have a-greed to hold things in Com - mu - nion

And as-sist each o - ther in dis-tress, then let us praise the U - NION

You heroes all attention give of every rank and station,
See what a piece of work there is all over this great nation,
Because the people have agreed to hold things in Communion
And assist each other in distress, then let us praise the UNION.

(Spoken.) Can you inform me Mr. Bull, what is to be done by the Unions? Why friend they are determined to stand together, and assist each other in distress. I have an idea Mr. Bull that the ministers have formed and humbugged the people. R__'S pills don't purge very clever, A__e say's "Patience", E G__y has union'd his family with good preferment's; and old Sir Andrew Hang the Devil wishes to again bring the people into a union to starve all day on a Sunday, and live by fasting all the week. If he had all the gas-lamps in London down his throat, I have no doubt that he would think of the Sabbath, and praise the Unions until every river in the islands of Scotland is over flowed with oatmeal porridge and prayer books.

They are so strong united now, they do not care a farthing,
They may do their best & do their worst they will find they got a
    bargin —
We are all aware the nation through There has been great confusion,
Let every Briton shout success to them that join the Union —

I understand there was a meeting held, who were the delegates that went up? Why the meeting was held in Charlotte–street. Rathborn Place, and the delegates were Dr. Wade, Mr. Johnson. And 15 others, they were received kindly by Lord Melbourne, who promised to go to the King immediately & get the poor men's sentence altered — and if the unions never do another good thing, their conduct in this case will be enough to immortalize their names for ever, so success to the Unions.

On Saturday 30,000 of the Unions met the paper did declare it,
To partition our King himself against that horrid verdict;
Again they met on Sunday morn 10,000 waited steady,
For the delegates to return, who said Lord Melbourne's ready.

12,000 I am told was at the funeral of one of the members. Yes there was indeed, and although they were only mechanics, whom the dandies of the west seem to despise, their conduct was good, and they looked the most creditable set of men you ever see! — why, do you know that the women were so pleased, That they intended to have a Union also, and declare also that while the Unions act so much like true men, they will do all in their power to assist them, and leave off drinking gin and taking snuff, so as to render all the assistance they can.

Then how glorious it was to see in Bunhill Fields the men who met,
With what respect the whole body does each member ever treat;
12,000 at a funeral of a brother did attend,
Which proves they are true Unionists, for each one is a Brother's friend.

Printed by G. Hunt. (late Quick) Little Paternoster Row, Spitalfields

Concern over continually lowering wages brought together agricultural workers of the tiny village of Tolpuddle in the county of Dorset. Their "Friendly Society" had met only a few times during the 1833–4 winter when the local magistrate contacted Lord Melbourne, the Home Secretary, to report that workers were "combining" to complain of wage cuts. The Combination Acts that had previously prevented union activity had been withdrawn in 1824 but partially replaced in 1825, so Melbourne resorted to an old law from the 1797 Naval Mutiny (see Chapter 4) to convict these workers of swearing an illegal oath as part of the initiation to their union. Members were quickly rounded up on February 24, 1834. Six workers, including Methodist pastor George Loveless, were brought to trial in Dorset and sentenced to seven years' transportation to Australia. The response of urban trade unions to the transportation of the Tolpuddle laborers was immediate and overwhelming. (Thompson: 1996, 229)

This broadside discusses, in part, a union gathering called on short notice to protest the Tolpuddle sentencing. The meeting attracted five to ten thousand men to the National Institution Building in Rathbone Place to petition the legislature against the cruel and oppressive sentence. This song reflects much of the thinking of the time and describes, optimistically, the effectiveness of the proceedings. First, it criticizes the ministers who humbugged the people with the First Reform Bill ("Russell's pills"). It also cites Althorp's pleas for patience, Earl Grey's appointment of his son-in-law to his Cabinet, and discussions in the House of Lords on the public's desecration of the Sabbath by holding a national fast on most workers' only day off. In the chair was Dr. Arthur Wade DD, Chaplain to the Metropolitan Trade Unions. The principal speaker and organizer was Robert Owen, founder of the National Consolidated Trades Union.

On March 30, after the meeting, a deputation took a petition to Home Secretary Lord Melbourne, while a crowd of up to twelve thousand waited to hear the results. They were rewarded with the good news that Melbourne had assured them that the sentence would not be carried out until the petition was in the King's hands. This appeared to be a step forward and to substantiate the parliamentary statement that the government was considering recommending mitigation to the King. (Marlow: 1971, 115) The last verse refers to Burnhill-Fields, a Methodist cemetery in London, where Dr. Wade and the delegation met with the membership to report on the positive response of Melbourne.

After the activities described in this song, Melbourne completely reneged on his commitment to the workers. All six of the Tolpuddle Martyrs were already at sea, bound for Van Diemen's Land, when, on April 21, 1834 a massive trade unionist gathering involving tens of thousands of workers was held at Copenhagen Field. The assembly was to carry a petition with 800,000 signatures to Melbourne at the Home Office for remission of sentence on the Dorchester Unionists. The procession went off without any troubles and waited at Kennington Common for the delegates to arrive from their meeting with Melbourne. When they got there, the crowd was advised that Lord Melbourne had refused to accept the petition. "Neither frenzy nor uproar greeted the news of Melbourne's refusal. The crowd ultimately dispersed peacefully. This had been the day when labour put its hat on and walked towards the throne; and that it walked in a sober, decorous, disciplined manner." (Marlow: 1971, 134)

This interesting mixture of song and prose is the only contemporary ballad material that has been found covering this important incident. The Tolpuddle Martyrs received an enormous amount of press coverage, and this disgraceful affront to workers should have caused many more broadsides to be printed. Perhaps a huge cache will be found somewhere soon.

In 1836, Lord John Russell secured free pardon for the "Tolpuddle Martyrs" and arranged for their first class passage back to England.

JAMES BRINE, Aged 25.   THOMAS STANFIELD, Aged 51.   JOHN STANFIELD, Aged 25.   JAMES LOVELESS, Aged 29.

GEORGE LOVELESS, Aged 41.

Tolpuddle Martyrs, on their return to England

## 91 The Fatal English Poor Law Bill
## Or, The Ways of the World

Sir Frederick Madden's Collection of Broadside Ballads, 11/7485 – Roud V12209

*Tune: The Vicar of Bray; The Quaker's Opera, 1731*

Come all you gallant Englishmen,
And listen to my rhymes,
A word or two I will unfold,
About these present times;
Enforcing of the Poor Law Bill
Has caused great discontent,
And through the country far and near,
Some hundreds do relent.

    CHORUS
    Go when you will both day and night,
    They are complaining still,
    About the awful measure
    That is called the Poor Law Bill.

In Kent and Sussex riots have
Occurred for miles around.
Since passing of the Poor Law Bill
In Country and in Town.
If for relief you're forced to go,
They'll part I do declare,
The father and the Mother from
The infant children dear.

In Steyning Town near Brighton,
There of late occurred a row,
And how this riot did take place,
I really can't tell how;
But as far we can understand,
To wound each bleeding heart,
The Children from their parents
They did send for miles apart.

There is many a Man no work could get,
And walked about in pain;
Then ventured off to foreign parts,
To Portugal and Spain;
There for Spaniards and for Portuguese,
In battle lost his life,
And left his family behind,
His Children and his Wife.

Some early in the morning rise,
Seeking work for miles he goes;
And how one half the world does live,
Some thousands never knows;
From morning light till dark at night
He for employment roams,
While his tender Children and his Wife
With hunger pines at home.

Some others in a prison pine,
And others do bewail,
And many a prattling Infant says—
My father is in Goal,
Which makes the tender mother weep,
And sit and cry her fill,
And say he never would'v been there
But for the Poor Law Bill.

Now don't you think it's very hard,
Poor people's rights to smother,
To send the husband from the wife
The Children from the Mother.
It's done to keep poor people down,
As you shall understand:
It never was the Laws of God,
These Laws were made by Man.

In Bedfordshire and in Kent,
And down in Sussex too,
In Surrey, Hampshire, and Dorsetshire,
And all the country through.
But Steyning town near Brighton
There was the other day,
All through the English Bill.
A terrible affray.

Wm. Thomas.
Printed by Phillips and Co. 13, Poplar Place,
Lanes, Brighton. Travelers Supplied.

Printed in Brighton, at least one year after passage of the unpopular Poor Law Amendment Act in 1834 and just three years after passage of the Reform Act, this ballad shows that it soon became clear that the 1832 Reform Act was not going to improve the working man's lot. In his fabulous *A Book of Scattered Leaves*, James Hepburn writes, "No other piece of English legislation was so reviled in nineteenth-century broadside literature as the 1834 act." (Hepburn: 2000, 161) The Poor Law Amendment Act had been many years in the making before its adoption, since a majority did not exist before the Reform Bill was passed. Given the strength of the empowered social class system, it was not surprising that something so draconian was enacted at that time. The passage of the Poor Law Amendment Act is seen by Gertrude Himmelfarb as "a direct consequence of the reform act of 1832, an act which, it has been said, brought to power a 'new and self-conscious middle class' eager to promote its interests." (Himmelfarb: 1985, 153)

The Act of 1834 ended welfare for the workers of Britain as it had existed since Queen Elizabeth. It had been the responsibility of each local parish to provide relief to households in need, mostly in funds to see them through hard times, but people could stay in their own homes. Some parishes additionally provided a poor house for those who had no other place to go. The system was not great for the poor, but it was good for the landowners, because it did keep a local supply of low-cost workers available when the landed gentry needed them. Tax rates paid by landowners varied greatly between parishes, depending on their local unemployment and poverty situation. The new Act dealt with that problem by pressuring parishes to join together, forming a union that created the dreadful workhouses. The only form of assistance was then to be provided by admission to the Union Workhouse, and the system was designed so that no one would enter the workhouse unless they had no other option. All able-bodied workhouse residents were required to labor long hours doing hard, monotonous, unpaid, degrading work. Families were split up with men, women, boys, and girls housed in separate buildings. Food was marginal and sparse, all heads were shaved, and all were forced to wear uncomfortable uniforms that labeled them as from the workhouse. Working people called the workhouses "Bastilles," and the Act itself became known as the Starvation or the Robbery Bill. E. P. Thompson wrote that the Act "was perhaps the most sustained attempt to impose an ideological dogma, in defiance of the evidence of human need, in English history... The impractical policy of systematic starvation was displaced by the policy of psychological deterrence: 'labour, discipline, and restraint.'" (Thompson: 1966, 267)

The first Union workhouses were established in the agrarian south where the Swing demonstrations had happened and their establishment was cause for more unrest. This ballad refers to riots in Kent and Sussex. Some of the earliest risings took place within the Milton Union in Swale. Police were called from London and over twenty were arrested. (Edsall: 1971, 28) The song tells of another documented disturbance over separation of children from their parents in Steyning Town, Sussex near Brighton (where King William IV lived much of the time).

This author's great-grandmother and her eight children were interred for several years in the Maidstone Workhouse, and he sang Christmas carols with his church choir to residents of the Milton Union Workhouse annually in the mid 1940s.

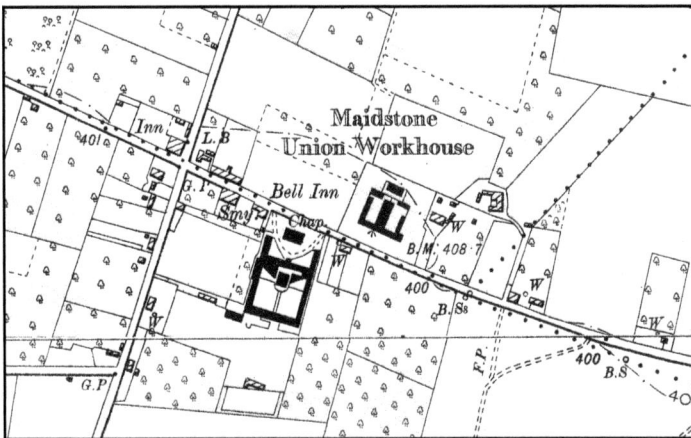

Maidstone Union Workhouse built 1833

## 92 "All round my hat," or a Corporation Turn-Out

Bodelian Library: Firth Collection, c.16(37) — Roud 22518

Tune: All Around My Hat; Bell's Life in London, 1835

"All around my hat I vill vear a green villow" —
All around my hat for twelvemonth and ay,
If any one should AX the reason vy I vears it,
Tis cause corporations will be soon purg'd away.
Oh, vy did Lord John Russell seek so cruelly to dish us,
For sartinly such treatment ve never met before;
My Kids look very glum, and my wife looks wery wicious
And she never, I'm afear". Will be May'ress anymore!
       For its all around my hat.

Oh, ven at table seated, she cut a dashing figure;
And none like her a chicken or a pair of ducks could carve.
Oh, vicked Lord John Russell, you have treated us with rigour.
To take away our comforts, and to turn us out to starve,
For ever Corporations feeds, and us alas, are parted:

The House of Commons gives the vord and ve must all obey,
Bad luck to Lord John Russell, For he's very cruel hearted,
And with this here Bill swept our comforts all away.
    And its all around my hat.

A curse upon the Committee who expos'd our evil doing:
Vy couldn't they quiet and enjoyment let us be.
Now nothing stares us in the face but wretchedness and ruin,
Instead of turbot, venson, calipash, and calipee,
Oh, never no more shall ve rest on our pillow;
Our glory is departed, our hoccupation's gone:
And all around my hat I vear a green villow,
Because we're flaxed by that ere precious Bill of Lord John
    Its all around my hat.

Following the Reform Act of 1832 came efforts to clean up the governance of municipalities, corporations, and boroughs throughout the British Isles. This song, with an unflattering imitation of a cockney accent and set to the traditional melody popularized by Steeleye Span's smash hit "All Around My Hat," derides local governments that operated with impunity and often had grossly corrupting, exclusive administrations. Many local offices were controlled by individuals who held their position for life. The song jokes that Lord Russell's committee should not be removing the cover under which they have been hiding. One part of the joke laments the pending demise of the singer's super dinners and his wife's tenure as Mayoress.

The most important immediate step in governance cleanup was the reform of the municipalities, which took place in Scotland in 1833 and England and Wales in 1835. (Cole & Postgate: 1938, 272) The sweeping but incomplete bill of 1835 did result in the democratization of many municipalities by an election of unpaid councilors every three years who would, in turn, elect a mayor and hold open meetings. It was applied to 178 old corporations, but not to all 246. (Pearce, Stearn: 1994, 87)

A Tory government would not have passed it, but the new Whigs saw the need and passed The Municipal Corporations Act of 1835, making a good start and undoubtedly cleaning up a number of unruly jurisdictions. But as councilors were now to be elected by rate payers, most lower-income people still had no voice in their local government.

**93** Dialogue and Song, Between Captain Swing and Joan o'Greenfield On The Burning of Both Houses of Parliament.

Bodleian Library: Broadside Ballads, 2806 c.16(173) – Roud V31837

Tune: *The Girl I Left Behind Me; Maurice Hime, 1810*

Did you hear the dreadful news of late, A—
On October the sixteenth, late at night, It was

bout the British Great Senate, That den of thieves has
awful, but a glorious sight, The senate house gave

met its fate, And lost its situation;
such a light, Like sun at noon it shone so bright.

The people in all directions run, On
CHORUS Sing Swing away the thing is done, For

horses, coaches, gigs did come To see the mischief
my part I can blame no one, The Parliament house has

swing had done, By this great conflagration.
reached the ground, By this great conflagration.

**JOAN,** — Well Swing, aw year yov bin at wark ogenith Parlement hewse jov bin very busy, where mun't Lord's anth big-whigs sit new to do their dirty wark?

**SWING,** — Why Joan, they may sit at home for what good they ever did, or ever intends to do, unless it's to Tax & *impoverish* this nation, and all others if they can.

**JOAN,** — Wha Swing. They towd me of it wur Guy Fawks os set it on fire.

**SWING,** — No Joan, Guy Fawkes (if ever there was such a man) thought of sending all of them to heaven in a body, Big-Whigs, Lords and Commons, and a pleasant ride they'd have had on the 5th of November, & if they all had been in when I put the match to the pile, and the doors all locked & barr'd, it had been no bad job, only the Devil would have been busy to gather them together, for some of them would have been for giving him the slip if they could, but he is pretty sharp, for he knows his subjects pretty well.

**JOAN,**—Wha, boh if tey should catcho' what ud be'th consequence?

**SWING,**—Catch me? No, no Joan, they'l ne'er catch me, like the bravo of Venice, I am here and there and every where, and still no where to be found; but however it may do some good for bricklayers & carpenters, and other tradesmen, but then the poor must pay for it, & no catch me, no have me, they often complained that it was too little, so they may build a bigger as soon as they like, or else stop at home. But Joan, I'll sing you a song about it, & then farewell.

Did you hear the dreadful news of late,
About the British Great Senate,
That den of thieves has met its fate,
And lost its situation: —
On October the sixteenth, late at night,
It was awful, but a glorious sight,
The senate house gave such a light,
Like sun at noon it shone so bright,
The people in all directions run,
On horses, coaches, gigs did come
To see the mischief swing had done;
By this great conflagration.

    CHORUS
    Sing Swing away the thing is done,
    For my part I can blame no one,
    The Parliament house has reached the ground,
    By this great conflagration.

But when they reached St. Stephen's square,
Both old and young they all did stare
Some thousands had assembled there,
In grief and consternation:
And some did shout with might and main,
Guy Fawks is come to 'th town again,
A plan of Government that's plain,
To hide some nasty dirty scheme. —
'Where are the Big whigs now' some cried,
I wish they all were back inside,
And P___l and Nosey by their side,                    *[Peel]*
In this great conflagration.

The flames still rag'd the engines play'd,
While every heart did seem dismay'd,
The Parliment house in ruins laid,
It caused great desolation,
Thousands, did shout it burned so free,
That den of THIEVES and misery,
Has ruined this blessed country,
And caused us all bond slaves to be.
But let us hope and still return,
Our RIGHTS we shall get back again,
Our LIBERTIES then we will maintain.
By this great conflagration.

The writings of the NATIONAL DEBT
I fear are not demanded yet,
If they were, the poor man need not fret,
But gaze with admiration:
If the National Dept and the Corn Bill
Were in the flames and burning well,
I'll jump for joy let weep who will,
The poor man then his belly might fill,
But books of old and ancient date,
And manuscripts have met their fate,
They soon will have a Tax Rate
Through this great conflagration.

So to conclude and end my song,
I don't know whether I'm right or wrong.
I fear we shall before it's long
Look out for new Taxation;
The King governs all true we say.
The soldier fights, the parson prays,
The farmer works for all he says,
But we know for all the poor must pay:
So let the poor themselves befriend,
Their rights and liberties all defend,
The hard times then they soon will it end.
By this great conflagration.

At the time of the great fire of the Houses of Parliament on the night of
October 16, 1834, government was held in lowest esteem by the working
people. It was clear that the two-year-old Reform Bill was not going to
improve the lot of the working man one bit. Wages remained devastatingly
low, Corn Laws helped keep food prices prohibitively high, and a run of
extremely cold winters anguished much of the population.

It was convenient to assume that the fire was started by starving agricultural workers, represented in this song by Swing, or by industrial workers denoted by the famous mechanic-turned-soldier, Joan of Greenfield. In this broadside, Swing and Joan air their grievances. The ballad describes the continuing public discontent with Peel and Wellington whom they wished were still inside the building. Caroline Shenton reflects that,

> For some, it must have seemed that the Apocalypse was near. St Steven's continued to burn away to its medieval core. At least one report of the effects of the fire on the Commons Chamber considered the sacrificial, purifying aspect of the blaze, almost as if the Authentic House of Commons were rising, phoenix-like, from the ashes of its own funeral pyre. (Shenton: 2012, 134)

The new Prime Minister, Lord Melbourne, took responsibility for saving the great hall by supervising the use of fire engines to control the fire. Further investigation suggested that the fire really began with the burning of old tally sticks that had ceased to be used over a hundred years before the fire. The sticks were burned in old stoves which ignited the building's wooden paneling. (Shenton: 2012, 240)

Parliament on Fire, October 16, 1834

Marching the Great National Petition to Parliament, 1842

Chapter 9

# CHARTER: 1837–1851

*Then, Hurrah for the Charter,*
*On, Shannon, Thames, and Tweed;*
*Now scythemen to the Harvest!*
*Reap you who sowed the seed.*
   —Ernest Jones, March 18, 1848

George Loveless, the first of the Tolpuddle Martyrs to be pardoned, arrived back to the London docks on June 13, 1837, aboard the *Eveline*, after
his ordeal as a transport to Australia.

> His return attracted no newspaper attention, even from the radical
> press... because Loveless landed in a week when national attention
> was focused on the King. William IV was gravely ill and a week
> later, on June 20th he died. The newspapers were then filled with
> obsequies for the dead, whom they were all able to love now he had
> departed, and hopes for the reign of the young, unknown Victoria.
> (Marlow: 1971, 215)

By 1837, it was completely clear to the un-enfranchised that the passage
of the 1832 Reform Act had done nothing to improve their desperate situation. Economic setbacks, high food prices, restrictive laws, and fear of the
dreaded workhouses hung as dark shadows over the workers of the British
Isles. Attendance continued to increase throughout the country at gatherings bent on fighting each of those issues. The question was how to extend
that energy into political reform.

Young princess Victoria's ascension to the throne on June 20, 1837 offered a slight ray of hope, but it occurred at the beginning of the longest
and worst depression of the 19th century, which lasted until 1842, as unemployment spread throughout the nation. (Parry: 1993, 141) Economic
necessity forced men, women, and children to take work, when available,

under slave-like conditions for twelve and fifteen hours a day at less than subsistence pay. Workplaces with poor ventilation, unsafe machinery, and unsanitary conditions shortened lives and brought on chronic illnesses with frequent devastating cholera outbreaks. Newspaper accounts chronicled the degraded and dehumanized conditions of British workers. Enquiry committees of the reformed Parliament were ineffectual. Of these enquiries, the German philosopher and socialist Friedrich Engels wrote:

> What have they done to prove their professed good-will towards you? Have they ever paid any serious attention to your grievances? Have they done more than paying the expenses of half-a-dozen commissions of enquiry, whose voluminous reports are damned to everlasting slumber among heaps of waste paper on the shelves of the Home Office? (Engels: 1845, 8)

In those hard times, The People's Charter emerged to relieve the hopeless condition of working people and offer a way to gain influence for needed change. The Charter was assembled in February of 1837 by a twelve-member committee, chaired by William Lovett, consisting of six members of the London Working Men's Association (LWMA) and six members of Parliament. The LWMA organized in 1836, attracting skilled workers as they promoted political education. The committee's Charter called for:

> A vote for every man twenty-one years of age, of sound mind, and not undergoing punishment for a crime;

> The secret ballot to protect the elector in the exercise of his vote;

> No property qualification for members of Parliament in order to allow constituencies to elect the man of their choice;

> Pay for MPs, enabling tradesmen, working men, or others of modest means to leave or interrupt their livelihood to attend to the interests of the nation;

> Equal constituencies, securing balanced representation for electors, instead of allowing less populous constituencies to have as much or more weight than larger ones;

> Annual Parliamentary elections, considered the most effectual check to bribery and intimidation, since no purse could buy a constituency under a system of universal manhood suffrage in each twelve-month period.

The plan was to establish a widespread organization to prepare for a national convention of working people. From May through September, 1838, large meetings were held throughout the country, the largest of which was held in greater Manchester on Kersal Moor just north of Liverpool on September 24. The meetings described the contents of the Charter, gathered signatures, and selected representatives to attend the Chartist National

Convention planned for February 1839. There were amazing turnouts to these meetings, which featured bands, old banners from Peterloo, many women's groups, and a wide array of speakers and leaders of the Chartist Movement.

Leading up to the convention, disagreements developed between the initial leadership, including William Lovett, who promoted the use of "moral force," and those who advocated "physical force." A lead advocate of physical force, if necessary, to achieve the Charter was Feargus O'Connor. A former Member of Parliament from Ireland, he emerged as one of the chief spokesmen of Chartism and published Chartism's main spokes-piece, *The Northern Star and Leeds General Advertiser*. He had been most influential in the northern industrial areas, but his popularity soon spread. This philosophical disagreement about force threatened to fracture the movement, "but for all the division exemplified by the stormy meetings held at Birmingham, London, Newcastle, Glasgow, and Renfrew... the approach of the convention gave Chartism at least the facade of unity." (Ward: 73, 111) Delegates selected at the public meetings started the Convention on February 4, 1839 in London, and on February 28 sent John Collins as missionary to spread the word and gather signatures to the petition. May 7 was the day that the 1,280,000-signature petition in support of the Charter was ceremonially delivered to the houses of Parliament. The convention relocated to Birmingham on May 13, but returned to London after the July 4th Police Riots in the Bull Ring for which Lovett and Collins were sent to Warwick Gaol, where they were grossly mistreated. Parliament defeated the motion to consider the Chartist Petition by 235 to 46 on July 12, 1839. As word got out, disturbances occurred throughout the country, the most notable being the catastrophic Newport Rising in South Wales. This first attempt by working people to obtain redress of their grievances by promoting the Charter ended with most leaders in prison, and its convention concluded in Fall of 1839, thus ending the first coalition of radical organizations working for Reform.

Chartism mostly continued through local organizations and trade unions, obtaining outcomes with variable success. A Chartist convention did convene in Manchester on July 20, 1840, with 23 mostly new Chartists. They continued discussion on what more could be done for the three Newport Chartists John Frost, Zephaniah Williams, and William Jones, who were convicted and transported for insurrection after the Newport Rising. This gathering was best known as the origin of the National Charter Association (N.C.A.), which ultimately came under the influence of Feargus O'Connor, who dedicated *The Northern Star* to promoting the N.C.A. and being the primary means of communication among the members. (Chase: 2007, 164) Lasting from 1840 to 1858, the N.C.A. peaked at 50,000 members in 1842, and masterminded a leviathan Charter Petition, which combined the original six points of the Charter with a call to repeal both the Poor Law Amendment Act of 1834 and the Act of Union of 1801. When the petition was grandiosely delivered in May 1842 it had 3,000,000 signatures and was so large it could not get into Westminster Palace even after attempts to enlarge the entryway. Eventually the petition and its fancy covering had to be split to get it in. The petition was rejected in May after another petition presented by the Complete Suffrage Union had been rejected in April by almost as great a majority. (Thompson: 1984, 280)

After the success of Daniel O'Connell's Catholic Rent Organization in securing the Catholic Emancipation Act of 1829, O'Connell redirected his attention to repealing the Irish Act of Union of 1801. In behalf of this cause, O'Connell held monster meetings of more than 100,000 people through-out Ireland during 1842–3, but the government of Robert Peel stopped them from holding a major meeting in Dublin in the fall of 1843. Shortly afterwards O'Connell was indicted for conspiracy to overthrow the govern-ment. His stunning self-defense was successful, but further rallies for repeal were banned. He persisted with his efforts and was convicted of conspiracy, was fined 2,000 pounds, and served three months of a twelve-month sen-tence. He continued to work for reform after his release, but his organiza-tion began to dissolve with the estrangement and disaffection of the Young Irelanders, who moved on to the use of physical force.

By early 1845 the economies of England, Scotland, and Wales began to improve; however, Ireland rapidly worsened as potato blight wiped out the poor people's primary source of food during the fall harvest. The continu-ing effects of the blight over the following years resulted in over a million deaths from disease and starvation, and more than two million Irish people migrated elsewhere, mostly to America. The government's attempts at mit-igation provided little or no relief from the devastation.

It took until 1848 for the Chartists to build enough support to prepare another petition for Parliament. To present it, a rally was set for London's Kennington Common on April 10, 1848. As the critical time approached for delivering the petition, government's fear of armed revolution grew; armed revolutions had already occurred in most European countries earlier that year. The government granted permission to meet on Kennington Common, but not to march into town with the petition. Twenty thousand soldiers and 150,000 specially sworn constables were assembled under the command of none other than Old Nosey (Lord Wellington) to assure that the Chartist mob could not gain access to the City. Feargus O'Connor agreed to aban-don the march and transported the massive petition to Parliament himself, in three hansom cabs.

As interest in the Chartist movement waned, O'Connor began to advo-cate a land reform plan, the "Chartist Cooperative Land Society," in which shares were sold to buy land to resettle factory workers. New members, in-cluding the articulate Ernest Jones, rallied to the O'Connor banner. It began to catch on and was moving along well until the disastrous Chartist episode of 1848. Parliament hurriedly passed a new Treason Felony Act, which pro-hibited advocating republicanism, and investigated O'Connor's land reform program. As a result, most of the leadership of the Chartist movement were jailed, and O'Connor was ordered to return funds gathered for the land scheme. After this last defeat, and with the exception of only a few minor activities in provincial areas in the north, the Charter Movement was dead.

The 1840s were not good years for the working class or parliamentary reform. Despite ten years of reformers' united efforts, their petitions were repeatedly rejected by Parliament. Working people throughout the British Isles were starved to death or served time in the dreaded workhouses, where they also starved or died of communicable diseases. Attempts by the Irish to peacefully obtain repeal of the Act of Union with England were unsuccessful. The middle class, however, now partially represented in Parliament, were pleased to see repeal of the Corn Laws and other tariffs that were thought to deter business.

To deal with the disappointment of the working classes over the setbacks of the 1840s and to extol the virtues of British ingenuity, Queen Victoria's husband, Albert, her German first cousin, planned and carried out the Great Exhibition of 1851 in the glass and cast iron Crystal Palace. The public showed up in tens of thousands each day via the new innovation of excursion trains to pay a shilling to view the glories of the imperial wealth, diversity, and technological innovation of the Victorian Era.

Chartists fired on by 45th Nottinghamshire Regiment at Newport

# 94 Queen Victoria

Charles Hindly, *Curiosities of Street Literature* (1893): 55 – Roud V1426

Tune: The Nut Girl; Broadside, 1819–44

WEL - COME now, VIC - TO - RI - A   Wel - come to   the   throne!

May all  the trades be - gin  to stir, Now you  are Queen of  Eng - land;

For your  most gra - cious Ma - jes - ty May see  what wretch - ed  po - ver - ty

Is   to  be found on Eng - land's ground, Now  you  are Queen of  Eng - land

CHORUS Of all  the flo - wers  in  full bloom, A - dorned with beau - ty  and per-fume,

The  fair - est is  the  rose  in June;  Vic - to - ri - a Queen of  Eng - land.

WELCOME now, VICTORIA!
Welcome to the throne!
May all the trades begin to stir,
Now you are Queen of England;
For your most gracious Majesty
May see what wretched poverty
Is to be found on England's ground,
Now you are Queen of England.

CHORUS
Of all the flowers in full bloom,
Adorned with beauty and perfume,
The fairest is the rose in June;
Victoria, Queen of England.

While o'er the country you preside,
Providence will be your guide,
The people then will never chide,
Victoria Queen of England.

She doth declare it her intent
To extend reform in parliament,
On doing good she's firmly bent,
While she is Queen of England.

She says, I'll try my utmost skill,
That the poor may have their fill;
Forsake them!—no I never will
While I am Queen of England;
For oft my mother said to me,
Let this your study always be,
To see the people blessed and free,
Should you be Queen of England.

And now my daughter, you do reign,
Much opposition to sustain,
You'll surely have, before you gain
The blessings of old England,
O yes dear mother, that is true,
I know my sorrows won't be few,
Poor people shall have work to do,
While I am Queen of England.

I will encourage every trade,
For their labour must be paid,
In this free country then she said—
Victoria Queen of England;
That poor-law bill, with many more,
Shall be trampled on the floor—
The rich must keep the helpless poor,
While I am Queen of England.

The Royal Queen of Britain's isle
Soon will make the peoples smile,
Her heart none can the last defile,
Victoria Queen of England;
Although she is of early years,
She is possessed of tender cares,
To wipe away the orphan's tears,
While she is Queen of England.

With joy each Briton doth exclaim,
Both far and near across the main,
Victoria we now proclaim
The Royal Queen of England;

Long may she live and happy be,
Adorn'd with robes of royalty,
With blessings from her subjects free,
While she is Queen of England.

In every town and Village gay,
The bells shall ring and music play,
Upon her coronation-day
Victoria Queen of England.
While her affections we do win,
And every day fresh blessings bring,
Ladies help me for to sing
Victoria, Queen of England.

W. & T. Fordyce, Printers, 48, Dean Street, Newcastle.

Queen Victoria's ascension provided a ray of hope in an increasingly bleak and tumultuous time. It was good to remain positive and to retain an open mind that the poor man's plight would improve during her reign. This ballad acknowledges the level of the nation's distress on June 20, 1837 when the young princess ascended to the throne. The first verse asks her to see what wretched poverty is to be found on England's ground. This broadside expresses great faith that her reign will advance abolition of the New Poor Law Bill and further parliamentary reform, but neither matter was mentioned in the Queen's first address to her new Parliament.

These prospects were further dampened when Lord Russell, who played a major role in passage of the Reform Act and now served as home secretary of the newly elected Parliament, declared on November 20, 1837 that he saw the 1832 reform bill as complete and final. As a result of this often-misquoted speech he was nicknamed Finality Russell, but during 1850s he submitted four new reform bills himself. (Lang: 2005, 50)

Queen Victoria

## 95 The Cotton Spinners Farewell
Bodleian Library: Johnson Ballads, 1945 – Roud V15587

*Tune: Bonnie Ship The Diamond; Europa Ship Log, 1868-70*

Ye work-ing men of Bri - tain, come lis - ten a - while,

Con - cern-ing the cot - ton spin __ ners who late - ly stood their trial.

Trans - port - ed for se - ven years, far, far a - wa',

Be - cause they were u - ni - ted men in Ca - le - do - ni - a

Ye working men of Britain, come listen awhile,
Concerning the cotton spinners who lately stood their trial,
Transported for seven years, far, far awa',
Because they were united men in Caledonia.

When first we were arrested, and lodged in Glasgow gaol.
They striped us of our clothing, left us naked in our cell;
No sympathy they showed to us, no not the least ava',
Because we were united men in Caledonia.

Our trial they postponed for time after time,
Indictment on indictment, and crime upon crime,
Which turned out all a humbug, for this was their claw,
To prevent combination in Caledonia.

Success to our friends in Ireland, who boldly stood our cause,
In spite of O'Connell and his support of whiggish laws,
Away with his politics, they are not worth a straw,
He's no friend to the poor of Ireland, or Caledonia.

Success to O'Connor who did nobly plead our cause,
Likewise to Mr. Beaumonty, who abhors oppressive laws,
But after all their efforts, justice and law,
We are banished from our country, sweet Caledonia.

Ye brave men of Northumbria we bid you all farewell,
Were our voices like trumpets, to our enemies we'd tell,
Your actions to us was noble, although your band was sma',
To crush the monster Tyranny from Caledonia.

Whigs and Tories are united we see it very plain,
To crush the poor labourer it is their daily aim,
The proverb now is verified and that you all know,
In the case of those poor spinners in Caledonia.

Adieu to those who are near to us, our wives and children dear,
Put your trust in the Lord, your enemies need not fear,
Although we are banished far far awa',
You will find friends in old England and Caledonia.

W. and T. Fordyce, Printers, Dean Street, Newcastle

Times were desperate all over in 1837, and this pathetic ballad about the wage slaves of Glasgow, who were trying to stop further reductions of their wages, tells it well. The strike of the Glasgow spinners happened around the time of the ascension of Victoria. The Whig government appeared to have learned nothing from their mistakes with the Tolpuddle Martyrs. They took months to officially charge the Glaswegians, and at the last minute they dragged out, among other things, the old illegal oath law from the Naval Mutiny of 1797.

The ballad describes the abuse of the prisoners: stripping them of their clothing, delaying trial dates, adding and changing charges—tactics still used by regressive regimes today. Eventually the jury unanimously found the strikers innocent of most counts: appointing "a secret committee" to do unlawful acts, attempting to set fire to houses and to factories, assaulting strike breakers (knobs) and invading their houses. By a majority of one the jury found them guilty of conspiracy to keep wages up, of disturbances at Oakbank Factory, and of molestation at Mile End Factory. The *Northern Star* and the *Northern Liberator* reported on the proceedings, presenting the prosecution of the spinners' committee as part of a planned attack on the whole working class. (Thompson, 1984, 21–22) The prisoners were sentenced to seven years' transportation but never left for Van Diemen's land. They were eventually pardoned after spending three years in hulks at Woolwich.

The fourth and fifth verses refer to the growing animosity between Daniel O'Connell and Feargus O'Connor. O'Connell had a solid role with the Whig Party, which he continued to cultivate in his struggle to repeal the Act of Union. It appeared that the spinners were being sent on trumped-up charges down the same path as the Tolpuddle Martyrs, and O'Connell, now considered the radical scourge of trade unions, fell from working-class favor. (Ward: 1973, 93) O'Connor, a former member of Parliament from Cork, originally owed his seat to O'Connell, and had championed the spinners' cause as part of his early advocacy of militant union support. Acting on his commitment to the industrial workers' issues, O'Connor remained a strong anti-Whig campaigner. This later led to his becoming the leader of the "physical force" wing of the Chartist movement.

The fifth verse thanks "Mr. Beaumonty, who abhors oppressive laws." Augustus H. Beaumont was born in New York and lived much of his adult life in Jamaica, where he was active in arranging details for ending slavery in the West Indies. In 1835 he resettled in Britain and established in Newcastle an important part of the radical press, *The Northern Liberator*, in November 1837. He died in 1838 at the age of forty.

The Glasgow Cotton Spinners

## 96 A New Song on the Great Demonstration, Which is to be made on Kersal Moor, September 24th, 1838

Bodleian Library: Firth Collection. c. 16(40) – Roud V33134

*Tune: Liverpool Girls; Palmer, c. 1840*

You reformers of England and Ireland attend,
To this song I have made which I lately have penn'd
Concerning a meeting which now has took place,
Our rights for to gain and to better our case
The time it is come boys, the work has begun
To be free, or forever be slaves.

You Lancashire lads, this day is the time,
Reformers will now both their hands and hearts join,
For Freedom and Liberty now is the cry,
To no longer be slaves but like freemen to die.
So let us be steady, determined and ready,
When met boys upon Kersal Moor.

The rich man he lives in his luxury at ease,
The poor man's degraded, death stares him i'th face,
The rich knows not now what to eat drink or wear,
The poor's clothed in rags, what does the rich care,
But our motto shall be, huzza for liberty!
Now we're met boys upon Kersal Moor.

From Macclesfield, Stockport, and Oldham they've come,
Ashton, Rochdale, and Middelton with music and drums,
Bury, Bolton and Leith, it is a grand show,
Reformers all marching, Thousands in a row.
With banners so free and loud shouts of huzza;
Now reformers join on Kersal Moor.

The Manchester lads now they lead on in front,
As they did in the days of brave HENRY HUNT*,
Annual Parliaments, Suffrage, determined to gain,
The Ballot without these we slaves must remain
Determined to be either bondsmen, or free,
United upon Kersal Moor.

The Birmingham lads and the lads of the North.
Have showed us great courage their valour and worth;
Will the brave men of Lancashire now behind lag,
All that do their heads ought to be stuck in a bag.
But no's! all the cry, we will fight till we die,
For Liberty on Kersal Moor.

There is Fielden, brave Attwood, and Oastler so free,
Fletcher, Stephens, O'Connor, who all do agree
Reform it is needed, Reform we will have,
For freedom's the cry of the honest and brave.
Be loyal and true boys, think on Peterloo.
Remember this on Kersal Moor.

You females of England all join the true cause
Your liberty's rights, brave freedom and laws.
That in after ages our children may say,
Our forefathers struggled, fought for liberty
And joined the throng now we bravely move on,
To the meeting held on Kersal Moor.

*The greatest reformer of the age

So up and be doing— in one union join,
That the bright star of freedom may brightly shine,
And Liberty's shout resound from shore to shore,
That Britons are free and will be slaves no more,
Huzza for reform, we shall weather the storm
At this meeting upon Kersal Moor.

J Wheeler, Printer Whittlestreet Manchester

Massive crowds turned out for all gatherings dealing with the primary issues of the day, including the Poor Law Bill, the newspaper tax, the ten-hour workday, the Corn Law, and trade unionism. It was now time to see if people would turn out in such large numbers for a meeting dedicated to just the Charter. By the summer of 1838, everything to establish an effective movement was in place. Unemployment and high food costs made it clear that the Reform Bill had not improved the desperate lot of the working poor. The ideal site for this outdoor meeting devoted to Chartism was Kersal Moor, near Manchester, and thousands assembled there on September 24, 1838. The ultimate purpose of the meeting was to enable the people to elect their delegates to a national convention to be held in London early the following year. (Royle: 1980, 22)

This ballad was a rallying cry from what is believed to have been the largest meeting yet in support of the Charter. Verse four cites some of the cities and towns represented in the crowd. The seventh verse lists the popular organizers and people who spoke on the issues. The eighth verse makes it clear that, as with other Chartist functions, women were welcome and active at the event. The gathering included twenty bands, some two hundred banners including many from Peterloo, and attendance estimated between 50,000 and 300,000.

This exciting event, however, has a backstory. By the time of the Kersal Moor meeting, the former Irish Member of Parliament, Feargus O'Connor, had been publishing *The Northern Star* for ten months, and had rapidly become recognized and loved as the leader of Chartist activities in the North of England. O'Connor was also seen as the leader of those who believed that to see adoption of the Charter, Chartists must be willing to resort to physical force. In contrast, the southern leadership advocated moral force, relying on education and rational persuasion. According to G. D. H. Cole,

> The real difference, in 1838, was between those who held that the method of working-class agitation should be educational and rational, and designed to elicit the sympathy of men of goodwill in other classes, and those who held that the governing classes would yield nothing except from fear, and that accordingly any and every method should be used to make the demand for Radical reform as formidable as possible in their eyes. (Cole: 1941, 313)

# 97 Frost, Williams, and Jones's Farewell to England

Bodleian Library: Johnson Ballads, 1480 – Roud V33008

*Tune: The Wandering Harper; Crosby's Irish Musical Repository, 1808*

As I walked through the town of Portsmouth,
I heard three wretched men to say,
Farewell our dearest wives and children,
We can with you no longer stay,
In agony and broken hearted,
We are compelled behind to leave,
Our native land, our friends and kindred,
For our awful fate to grieve.

CHORUS
Across the sea, Frost, Jones, and Williams,
Through tempest and dreadful gales,
We leave our native land behind us,
To end our days in New South Wales.

At Monmouth we were tried for treason,
And we were condemned to die,
Great and small throughout the nation,
For to save our lives did try,
England Ireland Wales, and Scotland,
Manifold for us did strive,
And through a deal perseverance,
Government did spare our lives.

Sad was the day we drew together,
Thousands of men from far and near;
Which caused grief and consternation,
In every part of Monmouthshire,
That fatal day we'll long remember,
Which caused distress on every mind,
Was the third of last November,
Eighteen hundred and thirty nine.

Tens of thousands have petitioned,
Overcome with grief and woe,
Every rank in all conditions,
A free pardon us to gain,
We anxiously each hour expected,
That some messenger to see,
To our dismal cell approaching
With the sound of liberty.

But ah! We were mistaken,
All hopes have proved in vain,
We forever now are banished,
Never to return again,
A long farewell our wives and children,
Adieu our friends and neighbors,
While in slavery we are pining,
Oft we'll think of Monmouthshire.

Happy with our wives and children,
We on our native land might be,
If the length of our misfortunes,
We could only once foresee,
O! For those we left behind us,
From our eyes runs floods of tears
Although from death they have reprieved us,
We think our sentence too severe.

Many a heart will beat in sorrow
Many an eye will shed a tear,
Many an orphan and its mother,
Will lament in Monmouthshire,
For the third of last November,
When their fathers went astray,
Many thousands will remember,
The sad disaster of the day.

We will conclude our mournful ditty,
Which fill our aching heart with pain,
Shed for us a tear of pity,
We never shall return again,
And when we've reached our destination,
O'er the rolling seas through storms and gales,
Oh! May you live at home in comfort,
While we lament in New South Wales.

Birmingham Printed and sold at Watt's 14, Snow Hill

This ballad imagines the feelings of John Frost, Zephaniah Williams, and William Jones, three Welshmen convicted of the crime of high treason for their leadership of the Newport Rising of 1839, and destined to be transported for life, but pictured here still in Plymouth awaiting transport to New South Wales. These very historic times are frequently referred to as the last armed insurrection in England and Wales.

The Newport Rising of 1839 followed a sequence of significant events starting with the Chartist Convention of that year. After its three-mile-long, 1,280,824-signature petition was delivered to Parliament on May 7, the Convention moved to Birmingham later in May, where Convention participants often gathered in the evenings at the Bull Ring area of the city. The City angered the Chartists by importing London Peelers who caused fights, labeled "The Bull Ring Riots," which were blamed on the Chartists.

It took until July 12 for Parliament to contemptuously reject the Charter by 235 votes to 46. Back again in London, the Convention debated a number of countermeasures, including a month-long general strike, smaller but focused work disruptions, major runs on the banks, widespread or focused insurrections, etc. Charter secretary William Lovett and three other officers of the Convention were arrested for sedition, charged with posting placards signed by Lovett. Authorities throughout Britain began to take action against the Chartists. Many of its major leaders were soon in jail, including Lovett, O'Connor, Vincent, Harney, and others. (Thompson: 1984, 69)

While the Chartist Convention remained in session, an area of Wales that still breathed uneasily over the Merthyr Tydfil Riots of 1831 was under severe watch. Magistrates from Llanidloes claimed that workers were arming and drilling, and asked for backup from London. Three policemen from London arrested three local Chartist leaders and held them in rooms at the Trewythen Hotel. Chartists stormed the hotel and released the prisoners, and Llanidloes was in Chartist hands for several days, until the military arrived and routed the mostly unarmed workers. (Cole: 1941, 142) Thirty-two Chartists, including three women, were apprehended and tried in Montgomeryshire Assize Court. Thirty received sentences of three months to one year. Two of the three originally jailed Chartists were transported to Tasmania, and one escaped to America.

All these events led toward the Newport Rising. Enough was enough, and it was time for citizens to take matters into their own hands. The target would be Wales's leading coal port on the Usk River at Newport, chosen because it had an active Chartist membership and was accessible to the entire area. One of the leaders was John Frost, a former Mayor of Newport who had served as a chairman of the Chartist Convention in London. He had been relieved of his position as a magistrate in March of 1839 by Home Secretary Lord John Russell (the reformer) who considered Frost to be allied with the "physical force" contingent of the Chartists. Also leading this mission were Zephaniah Williams, the active atheist and coal miner, and public house landlord William Jones. They planned to each lead a column of men from three different directions into Newport on November 5, 1839, and meet up with the local Chartist contingent there. Unfortunately, the pending overnight march was the talk of all the marchers' pubs for weeks before Guy Fawkes Day, and, as is often the case, the weather on the evening of the 4th was horribly wet. With all the advance warning, a small platoon of soldiers had moved in the day before and locked up the key Newport Chartists in the Westgate Hotel. Coming in through the rain, the marchers learned of the plight of their colleagues at the Westgate and went to help them regain their freedom. Upon arrival the column led by Jones was missing, but the size of the crowd, though wet, was huge. Right away the soldiers fired two rounds at the mostly unarmed Chartists, who turned and fled to the hills, leaving at least twenty-two of their number dead. (Thompson: 1984, 80)

Frost, Williams, and Jones were arrested and in January 1840 convicted of high treason. They were sentenced to be hanged, drawn, and quartered. It took heavy Chartist pressure and massive petitioning for their sentences to be altered to transportation for life; more people signed the 1840 petition for a pardon than had signed the 1839 Chartist national petition. (Chase: 2015, 94) Frost was eventually pardoned and returned to Britain in 1856. Williams found coal in Tasmania and became very rich. Jones remained in business in Australia and died a pauper.

## 98 Removal of Napoleon's Ashes

Bodleian Library: Harding Collection, B 15(256a) – Roud V497

*Tune: Princess Royal; Turlough O'Carolan, 1725*

At - tend you gal - lant Bri - tons bold, Un-to these ___ lines I
Who for cen - tu - ries that is gone by, for Eng-land fought most

will un - fold The deeds of va - lient he - roes
man - ful - ly And in the Bri - tish re - cords,

I am go - ing to ___ re - late
There you will find ___ the date.

But of a va - liant Cor - si - can as e - ver stood on
CHORUS And now a-cross the foam-ing waves, to ___ fetch from St. He -

Eu - rope's land, I ___ am in - clined to sing in praise; how
le - na's grave, The proud and gal - lant French - men, so

no - ble was his heart, In e - v'ry bat - tle
bold - ly do ___ de - part To bring a - way, as

man - ful - ly, he ___ strug - gled hard for ___ li - ber - ty, And
Bri - tons say, and con - se - crate with - out de - lay, In

to the world a ter - ror was, Na - po - leon Buo - na - parte.
Pa - ris town, the a - shes of Na - po - leon Buo - na - parte.

Attend, you gallant Britons bold, unto these lines I will unfold
The deeds of valiant heroes I am going to relate,
Who for centuries that is gone by, for England fought most manfully,
And in the British records, there you'll find the date.
But of a valiant Corsican as ever stood on Europe's land,
I am inclined to sing in praise; how noble was his heart,
In every battle manfully, he struggled hard for liberty,
And to the world a terror was, Napoleon Buonaparte.

CHORUS
And now across the foaming waves, to fetch from St. Helena's grave,
The proud and gallant Frenchman, so boldly do depart,
To bring away, as Britons say, and consecrate without delay,
In Paris town, the ashes of Napoleon Buonaparte.

We read of gallant Marlborough, we read of valiant Nelson,
We read of noble Jarvis, brave Howe, and gallant Blake,
Of Wolfe and Abercrombie, great men who fought by land and sea,
Back from the days of Wellington, unto Sir Francis Drake;
They were men of courage true, and fought like Britons of true blue,
Always was undaunted, so noble was each heart,
But Europe, we must understand, could not boast of late of such a man,
As the valiant little Corsican, Napoleon Buonaparte.

When at the Isle of Elba, Napoleon fought for liberty,
And when he went across the Alps, he did the world amaze,
He would never yield when in the field, but strive to gain a victory,
Europe will long remember how Moscow it did blaze;
But fatal June at Waterloo, did make Napoleon for to rue,
To see the tricks of Blucher, struck terror to his heart.
It was then he had to fight or run, he cried, alas! I am undone
Like a bullock sold in Smithfield, was Napoleon Bonaparte.

It was in the days of Castlereagh, brave Bonaparte was led astray,
And the battle of great Waterloo was bought by English gold
We long may recollect the day, when Grouchy did the French betray,
And brave Napoleon Bonaparte upon the ground was sold.
He in the field then valiant stood, saying, while I have life and blood,
I will not die a coward with his hand upon his heart,
I always proved myself a man, but now I can no longer stand,
My glass is nearly run, cried brave Napoleon Bonaparte.

He was by his friends forsaken, and prisoner he was taken,
And he was sent to England, just like a convict bound,
Far across the briny waves, a gallant soldier bold and brave,
On board the Bellerophon man-of-war, to Plymouth Sound;
Where he a little time did lay, and thousands flocked by night and day,
From here and there, and everywhere, in droves from every part,
They were struck with wonder and amaze, as anxiously they on did gaze,
That valiant little Corsican, Napoleon Bonaparte.

Then soon it was concluded. Napoleon should be banished
Unto some distant island, where he no more should smile,
And he was sent across the sea, a prisoner for life to be,
His days to end in misery on St. Helena's Isle;

Louisa for her husband wept, nor day nor night she seldom slept,
The briny tears rolled from her eyes to soothe her aching heart,
"Where is my Emperor?" she cried, "Oh! cursed be the gold that bribed
False Grouchy to betray my brave Napoleon Bonaparte."

Some years he lived in exile, and mourned on St. Helena's shore,
And there, alas! he was deprived of every bosom friend.
He respected was by high and low, through Europe wheresoever you go,
On the Isle of St. Helena, he there his days did end.
He cried, my glass is nearly run, I can behold the setting sun
And while he spoke he gently laid his hand upon his heart,
He looked around and gave a smile, and died upon St. Helena's Isle,
And there they laid the ashes of Napoleon Buonaparte.

Now to erect a monument, agreed has every soldier,
The Peer, likewise the peasant, every Frenchman bold and brave,
And in a very little while they'll bring from St. Helena's Isle,
The ashes of Napoleon that lays moldering in the grave.
In the city of great Paris, a tomb will be erected,
So splendidly, for to contain his ashes and his heart,
And rich and poor that pass that way, will joyfully a tribute pay,
To the ashes and the memory of Napoleon Bonaparte.

This ballad is credited to John Morgan who, according to James Hepburn, is "the significant figure among professional broadside ballad authors of nineteenth-century England." (Hepburn: 2000, 49) France's Marshal Nicolas Soult, representing France at the marriage of Queen Victoria to Prince Albert in 1838, took the opportunity to propose that France bring back the body of Napoleon from the island of St Helena, where he had died on May 5, 1821. With full authority of the British Government, a French contingent of Generals and close associates of the Emperor exhumed and identified Napoleon, reporting his body still in very good condition. The French naval vessel bearing the remains arrived in Cherbourg on November 30, 1840, and Napoleon was given what Will and Arial Durant called the "longest funeral in history." (Durant: 1975, 775) Bonaparte was ultimately placed in an extravagant shrine at Les Invalides in Paris. It took until 1942 for the remains of his only legitimate son (Napoleon II) to be buried alongside him, by none other than Adolf Hitler.

This song was one of the most widely printed pro-Napoleon songs. At least as many English broadside ballads were written about the disinterment of Napoleon as about Victoria's wedding. Under several titles, all of which mention the ashes of Napoleon, this broadside continued to be printed for many years. Ballads like this are strong on sympathy for Napoleon and for British naval and military heroes like Nelson. The Napoleonic wars left an indelible impression on those who lived through them. Did they still wonder what life would have been like if only Napoleon had won?

## 99 A New Chartist Song

*The Northern Star*, February 13, 1841

Tune: Bay of Biscay; Broadside, 1867

Loud roar'd the people's thunder,
And tyrants heard the storm,
They trembled, and knocked under,
And gave us mock Reform.
They felt the electric spark,
Which bared corruption's ark;
Rent their veil, they turned pale,
At the voice of freedom, O!

Then our good ship Britannia,
Amongst the breakers lay,
Poor Bark! we gladly mann'd her,
With Whigs and Gaffer Grey;
But lubbers all the proved,
And from the rocks ne'er moved,
There are they, till this day,
On thy rocks, corruption O!

At length the People's Charter
Shoots forth its beacon rays!
She deepens now her water,
The tide around her plays;
Soon shall her lubber crew,
Resign her helm to you;
Chartists brave, ye must save,
The good ship, Britannia, O!

The morn of freedom's breaking,
We hail it from afar:
And for a compass taking,
Our glorious *Northern Star*!
We'll soon the breakers clear,
The port we soon shall near;
Now, we sail, with the gale,
For the Bay of Freedom, O!

Our pilot, Brave O'Connor
We soon will get on board,
More sail we'll crowd upon her,
And get her richly stored;
Mann'd by a gallant crew,
Of Chartists staunch and true,
We shall ride, with the tide,
To the port of Freedom, O!

This song appeared in *The Northern Star* while plans were underway to submit the second Chartist petition to Parliament. One by one, the original Chartist leaders completed their prison sentences and organized their next moves. In Manchester on July 20, 1840 a conference of twenty-three delegates formed a new Chartist organization for England, the National Charter Association (N.C.A.). It was promptly blessed by Feargus O'Connor from his York Castle jail cell, where he was finishing up his 18-month term. (Royle: 1980, 27) The new organization was more democratic than the People's Charter, with positions elected directly by members of local chapters rather than at mass meetings, as had been the case in 1839. Distribution of representatives was more fair, with twenty-four from England and twenty-five divided between Scotland and Wales. In addition to the original six points from the first Charter, the N.C.A.'s new petition was more political than the previous one, demanding repeal of both the Poor Law Amendment Act (1834) and the Union of Britain and Ireland from 1801.

The Whig government continued to run up debts. In June of 1841, following a defeat of the government's budget in May, a general election was called and a vote of no confidence put forward by Leader of the Opposition, Robert Peel. The election resulted in a majority conservative government led again by Sir Robert Peel, who was also well known as the father of the British police (Bobbies and Peelers). Peel lowered the duty on corn and reduced the debt by reintroducing the income tax which had ended after the Napoleonic wars. It was to this new conservative government that the Chartists brought their second petition with its 3,317,752 signatures in early May, 1842, and, as expected, it was roundly voted down 287 to 46.

## 100 To the Chartists of Shropshire

*The Northern Star and Leeds General Advertiser*, May 27, 1843

*Tune: Cruel Mother; ballad tune, printed 1776*

Raise the Chart-ist ban-ner high, Plant it in the Wre-kin,

Let its mot-toes proud-ly fly, To the ty-rant speak-ing.

A - gi-tate each wood-ed vale, A - gi-tate each vil-lage,

Show the wife and or-phan pale, How the fac-tions pil-lage.

Raise the Chartist banner high,
Plant it in the Wrekin,
Let its mottoes proudly fly,
To the tyrant speaking.

Agitate each wooded vale,
Agitate each village,
Show the wife and orphan pale,
How the factions pillage.

Leave no spot in Shropshire wide
Until it owns the Charter;
Spare the man who would divide
Your ranks, or freedom barter.

Prove that in each vein now runs
The British blood of old;
And that— crushing freedom's foes
Ye dare be firm, and bold.

Cease not in your noble cause,
Until you freedom gain;
And liberty and equal laws,
Are England's own again.

Then bear the Chartist flag once more,
O'er mountain stream and vale;
A cause like yours so bright and pure,
Is never doomed to fail.

1842 was the year in which more energy was hurled against the British authorities than in any other of the nineteenth century. More people were arrested and sentenced for offences concerned with speaking, agitating, rioting, and demonstrating than in any other year, and more people were out on the streets during August 1842 than any other time. It was the nearest thing to a general strike that the century saw. (Thompson: 1984, 295)

While people's energy was spent seeking political reform, the working poor throughout industrial Britain were suffering from yet another devastating economic depression. Friedrich Engels traveled through the industrial region during this time and wrote about seeing numbers of starving, emotionally distraught, unemployed people. "This occurred in all the industrial districts from Leicester to Leeds and from Manchester to Birmingham. Here and there sporadic disturbances occurred, as in the Potteries of North Staffordshire. The greatest excitement prevailed among the workers and this culminated in severe rioting throughout the factory districts." (Engels: 1845, 102)

Thomas Cooper, respected poet and Chartist organizer, addressed a number of meetings in the Pottery towns of Shropshire as missionary for the Chartists, concluding with a huge open-air gathering at the Crown Bank in Hanley. Cooper seconded a motion that all work should cease until the Charter had become the law of the land. It appeared that this might become the beginning of the National Holiday that had been discussed in 1839.

It took Cooper several days to travel to another Chartist conference in Manchester, and on arrival he realized that smoke was not rising from the factory stacks. He learned that a conference of 358 delegates from the factory areas had voted to convert the almost random strikes into a grand national strike for the Charter. He later called upon workers throughout the country to join the strike, and it spread swiftly through the industrial areas of England and Scotland. It began to look like the movement that Chartists had spoken of for so long. Was this all spontaneous, and were the Chartists exploiting it to turn it into their political movement? Dorothy Thompson concludes: "Whether or not the Chartist leaders in the industrial areas had called for strikes, it seems inevitable that they would have occurred. In the Manchester district as in the Potteries and the Staffordshire coalfield, the articulate leaders in the strike movement were the Chartists." (Thompson: 1984, 290)

The National Charter Association called for a general strike in eight days throughout Great Britain with the manifesto ending: "Strengthen our hands at this crisis; support your leaders; rally round our sacred cause; and leave the decision to the God of justice, and of battle." (Cole, G.D.H.: 1941, 202)

# 101 The Tara Monster Meeting

National Library of Scotland, L.C.Fol.178.A.2(065) — Roud V28206

*Tune: The Girl I Left Behind Me; Maurice Hime, 1810*

On the fif-teenth day of Au - gust, in the year of For - ty - Three
That glo-rious day, I well may say, Re - cor-ded it will be,
On the ro - yal hill of Ta - ra where thou-sands did pre - vail __
In u-nion's bonds to join their hands, To sign for the re - peal

On the fifteenth day of August,
In the year of Forty Three,
That glorious day, I well may say,
Recorded it will be,
On the royal hill of Tara,
Where thousands did prevail
In union's bonds to join their hands,
To sign for the repeal.

Such a grand sight was never seen,
Nor will till time's no more;
Its lasting fame shall long remain
Around Hibernia's shore.
No pen or talent can describe
The glories of that day,
As there was seen on Tara's green,
A matchless grand display.

There was Wexford, Wicklow, and
Kildare, Sweet Dublin, and
Ardee, West Meath, King's County, and
Dundalk, most charming for to see,
Ba'intree, Trim, and Bective,
With Kellnaven and Kinsale,
On the royal hill of Tara stood.
To sign for the Repeal.

I topped the hill with heart and will,
And cast my eyes around.
With a charming consternation,
I viewed from the rising ground,
The approaching legions of the earth
Advancing from afar.
With floating flags and beating drum,
Like thundering claps of war.

I thus proceeded farther.
Through a splendid arch did past,
Where I behold some thousands
On the hill attending mass.
So many being uncovered
In a pious holy strain,
For to describe the charming sight
It fluctuates my brain.

To see the flags of Drogheda,
With their harmonious band.
With sacred pious music
Round the corpses' grave did stand.
Where is the heart that could not feel
Or eye refuse a tear,
To see these murdered victims
For their country sleeping there

Hundreds of thousands of people, many travelling hundreds of miles on foot, attended "monster meetings" throughout Ireland in 1843. Daniel O'Connell held these meetings to show the British government that the people of Ireland were united in wanting to leave the United Kingdom and to re-establish the Irish Parliament that had been abolished in 1801. This song describes the largest of these gatherings, held on Lady Day, August 15, 1843 on the Hill of Tara, sacred home of the ancient kings of Ireland, located some twenty miles northwest of Dublin. According to legend, as many as 142 kings had reigned from this place, and it was considered to be the dwelling of the gods and the entrance to the other world. To this day monoliths, mounds, and many archeological features are still visible. The murdered victims in the last verse, sleeping on the Hill of Tara, were patriots buried there during the 1798 rebellion.

Such an enormous crowd from as far away as Kinsale must have inspired high hopes for removing the yoke of Britain's Parliament. The site is staggeringly beautiful. On a clear day it is possible to see half of the counties of Ireland from the top of that hill. Tara was covered on that day with hundreds of thousands of like-minded people holding out hope for repeal. "Headed by bands and banners, and marshalled by horsemen, no such gathering as that at Tara was ever seen before, and may never be seen again." (MacManus: 1966, 581)

The initial six points of the Charter had been drafted in 1837 by a twelve-person team including Daniel O'Connell, who subsequently lost the confidence of the working men with his attacks on trade unions and support of the new poor law. (Royle: 1980, 19) O'Connor had severely disagreed with O'Connell over the moral versus vs. physical force issues, and O'Connor found fault with O'Connell's limited goal of seeking the repeal of the 1801 Union, because it did not include total independence for Ireland. The growing Young Ireland Movement added its opposition to O'Connell's repeal efforts, driving him to focus more on his alliance with the Whig party. (Ward: 1970, 173) Later in 1843, for his trouble, O'Connell was jailed for twelve months. The House of Lords had him released after three months, but the trauma weakened his health, essentially ending his battle for repeal. He died during a pilgrimage to the holy land in 1847.

Monster Repeal Meeting on Tara Hill, Co. Meath, 15 August, 1843

## 102 The Chartist Song

Bodleian Library: Harding Collection, B 15(43a) – Roud V28520

*Tune: A Man's a Man for a' That; Robert Burns, 1795*

Art thou poor but ho - nest man, Sure - ly op-press'd and a' that,

At - ten - tion give to Chart-ist Plan, 'Twill cheer the heart for a' that

For a' that, a' that; Though land - lords gripe and a' that;

I'll shew thee, friend be - fore we part, The rights of men and a' that.

Art thou poor but honest man,
Surely oppress'd and a' that,
Attention give to Chartist Plan,
'Twill cheer the heart for a' that
For a' that, a' that;
Though landlords gripe and a' that;
I'll shew thee, friend before we part,
The rights of men and a' that.

The Bible friend, will plainly show,
How God gave his laws and a' that
And land and springs he did bestow,
To families and a' that,
Yes a' that and a' that,
To Have and hold for a' that
That with his gift they should not part
The text will plainly show that.

The rights of man then is in the soil,
An equal share and a' that
For landlords no one ought to toil—
'Tis imposition and a' that,
Yes a' that and a' that
Their title-deeds and a' that
Howe'er they got them matters not,
The land is ours for a' that.

Cursed be he who shall remove,
The poor man's bounds and a' that,
Or covet aught should he improve
His house, or stock, and a' that,
Yes a' that and a' that
His cattle goods and a' that
Could but be mortgaged for a term,
Till Jubilee and a' that.

Brave Chartist has shown the way to fix
Man's happiness and all that,
His freedom with his interest mix,
Their Charter plan will show that.
Yes a' that and a' that,
Divide the rent and a' that
What god has gave all should enjoy,
And all the world should know that.

Then let us pray, that come it may
As come it will for a' that,
This Christian plan o'er a' the earth
Shall bear the gree and a' that.
Yes, a' that and a' that,
As come it will for a' that;
The man and man the world o'er
Will brothers be and a' that.

This song borrows the melody and repeating motif of one of the most beloved songs of Robert Burns. Land reform, idealized in this song, became a centerpiece of the latter years of the Chartist movement. Feargus O'Connor wanted to enable factory workers to return to living off the land. He proposed to sell shares in a fund that would buy large tracts of land, to be divided into small (2- to 4-acre) farms each with a small cottage. Participants would own their land and, according to O'Connor, be able to survive comfortably and produce surplus food to meet Britain's needs. He advocated this approach in *The Northern Star* starting in 1843 and in his book, *A Practical Work on the Management of Small Farms*. Somewhat at the expense of the Charter itself, O'Connor diverted most of his attention after 1843 to this land scheme.

The Chartist Cooperative Land Society plan was launched publicly in April 1845 with O'Connor completely in charge. Amid much controversy, several plots of land were acquired with large donations from wealthy supporters and made available for workers. On this basis, some hundreds of households were settled on the estates brought by the land company. (Cole: 1941, 329)

Later Chartists and biographers of O'Connor were dismissive of the plan, but many of the ideas expressed during this experimental period were in step with today's back-to-the-land movements. "The comfortable small houses which were built under O'Connor's direction remain, many of them, to this day as monuments to the integrity of Chartist planning in an age increasingly devoted to shoddy." (Thompson: 1984, 303)

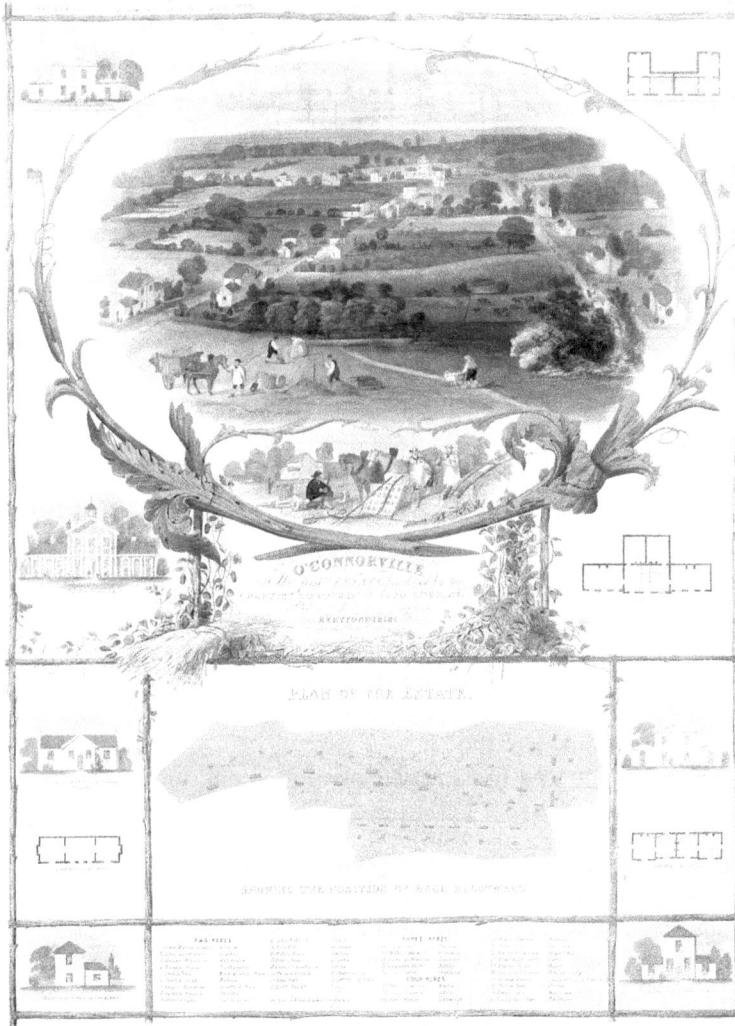

From the 1847 Map of O'Connnorville

# 103 A New Song Called the Tradesmen's Lament

Bodleian: 2806 b.11(282) – Roud V11588

*Tune: Irish Stranger; Broadside, 1813-38*

On a cold win - ter's morn - ing as the day was a dawn - ing

A voice came both hol-low and shrill. When the bit-ter winds did blow and the

snow was fast fal-ling, A stran - ger came o - ver the hill,

The cloth - ing he was wear - ing was all tat - ter'd and torn

La - men - ting for plea - sure I fear ne - ver will re - turn.

His face be - wil - dered and For - lorn

Old Ire - land what have you come to?

On a cold winter's morning as the day was a dawning
A voice came both hollow and shrill.
When the bitter winds did blow and the snow was fast falling,
A stranger came over the hill,
The clothing he was wearing was all tatter'd and torn
Lamenting for pleasure I fear never will return.
*His face bewildered and Forlorn\**
Old Ireland what have you come to?

There once was a time I could find friends plenty
To feed on their bountuous store,
But now my friends are few since my portion is scanty
But providence may open the door,
It nearly breaks my heart when my cottage I behold,
It is claimed by another who has plenty of gold
And I passing by shivering with cold,
Old Ireland what have you come to?

There is those nobles and commedians who daily assemble
And try their exertion and skill,
But alas? After all on the land they will tremble
For all trade is now standing still,
If the great god of war should on us call
I would break my chains of galling and boldly face a ball
To see my children starving it grieves me more than all,
Old Ireland what have you come to?

There is Dublin, Cork and Limerick and Belfast has fell to ruin
In fact all the country is at a stand,
Our work it is all gone, Oh alas there is nothing doing
While thousands are starving in the land,
It would break the heart of monarks bold
If they could rise again to view our desolation it distract their brain,
So pity us poor tradesmen or death will ease our pain,
Old Ireland what have you come to?

*Missing line on broadside supplied by the author.

The dreadful Irish Potato Famine of 1845–51 is the subject of this ballad lamenting the distress of the poor starving people of Ireland. The Irish potato crop of 1845 was completely destroyed by the wet mold *Phytophthora Infestans,* known as potato blight or late blight, which was first encountered in the U.S.A. in early 1843 and soon spread to all of the potato-growing countries in Europe. The blight hit Ireland the hardest because of the country's disproportionate dependency on a single variety of potato, the Irish Lumper. Due to the lack of genetic variability, the crop was susceptible to damaging organisms such as this mold. Over a million Irish died from starvation or from illnesses related to the blight.

While hundreds of thousands of Irish were dying from starvation, the governing landowners were exporting tens of millions of tons of food from Ireland. In the second verse the tradesman tells of shivering in the cold while passing by what had been his cottage, now repossessed. Many tales were told of families who had lived hand-to-mouth and were evicted by the landlord to enable growth of more lucrative crops.

Thousands attempted to escape the horror of the famine by emigration to England, Australia, Canada and, mostly, the U.S.A. Steerage passengers could gain passage to England for a few shillings or to the U.S.A. and Canada for £5 6s, which included a daily gallon of water and one pound of bread. Passengers were responsible for all else, including bedding, food, and cooking utensils. The Colonial Land and Emigration Commission paid the fare of emigrants to Australia. (Dodds: 1952, 293) It took more than 40 days to cross the Atlantic to the U.S.A. or Canada and four months to reach Australia.

## 104 The Corn Laws

Bodleian Library: Firth Collection c.16(49) – Roud V38870

Tune: Auld Lang Syne; Robert Burns, 1797

Ye mil - lions that so keen - ly feel The pres-sure of the times,
In vain you la - bour night and day. The own - er of the soil,

To you I do___ ear-nest-ly ap-peal, Then lis - ten to my rhymes,
By Corn Laws take the bread___ a - way, That should re - ward your toil.

CHORUS

Then o - pen ev - ery Bri - tish port, and let the poor be fed,

No long - er see your child - ren starve, And die through want of bread.

Ye millions that so keenly feel
The pressure of the times,
To you I do earnestly appeal,
Then listen to my rhymes,
In vain you labour night and day,
The owner of the soil,
By Corn Laws take the bread away,
That should reward your toil.

    CHORUS
    Then open every British port,
    and let the poor be fed,
    No longer see your children starve,
    And die through want of bread.

The haughty possess the land,
And wield oppression's rod,
Inspite of that divine command,
Found in the word of God;
The Corn Laws petrify their hearts,
And make the nation groan,
For when the people cry for bread
They only get a stone.
    Then open every, &c

Down, down with the starvation laws
And no more be beguiled,
Cheap bread must surely be the cause
Of woman man and child:
All property is insecure,
And insecure must be,
Till they our plunder rights restore
And make the Corn Trade free.
   Then open every, &c

The Corn Laws are the greatest scourge
That has been since the flood,
Enacted since the time of George,
Whose reign was that of blood!
But we have now a Queen beloved,
Oh! let it not be said,
That she can see and hear unmoved,
Her people cry for bread.
   Then open every, &c

By Allen Davenport<br/>"Author of all the Songs and Poems under the signature of Alphus"

As the Potato Famine expanded, Peel's government had to seek ways to achieve relief, including increasing public works projects, making available large amounts of American Indian corn, and in 1846 attempting to lower food prices by phasing out the Corn Laws over three years.

Corn Laws, restricting or taxing import of all types of cereal grain, had played to mixed reviews since first passed in 1815. This tariff game assured a continuing high income for the landed gentry who rented their land to farmers at outrageous rates. Landed gentry wanted to keep foreign grain out and domestic prices high. Farmworkers needed low prices to feed their families. Industrialists wanted prices low to keep wages down and workers fed. In 1841, when Robert Peel began his second term as Prime Minister, he embarked upon a plan to end the Corn Laws. Urged anew by the Irish Famine, Peel's Importation Act of 1846 was approved in Commons, 327 to 229. On June 25, the Duke of Wellington persuaded the House of Lords to pass it. The trauma of the Corn Laws finally ended.

Peel had also proposed an Irish Coercion Law to expedite prosecution of high crimes such as stealing food, committed by starving famine victims, but it also contained inflammatory clauses like a curfew law which punished by transportation anyone caught out between sunset and sunrise. (Dodds: 1952, 242) On the same date that the Importation Act of 1846 passed the House of Lords, the Irish Coercion Bill was defeated in the Commons, 292 to 219, by a combination of Whigs, Radicals, and Tory protectionists. With this defeat Peel resigned as Prime Minister.

## 105 The Men of Forty Eight

IU. V. Kovalev, *Anthology of Chartist Literature* (1956): 208

*Tune: Oh! Susanna; Stephen Foster, 1848*

They rose in Freedom's rare sunrise,
Like giants roused from wine!
And in their hearts, and in their eyes,
The God leapt up divino!
Their souls flashed out like naked swords,
Unsheathed for fiery fate;
Strength went like battle with their words,
The men of Forty-eight.
Hurrah!
For the men of Forty-eight.

Dark days have fall'n! yet in the strife,
They bate no hope sublime,
And bravely works the fiery life,
Their hearts' pulse thro' the time.
As grass is greenest trodden down
So suffering makes men great;
And this dark tide shall grandly crown
The men of forty-eight.
Hurrah!
For the men of forty-eight.

Some, in a bloody burial sleep,
Like Greeks, to glory gone!
Swift in their steps, avengers leap
With their proof armour on!
And hearts beat high with dauntless trust,
We'll triumph soon or late,
Though they be mouldering in the dust,
Brave men of Forty-eight.
Hurrah!
For the men of forty-eight!

O! when the world wakes up to worst,
The tyrants once again;
And Freedom's summons-shout shall burst
In music on the brain.
With heart to heart and hand in hand,
Ye'll find them all elate,—
And true as ever Spartan Band!
The Men of Forty-eight!
Hurrah!
For the Men of Forty-eight.

The Friend of the People January 25, 1851

This nostalgic song reflects on the last notable attempt to submit the Chartist petition to Parliament. The last National Chartist Convention was held on Kennington Common, London, on Monday, April 10, 1848. During that same year, revolutions took place to achieve independence and democracy in France, Italy, Denmark, Austria, Sweden, Switzerland, Belgium, and in German states. An unsuccessful uprising was also attempted that same year by the Young Irish.

The government feared violent action, and the royal family was hastily evacuated to the Isle of Wight. The Duke of Wellington, at age 79, was called back to lead the heavily guarded cadres of policemen, soldiers, sailors, special constables, and armed civil servants, with cannon at the ready to face the crowd. Early that morning people began to pour in to Kennington Common, many arriving from other towns by train. The meeting had been approved by Home Secretary Lord Russell, but the assemblage was forbidden to march to the houses of Parliament. Estimates of the numbers on Kennington Common on that day ranged from O'Connor's claim of 500,000 to Lord Russell's government's estimate of 12,000–15,000. (Royle: 1980, 42) Since the crowd was not allowed to march across the River to deliver the petition, O'Connor took the massive document to Parliament in three hansom cabs and then took another cab to the Home Office to assure Lord Russell of the legality of the proceedings.

This last submission of huge petitions by the Chartists to Parliament fared no better than the earlier two. Shortly after its presentation, clerks of Parliament reported that there were less than two million legitimate signatures collected rather than the six million claimed. This meant that the clerks had managed to discount more than four million signatures. The government simply made up a number to undermine the cause. But whether its figures were true or not, the government's line was reported by the newspapers and the petition was discredited. The petition was quickly packed off to a committee where it was denounced as a fake and never even debated. (Foot: 2005, 109)

Kennington Common Meeting to deliver third version of the Charter

## 106 The Silent Cell

Peter Scheckner, *An Anthology of Chartist Poetry* (1989): 197

Tune: Lady Isobel and the Elf Knight; ballad tune, printed 1776

THEY told me 'twas a fearful thing
To pine in prison lone:
The brain became a shriveled scroll,
The heart a living stone.

Nor solitude, nor silent cell
The teeming mind can tame:
No tribute needs the granite-well;
No food the planet-flame.

Denied the fruit of others' thought,
To write my own denied,
Sweet sisters, Hope and Memory, brought
Bright volumes to my side.

And oft we trace, with airy pen,
Full many a word of worth;
For Time will pass, and Freedom then
Shall flash them on the earth.

They told me that my veins would flag
My ardour would decay;
And heavily their fetters drag
My blood's young strength away.

Like conquerors bounding to the goal
Where cold, white marble gleams,
Magnificent red rivers! roll!—
Roll all you thousand streams!

Oft, to passion's stormy gale,
When sleep I seek: in vain,
Fleets of Fancy up them sail,
And anchor in my brain.

But never a wish for base retreat,
Or thought of a recreant part,
While yet a single pulse shall beat
Proud marches in my heart.

They'll find me still unchanged and strong,
When breaks their puny thrall;
With hate—for not one living soul—
And Pity for them all

By Ernest Jones
Composed during illness, on the sixth day of my incarceration in a solitary
cell, on bread and water, and without books, —August, 1849.

Many hundreds of Chartists were transported or jailed during the decade
that the Chartist movement prevailed. The last of the Chartist rallies was
held on Kennington Common, on April 10, 1848, and it was on that very
evening Parliament held the first reading of the Crown and Government
Security Act. The act created new offences of "treason felony" for which
the penalty was imprisonment or transportation for life. (Chase: 2015, 166)
Subsequently, as Chartist activities began to surge, the new act was employed to arrest more of the remaining Chartists. Among the some 300
people arrested was Ernest Jones, a rising spokesperson for Chartism.

Jones, author of this ballad, was educated in Germany and known as
a young man of wealth and fashion. He was presented to Queen Victoria
by his family and called to the Bar in 1844. Soon after becoming an attorney, Jones became a strong supporter of the O'Connor faction of the
Chartist Movement. After the Kennington Common meeting, Jones went to
Manchester on June 6 to address a Chartist gathering, where he was arrested for violation of the new Treason Felony Act for his speech at London's
Bishop Bonners Field on June 4. He was convicted and sentenced to two
years of solitary confinement. Two other Chartists who drew similar sentences died during their prison terms.

Jones told of the cruelty of the British penal system in this song but he
chose other opportunities to describe the increased severity of bad treatment given to Chartists. It was several years later that he described the
details of this time in jail:

> I was kept for more than two years in separate confinement on the
> silent system, most rigidly enforced—so rigidly that for an invol-
> untary smile I was sent for three days to a dark cell on bread and
> water. For the first nineteen months I was kept without books, pen,
> ink, or paper, and had to sit out that time in a cell, twelve feet by
> seven, locked up in solitude and silence, without even a table or a
> chair. To this cell (the day cell) were three windows, two without
> glass but with rough wooden shutters, through which the wind and
> snow and rain of winter blew all over the place. My night cell was

of far smaller dimensions, 9 feet by 4 feet. Its window was unglazed its shutters did not meet the window frame nor each other by one or two inches. There was an aperture over my bed 18 in. by 12 in., through which the snow and rain fell on me as I slept, saturating my clothes with moisture, so that often the water dripped on them as I put them on. The bed itself was a sack of straw with a piece of carpeting. (Cole: 1941, 346)

This song conveys the intellect and courage of Jones who went on to become active in the struggle for the Reform Bill of 1867. Despite the commitment and hard work of all the thousands of people who worked to achieve Parliamentary Reform, it was not yet the time. But the groundwork was laid and the path was ready to be taken.

Ernest Jones

J. B. (*to the Workingmen of England*). "If we do grant this privilege of suffrage, it must be taken as a privilege, not a *right*—you understand."

Uncle Sam. "Stick to him, boys. The mountain is giving way by degrees."

Chapter 10
# REFORM: 1851–1868

*The class that has hitherto ruled in this country has failed miserably. It revels in power and wealth, whilst at its feet, a terrible peril for its future lies the multitude which it has neglected.*
— John Bright, 1866

Working class people learned from the Chartist Movement that they were not going to achieve the improvements they desperately needed through adoption of the Charter. The organizing skills they had acquired in Chartist activities were, however, adapted to trade union activities and other essential issues of the times. Despite the recently invigorated Treason Felony Act's gagging capabilities, significant union activity boiled up in the mills in the early 1850s, resulting in strikes and other action throughout most British industrial areas. Liberal MP for East Surrey, Peter Locke King, forwarded a reform bill that would in effect extend the vote to all those living in unrepresented towns and counties and who occupied homes that they rented annually for £10. This bill rectified only a few defects of the 1832 Reform Bill, and it rapidly died during its second reading. (Smith: 1966, 30) It did, however, inspire Prime Minister Russell to break his earlier "finality" vow, and to put forth a reform bill the next year. Russell's bill contained several realignments of boroughs, but did little to increase eligibility to vote. This bill of 1852 was not pressed because of the change in ministry during that year. It was 1854 before Russell brought forth another reform bill, which this time contained several special franchises to give the vote to middle class doctors, lawyers, educators, and successful merchants. He believed the bill might have passed, had it not been for the Crimean War. (Seymour: 1915, 242)

The years of warfare that followed served as an acceptable excuse by Lord Palmerston (as Home Secretary, then Prime Minister) for delaying further attempts at reform. During the Crimean War (1853–56), British soldiers were plagued with incompetent officers, inferior equipment, inadequate medical support, and incredibly bitter winters. Cholera raged through the war camps, so only one in ten of the 19,584 British troops lost in the Crimean War actually died in action. Most died of illness and disease. (Royle: 2000, 502) News of the soldiers' suffering arrived rapidly in Britain through the new telegram system, with daily communiqués from William Howard Russell of the *Times*. The British public remained loyal to its soldiers and rejoiced their return home. Immediately after the Crimean War, the British Second Opium War opened up to expand opium addiction in China through gunboat warfare. Yet another major conflict arose in 1857–58, known by the people of India as the Indian War of Independence and by the British occupiers as the Sepoy Rebellion or Indian Mutiny. All three of these conflicts were convenient to the administration of Palmerston, who — despite his affiliation as a Whig and Liberal — opposed expansion of the franchise.

Most elections during the 1850s ended with the winning party holding less than a majority and having to form a coalition with other parties to obtain a majority of all members of Parliament. Because of this situation the government frequently changed between Tory and Whig, with Conservative and Liberal party identities emerging. During the two brief periods that Derby/Disraeli Governments were in power, and despite their conservatism, they accomplished some welcomed reforms: practicing Jews were admitted to the house of Commons in 1858, and in the same year the first and least important of the Chartists' demands were met, the abolition of the property qualifications for MPs. (Beales: 1969, 187) Then in 1859, Benjamin Disraeli submitted a cynical bill that was similar to, but briefer than, those previously written by Russell. "It was, as MP John Bright put it, *A Country Gentleman's Bill*." (Hall: 2000, 87) As with all the previous unpassed bills, this one was designed to maintain a minimum level of property ownership or rental value to be held by the head of a household in order to achieve enfranchisement, with lower minimums in cities (boroughs) than in the counties. Disraeli's Bill was defeated by only 39 votes in a full house of Commons. At the request of PM Derby, another election was held.

This 1859 election replaced the Derby Government with yet another Palmerston Government that some labeled as the "First Liberal Government," with Russell serving as foreign secretary and Gladstone as Treasurer. Russell had been in Europe for four years writing books. In order to get him to return so that a viable administration could be assembled, Palmerston offered Russell another chance to move a second Reform Bill — despite Palmerston having no interest in realizing reform. So in 1860 Russell assembled another proposal that looked a lot like the previous failed bills. This measure, like its predecessors, kept control in the hands of the upper classes, but would have given the vote to more middle class tradesmen and higher paid workers in cities. But wars, imperialism, economics, and lack of compelling pressure from the people all meant that, like previous attempts, this bill was destined to fail. As long as the country remained quiet it seemed easier for the Whigs and Tories to force ministers to drop Reform; the members compelled Russell to abandon his bill in 1860 and "the public received its demise as apathetically as it had accepted its introduction." (Smith: 1966, 46) And then the monarchy was shaken: Prince Albert's death from typhoid fever in December of 1861 sent Queen Victoria into prolonged depression and mourning.

The American Civil War (1861–65) had deep economic impact on British industry, motivating British merchants to clandestinely provide the Confederate Navy (South) with armed vessels to help run shipments of cotton through the blockade of the Union Navy (North). Areas like Liverpool, as well as several members of Parliament, favored the South, but Britain had resolved to maintain a neutral stance on the Civil War. From the start its people could not ally their feelings with slavery, and on that issue alone, the British public would not side with the South, even though the blockade was taking a high economic toll.

Seizing opportunity afforded by the death of Palmerston in October 1865, the succeeding Russell/Gladstone Government submitted yet another uninspiring reform bill in March 1866. Once again a bill was quietly making its way through Commons with little public support and strong Parliamentary resistance, when suddenly the situation changed. Robert Lowe from the Liberal back bench, "a virulent and doctrinaire critic of any approach to democracy," (Beales: 1969, 202) spoke up: "If you want venality, ignorance, drunkenness, — if you want impulsive, unreflecting, and violent people, where do you look for them in the constituencies?" (Seymour: 1915, 250) A group of some forty reactionary Liberals gathered around Lowe, joining with the Tory opposition to defeat the bill altogether. They became known as "Adullamites," a name coined by John Bright that alluded to the Biblical "Cave of Adullam" (1 Samuel 22) where David was joined by the discontented. The insinuation of Lowe and the Adullamites was the straw that broke the camel's back. Adullamites' negative statements about class were repeated in news reports and at rallies and meetings through the rest of 1866. Russell resigned as Prime Minister, and his government was replaced with another Derby/Disraeli Conservative Minority Government. It had taken the "Cave of Adullam" to reawaken thousands of people, especially in the industrial areas, and start them clamoring anew for change.

Since 1864 the predominantly middle class National Reform Union had worked with John Bright in Manchester. In 1865 a wider-based working class Reform League pressed for manhood suffrage under the chairmanship of Edmond Beales. Then in 1866, fueled by the Adullamite uproar, huge gatherings in support of manhood suffrage met throughout the country. Much like Cobbett, Attwood, and Hunt during the battle for passage of the 1832 Reform Bill, Beales, Bright, and Gladstone drew large crowds everywhere they went. The expanded rail service sped them from town to town, assuring a groundswell of sentiment for change, including a famed

meeting in Trafalgar Square. On July 23, when Hyde Park had been closed
to a vast meeting scheduled to take place there, the much larger than expected crowd arrived at the huge closed gates and were met by large numbers of police equipped with truncheons. Beales then moved the gathering
to Trafalgar Square. However, a sizable minority tore up the railings of the
park, swarmed into it and engaged in a long and furious battle with the
police. (Foot: 2005, 148–49) Authorities feared that disturbances would increase as they had before passage of the 1832 Reform Act. The Queen herself called for reform in 1867 when she opened Parliament for the first time
after the death of the Prince Consort, and Prime Minister Derby charged
Disraeli to submit a viable Reform Bill.

On March 18, the "Representation of the People Act 1867" was presented to Parliament by the Tory Government. As first submitted, it was
not much different from the previous year's Liberal Bill that Disraeli had
worked to defeat. Though attempting to imply democratic content by mis-
use of the phrase "household suffrage," with this new bill Disraeli so wa-
tered down this principle that the Bill as first introduced was not democratic. It added to the upper-class vote, but enfranchised only a portion of
the working class householders. It excluded from the franchise not only all
"lodgers," but the large class of so-called "compound householders" whose
taxes were paid by their landlord. (Trevelyan: 1913, 372)

The Liberal Party met and decided, over objections of Bright and
Gladstone, to support the Bill through the second reading and see what improvements could be made in Committee. "So was wrought the most unin-
tentional revolution in the history of British politics. The Bill was amended
in line with Liberal thinking in these areas but from the baseline of borough
suffrage." (Parry: 1993, 216) Surprisingly, amendment after amendment
was submitted to and, for the most part, accepted by Disraeli, gradually
reshaping the bill into a democratic document.

Amendments that improved the Bill included the Hodgkinson
Amendment, strengthening the concept of "household suffrage," under
which renting (male) heads of household would now pay their taxes directly, be identified on public record as taxpayers, and therefore have the right
to enfranchisement. Bothersome special franchises were eliminated from
the Act. Rate payers with property in both town and country were now
allowed only one vote. All clauses containing restrictive conditions denying
the vote to workers were dropped. One amendment that was not accepted
was that proposed by John Stuart Mill, which would substitute the word
"person" for "man." Mill argued that as tax-payers, women had as much
claim as men to the franchise. (Smith: 1966, 204) The Bill made corrections
that increased the number of Parliament members from several larger cities,
eliminated one of two members from boroughs with populations under
10,000, added thirteen new county divisions with two seats each, added ten
new boroughs, and gave the University of London a seat. Many unresolved
inequities in voting districts were dealt with by this bill. Earl Stanhope had

a clause inserted which removed the necessity for Parliament to dissolve upon the death of the Sovereign. (Smith: 1966, 201)

Bright wrote in his diary on July 15, 1867: "3rd reading of Reform Bill. Spoke briefly. Amusing recriminations between Lowe, and Disraeli, and a severe speech from Lord Cranborne against Disraeli. Bill passed with cheers from our side." (Walling: 1931, 310) Although Disraeli argued that the amended Tory Bill would increase the Conservative electorate, most Tories only reluctantly voted for it. Charles Seely, MP for Lincoln, said he supported the bill because it is "better to have these matters settled by Disraeli and Derby than by Beales and Potter." (Foot: 2005, 153) The bill sped through the House of Lords with only one further amendment, which limited residents of boroughs with three representatives to casting only two votes. Reform Acts for Scotland and Ireland were passed in 1868, with an increase of seven new Scottish members of Parliament that were transferred from English and Welsh dissolved constituencies. The subsequent General Election of December 7, 1868 failed to reap the rewards the Conservatives had hoped for, since it returned a Liberal majority of 116.

The outcome of this long battle for Reform enabled some working men to participate in the democratic governance of their country by voting. The new electorate was almost twice as large as before but still included only 17% of Britain's males over the age of 21.

People queueing for food and coal tickets at a district Provident Society office

**107** The Song of the Lower Classes

John Ashton, Modern Street Ballads (1968): 338 – Roud V39520

*Tune: The Vicar of Bray; The Quaker's Opera, 1731*

We plough and sow we're so ve-ry ve-ry low that we delve in the dir - ty clay.

Till we bless the plain with the gold - en grain and the vale with the fra - grant hay.

Our place we know. We're so ve-ry low 'Tis down at the land-lord's feet; __

CHORUS We're not too low the bread to grow, but too low the bread to eat.

We plough and sow—we're so very, very low
That we delve in the dirty clay,
Till we bless the plain with the golden grain,
And the vale with the fragrant hay.
Our place we know we're so very low,
'Tis down at the landlord's feet:
We're not too low—the bread to grow,
But too low the bread to eat.

    We're not too low—the bread to grow,
    But too low the bread to eat.

Down, down we go we're so very low,
To the hell of the deep sunk mines,
But we gather the proudest gems that glow,
When the crown of a despot shines.
And whenever he lacks—upon our backs
Fresh loads he deigns to lay:
We're far too low to vote the tax,
But not too low to pay.

We're low, we're low mere rabble, we know,
But, at our plastic power,
The mold at the lordlings feet will grow
Into palace and church and tower.

Then prostrate fall—in the rich man's hate,
And cringe at the rich man's door;
We're not too low to build the wall,
But too low to tread the floor.

We're low,—we're low—we're very very low,
Yet from our fingers glide
The silken flow—and the robes that glow
Round the limbs of the sons of pride.
And what we get and what we give—
We know and we know our share;
We're not too low the cloth to weave,
But too low the cloth to wear!

We're low,—we're low—we're very very low,
And yet when the trumpets ring,
The thrust of a poor man's arm will go
Thro' the heart of the proudest King.
We're low,—we're low—our place we know,
We're only the rank and file,
We're not too low—to kill the foe,
But too low to touch the spoil.

Ernest Jones remains famous today, mostly as the author of this song. The earliest copy of it seems to have been printed in his paper, *Notes to the People*, in 1852. Scheckner prints it with one more verse than the Ashton version used here, including the lines: "The rich are high—for we make them so and a miserable lot are we!" (Scheckner: 1989, 209) Other later printings did not include this verse. Current recordings today use several different melodies, but none I know use the melody of the "Vicar of Bray" as is chosen here.

This anthem captures well the resentment that the British working class felt toward the middle class and aristocracy. Jones was from the upper class, but he was a Chartist who promoted its tenets long after others gave up. After completing a two-year jail sentence for seditious speeches in 1850, Jones began publishing *Notes to the People* and continued to earn modest amounts from his political writing. He stood for Parliament five times, in 1847, 1852, 1857, 1859, and 1868, without success. Not even the Chartists voted solidly for him, as infighting had destroyed the solidarity of the Chartist movement. Jones and others kept the concept of the Charter limping along, and eventually combined resources with the Reform League to help achieve passage of the Second Reform Bill.

## 108 Striking Times

Bodleian Library: Harding Collection, B 11 (3680) – Roud V15590

*Tune: Bonnie Ship The Diamond; Europa Ship Log, 1868-70*

Cheer up cheer up you sons of toil and listen to my song,
While I try to amuse you and I will not take long.
The working men of England, at length begin to see,
They've made a bold strike for their rights in eighteen fifty-three.

CHORUS
It's high time the working men should have it their own way.
And for a fair days labour receive a fair day's pay.

This is the time for striking. At least it strikes me so.
Monopoly has had some knocks, but this must be the blow.
The working men by thousands, complain their fate is hard,
May order mark their conduct, and success be their reward.

Some of our London printers their glorious work began,
And surely they've done something, for they've upset the sun.
Employees must be made to see they can't do what they like,
It is the master's greediness causes the men to strike

The labouring men of London on both sides of the Thames,
They made a strike last Monday which adds much to their names.
Their masters did not relish it, but they made them understand
Before the next day's sun had set, they gave them their demand.

The unflinching men of Stockport, with Kidderminster in their train,
Three hundred honest weavers have struck their ends to gain.
Though the masters find they lose a deal, the tide must soon be turning
They find the men won't quietly be robbed of half their earning.

Our London Weavers mean to show their masters and the trade,
That they will either cease to work, or else be better paid.
'Twas in Spitalfields the weavers workd with joy in former ages.
But they're tired out of asking for a better scale of wages

The monied men have had their way large fortunes they have made,
For things could not be otherwise, with labour badly paid;
They roll along in splendor, and with a saucy tone,
As Cobbett says they eat the meat, the workman gnaws the bone.

In Liverpool the postmen struck, and sent word to their betters,
Begging them to recollect that they were men of letters,
They asked for three bob more a week, and got it in a crack
And though each man has got his bag, they have not got the sack.

The Cabmen and their masters made up their mind last week
To stop the cabs from running now is not that a treat,
The Hackney Carriage Act has proved a bitter pill.
It's no use to call out, Cab, Cab, drive off and show your skill

The coopers and the dockyard men are all a going to strike,
And soon they'll be the devil to pay, without a little mike,
The farming men of Suffolk have lately called to go,
And swear they'll have their wages rose, before they'll reap or sow.

E. Hodges, Printer, &c Seven Dials London

Although the Chartist movement gradually declined, multiple small union actions kept the working man's struggles for reform alive. Prices were going up, the industry was prosperous and demands for higher wages were made in almost every town. Smaller unions had to rely on the strike to seek their goals. This song from 1853 describes a number of separate actions for improving wages and working conditions. Karl Marx, a resident of London at this time, wrote on July 29, 1853 in the *New York Tribune*:

Strike is the order of the day. During the present week 5,000 miners have struck in the northern coal district; 400 to 500 journeymen cork cutters in London; about 2,000 laborers employed by the different wharfingers on the Thames; the police force at Hull, similar attempts being made by the City and general Metropolitan Police; and finally the bricklayers employed at St. Stephens, under the very nose of Parliament.

The actions listed in this song appear to be local. In the following years, movements would become broader and larger. Consolidations and combinations of workers in the individual trades were already underway. This was especially true of the Amalgamated Engineers who gradually won recognition from the employers and saw a rapid increase in membership. (Pelling, 1976, 51) Note that in this song William Cobbett was still being quoted, eighteen years after his death.

Factories Looming, Preston Skyline

## 109 The Cotton Lords of Preston

Sir Frederick Madden's Collection of Broadside Ballads, 10/6645 — Roud V38682

*Tune: The Miller of Dee; Village Opera, 1729*

Have you not heard the news of late a-bout some might-y men so great?

I mean the swells of Fish-gate. The cot-ton Lords of Pres-ton

They are a set of stin-gy blades. They
So with our bal-lads we've come out to
CHORUS: Ev'-ry-bo-dy's cry-ing shame on

locked up all their mills and shades, So now we've no-thing
tramp the coun-try round a-bout And try if we can-not
these gen-tle-men by name Don't you think they're

else to do, but come a sing-ing songs to you.
live with-out the cot-ton Lords of Pres-ton.
much to blame the cot-ton Lords of Pres-ton.

Have you not heard the news of late
About some mighty men so great?
I mean the swells of Fishgate.
The cotton Lords of Preston
They are a set of stingy blades,
They've locked up all their mills and shades,
So now we've nothing else to do
But come a singing songs to you,
So with our ballads we've come out
To tramp the country round about,
And try if we cannot live without
The cotton Lords of Preston.

CHORUS
Everybody's crying shame
On these gentlemen by name.
Don't you think they're much to blame
The cotton Lords of Preston.

The working people such as we,
Pass their time in misery
While they live in luxury,
The Cotton Lords of Preston,
They're making money every way,
And building factories everyday,
Yet when we ask them for more pay,
They had the impudence to say:
"To your demands we'll not consent;
You get enough to be content" —
But we will have the ten percent
From the cotton Lords of Preston.

Our masters say they're very sure
That a strike we can't endure;
They all assert we're very poor,
The cotton Lords of Preston
But we've determined everyone
With them we will not be done,
And we will not be content
Until we get the ten per cent
The Cotton Lads are sure to fall,
Both ugly handsome, short or tall;
For we intend to conquer all
The Cotton Lords of Preston.

So men and women all of you,
Come and buy a song or two,
And assist us to subdue
The Cotton Lords of Preston
We'll conquer them and no mistake,
Whatever laws they seem to make,
And when we get the ten-percent
Then we'll live happy and content.
Oh then we'll sing and dance with glee
And thank you all right heartily
When we gain the victory
And beat the Lords of Preston

In August of 1853 the weavers of Preston in Lancashire went on strike to get back the cuts from their wages — some 10–20% — that had been taken during the Irish famine in the 1840s. This song was obviously written to be sung at gatherings to solicit assistance with the strike. The well-organized and disciplined conduct of the Preston strikers won support and admiration throughout the country and they obtained help from other labor groups amounting to £100,000. The story of their struggle was favorably treated in most newspapers nationwide. Charles Dickens came to observe the situation and included many of his observations as background for his highly successful novel *Hard Times*.

The struggle turned, though, when on October 15 the manufacturers united to lock out over 18,000 workers. In February 1854 the manufacturers brought in men and women from agricultural districts and from Ireland to break the strike. Union leadership worked hard to avoid violence against the scabs, and few disturbances took place.

In March the strike was already failing when the masters persuaded the local magistrates to arrest the strike leaders on charges of "molesting and obstructing" some of the imported laborers whom they had persuaded to return to their homes. In May the strike finally collapsed, and the charges which were due to be heard at the autumn sessions were dropped. (Pelling: 1977, 48)

Factory Operatives Meeting, Preston

## 110 The Suffering of the British Army in the Camp Before Sebastopol

Bodleian Library: Harding Collection, B 15(322a) – Roud V16516

*Tune: Three Merry Men of Kent; The Jovial Crew, 1731*

All you who live at home at ease, and sleep on beds of down

Pray think of our brave sol - diers who lie fro-zen on the ground.

In the camp be-fore Se - bas - to - pol, in mud up to — their knees,

The flo - wer of our Ar - my there, has per - ished by dis - ease

CHORUS For Eng-land's gal - lant sol - diers you will sym-pa - thize I'm sure

No pen can write or tongue can tell the hard - ships they en - dure.

All you who live at home at ease, and sleep on beds of down
Pray think of our brave soldiers who lie frozen on the ground,
In the camp before Sebastopol, in mud up to their knees,
The flower of our Army there, has perished by disease.
    For England's gallant soldiers you will sympathize I'm sure
    No pen can write or tongue can tell the hardships they endure.

From the camp to Balaklava like horses they work,
Up to their knees in mud and snow, with neither shoes or shirt,
Then starving in the trenches and guarding of the ground,
Crushed with fatigue and hunger they in deaths cold arms are found.

Fathers cry my dearest son then weep in grief and woe,
Mothers cry my darling boy has perished in the snow,
Wives in agony lament in sorrow and despair
While the pretty little children cry where is my father dear.

I heard a maid lamenting, in grief she scarce could stand,
Saying my father died at Alma and my love at Inkerman,
My brother dear was wounded by the cursed enemy,
And now lies in the hospital at the town of Scutari.

The glory of Britannia, England's gallant soldiers bold,
Endured the greatest misery before Sebastopol,
Crushed with fatigue and hunger they braved danger with a smile,
No nation in the world can match the sons of Britain's Isle.

In filth and dirt without a shirt to shield them from the cold,
A wet blanket wrapped around them, how dreadful to behold,
Without a bed to lie their head but are compelled alas—
To lie fatigued and hungry upon the frozen grass.

The French are well provided for, their wants into are seen,
They have a friend a Bonaparte, and not an Aberdeen,
But Britons are neglected, and doomed in youth and bloom,
To die an early death and lay within the silent tomb.

Oh God protect our soldiers with thy Almighty hand,
Grant them a victory and guide them to their native land,
Befriend their wives and children since war caused them to part,
Protect their aged parents, and ease their aching heart.

Come sympathize with me my friends, refuse you'll not I'm sure
For our gallant British soldiers who such hardships do endure,
Who bear it all with patience and meets danger with a smile,
May God protect our soldiers bold, the sons of Britain's Isle.

John Marks, Printer, 206 Brick Lane, Whitechapel
G. Mason, 38 Kent Street, Borough.

Lord Russell brought forth two Reform Bills in 1852 and in 1854; the first was dropped due to apathy, causing his government to fail, and the second was dropped when the Crimean War began. Few completely understood the causes and objectives of the Crimean War, yet the word on the street was not only favorable, but ecstatically in favor of going to war. "Waterloo and Trafalgar were on every lip, crowds paraded the streets delirious with excitement, inflated with national pride... and so in March, 1854, shouting, cheering, singing, the nation swept into war." (Woodham-Smith: 1953, 144)

This song, written by the prolific broadside ballad writer John Morgan, makes clear that Britain was not prepared for such warfare. Its army was ill equipped for the cold winter and was led by incompetent officers who had purchased their commissions. The purchase system, under which a man first bought his commission and then paid for each subsequent step in rank, and which enabled a rich man to buy the command of a regiment over the heads of more efficient officers, seems so unjust, so disastrous, that it is almost impossible to believe that sensible people ever tolerated, much less supported it. (Woodham-Smith: 1953, 25)

The aristocrats commanding these hostilities oversaw such fiascoes as the Charge of the Light Brigade, trench warfare in subzero weather, and casualties from disease exceeding those in battle, all while the Generals slept most nights on a yacht just off the coast.

Warfare also encountered the modern age. For the first time, the newly installed telegraph system kept the British public abreast of these failings. Frequent dispatches from the front covered the badly managed Crimean War extensively. Additionally, the horrors of war were first recorded by photography in Crimea. On October 12, 1854, Thomas Chenery reported from Constantinople in the *Times*: "Here laid bare was the first stark evidence of the revolting conditions, faced by the sick and wounded at the British Military Hospital at Scutari." (Royle: 2000, 246) His article and the resulting outpouring of concern motivated the establishment of Florence Nightingale's Nursing Corps. William Howard Russell's communiqués from the front kept the nation aware of the war's many "unpleasantness's." As dissatisfaction with the conduct of the war increased, Parliament called for an inquiry in January 1855. Prime Minister Lord Aberdeen, seeing this as a vote of no confidence, resigned and never returned to public office. Both sides of this conflict desired peace and initiated the Congress of Paris in February of 1856. The treaty was quickly signed in March. Despite the public awareness of the horrors of this war, however, it remained popular with the British people.

The *Retreat* of January 1855 by Constantin Guys.

# 111 England Demands Reform And Reform She'll Have

Bodleian Library: Firth Collection, c.16(193) — Roud V33115

*Tune: The White Cockade; Broadside, 1846-54*

Cheer up! cheer up, Bri-tan-nia cries, And gain our rights we sure-ly will,

It does the cats and dogs sur-prise, To lis-ten to the To-ry Bill.

It __ is a bill and no mis-take, They must think the peo-ple fools I'm sure

Give us our rights, says John-ny Bright. Re-form my boys, and no-thing more.

CHORUS

Stick to em lads, old John Bull cried, Treat their mea-sure with dis-gust and scorn,

Old Eng-land won't be sat-is-fied, Un-til she gets a right re-form.

Cheer up! cheer up, Britannia cries,
And gain our rights we surely will,
It does the cats and dogs surprise,
To listen to the Tory Bill.
It is a bill and no mistake,
They must think the people fools I'm sure.
Give us our rights, says Johnny Bright.
Reform my boys, and nothing more.
   Stick to em lads, old John Bull cried,
   Treat their measure with disgust and scorn,
   Old England won't be satisfied,
   Until she gets a right reform.

When Disraeli brought in his bill,
He nearly frightened all the lot,
Finality Johnny, hollowed Ben,
Oh what a stunning nerve you've got.

Hang your Reform bill round your neck,
Oh cut it Ben, the members brawled,
Why the people won't be satisfied,
You had better made no bill at all.

One member who had seldom spoke,
Said, well I never knew such rigs,
If I had my will the cats should vote—
The bullocks, jackass's and pigs
And every female in the land,
Who was not drunk and in her mind,
Should have a vote if she
Would never wear a crinoline.

The costermongers want Reform,
And so does all the lasses too;
The tailor, snob, and dusty Bob,
The coal-heaver, chimney sweep and Jew;
And if we do not get Reform,
The Emperor of the French will bawl,
I'll rule the roast of the English coast,
We'll toddle now and eat them all.

The Tories say throughout the land,
The people are not fit to vote;
And why should they despise a man—
Because he wears a ragged coat.
There's an honest heart perhaps 'neath that coat,
You might depend on that man's word
Why should he not be as good a man
As the bastard son of any Lord.

I think old Israel will look queer
If he his p's and q's don't mind;
He'll be running down to Buckinghamshire,
With his muslin hanging out behind.
Old Derby he will get the sack—
Or else he'll have a stand up fight,
I will bet a sovereign he'll get whacked,
Give him a pepper Jackey Bright.

Old Southwark Charley where are you?
How is it you don't want to fight?
Go at old Israel the Jew
And fire your guns for Johnny Bright.

Be quick and man the ship REFORM,
And to the coast of Freedom steer;
Guide the helm-weather the storm,
Sing,—Britons won't be slaves!—Napier!

Be up and do the thing that's right
And Britons grievance to them tell;
Come Duncombe, Roebuck, Gibson, Bright:
Stand forward Williams and Roupell!
Every man demands his right:
Treat the Tory bill with scorn
Stick like bricks to Johnny Bright
And shout—Old England wants Reform!!

                               Taylor Printer, 93, Brick Lane

Lord Derby's Tory minority government was barely clinging to power.
Its poster boy, popular author Benjamin Disraeli, introduced a reform bill
that would have extended franchise to more affluent members of the middle class by adding so-called "fancy franchises." But this Bill did nothing
to lower the ownership requirements of the First Reform Bill, designed to
shore up and strengthen the conservative position in the counties. (Hall:
2000, 87) The Russell Bill of 1854, that had been withdrawn due to the
Crimean War, had also included fancy franchises for people with over £60
in a savings bank or £20 in armed forces pensions, or graduates of universi-
ties and members of learned professions—none of whom, without owning
real estate, were able to vote. No wonder then that this song was written to
bring out the insincerity of Disraeli's Bill. The Bill failed 330 to 291, which
ended the Derby administration, dissolved the Tory Government, and replaced it with Britain's first Liberal Party government, led by Conservative
Whig Lord Palmerston.

It is hard to believe that this government formed under the leadership of
Palmerston was considered a "Liberal Party Government," since he was an
aristocrat statesman and never supported Parliamentary reform. Over the
years he was noted for his gunboat diplomacy and was nicknamed "Lord
Pumice Stone." This new government, like previous Conservative and Whig
governments, did include John Bright, who remained "a moving force for
radical reform within the new party; but he abused Palmerston's government as 'a sham,' dominated by 'class prejudices' and vested interests."
(Parry: 1993, 210) It also included the zealous William Ewart Gladstone,
who was its reforming Chancellor of the Exchequer.

This song encourages a list of leading radical members of Parliament
to defeat Disraeli's Bill. Admiral Sir Charles Napier was elected MP for
Southwark in February 1855 and remained a strong advocate for reform
and sailor's relief until his death in 1860. Bright, a former spokesperson for the Anti-Corn Law league, had served in Parliament since 1843,

representing most radical causes, especially Parliamentary reform; during 1858 he had made several speeches to large groups in northern industrial cities on the subject of reform. The dandy Thomas Duncombe was a radical advocate for reform who fought to keep the Post Office from opening private mail. John Arthur Roebuck was a radical Member of Parliament who helped draft the Charter and pressured the government over excesses in the Crimean War. T. Milner Gibson was Russell's President of the Board of Trade and a leading opponent of the tax on knowledge. William Williams was a Lambeth radical MP, who fought for education in his native Wales. William Roupell, another Lambeth radical MP, served from 1857–62, then was convicted and sentenced to twenty years for forging his father's will.

THE LAST PANTOMIME OF THE SEASON.

## 112  When We Get Johnny's Reform

Bodleian Library: Johnson Ballads, 336 – Roud V7537

*Tune: Van Diemen's Land; Francis Forbes, 1812*

Oh! Is there not a fuss and bo-ther A-bout Re-form, Re-form?

From one end of Eng-land to the o-ther It's Re-form, Re-form.

They say it's to place us in a po-si-tion, That we may bet-ter

our con-di-tion And be so jol-ly hap-py When we get John-ny's Re-form.

Oh! is there not a fuss and bother
About Reform, Reform?
From one end of England to the other
It's Reform, Reform.
They say it's to place us in a position,
That we may better our condition
And be so jolly happy
When we get Johnny's Reform.

Little Johnny bless the darling boy
Love's Reform, Reform.
Long time he has nursed his favourite toy,
Reform, Reform;
And the dunderheads say now really
Is not it a fine grown baby,
Shan't we be jolly happy,
When we get Johnny's Reform

There is old friend Jacky Bright,
Say's that Reform, Reform,
Is just the thing that's right,
Reform, Reform;
To the seven pound franchise he will stick,
And send all opponents to old Nick,
And make all jolly happy
When we get Johnny's Reform

Now our pauper system load does call
For Reform, Reform;
and the great as well as small
Need Reform, Reform;
For the poor are not the only ones,
That feed upon the nations crumbs,
But never mind be happy,
When we get Johnny's Reform

The teetotalers they will preach
Up Reform, up Reform;
And the water drinking dodge they teach,
Reform, Reform;
But the tipplers they all do say,
They will get tight three times a day,
And be so jolly happy
When they get Johnny's Reform

The Little Boys and girls they say,
Reform, Reform,
They expect it's coming some fine day,
Reform, Reform;
Their bellies then they will be stuffing,
With almond rock and cakes for nuffin,
And be so jolly happy
When they get Johnny's Reform.

The farmers all throughout the nation,
Want Reform, Reform,
For they stand in need of reformation
Reform, Reform;
But must not they have tidy cheek,
To give their men eight bob a week,
And tell them to be happy
When they get Johnny's Reform

Many they aloud will shout
For Reform, Reform,
Scarcely knowing what it's about,
Reform, Reform;
They think no poor there will be then,
But all be ladies and gentlemen,
And be so jolly happy,
When they get Johnny's Reform

Now if the Bill should pass,
This Reform, Reform;
Now little Johnny he will laugh
At, Reform, Reform;
His little body he will strut, sir,
Like a crow along the gutter
And be so Jolly happy
When we get Johnny's Reform.

Then let us hope that we shall see
This Reform, Reform,
Do some good for you and me
Reform, Reform
But liberty give to your thought,
If it don't do good, why then it ought,
And make us jolly happy,
When we get Johnny's Reform

H. Disley, Printer 57 High Street St, Giles

This satirical song refers to the moderate reform act submitted by Lord Russell in 1860, his third try to pass a second Reform Bill. Russell had left Parliament four years earlier in a rage at Palmerston and had taken that time to write two books on his hero Charles James Fox. He had to swallow his pride to rejoin his old adversary in Palmerston's new Liberal Government as Foreign Secretary. He soon proposed another Reform Bill to extend the vote to £6 borough and £10 county householders, reducing the £10 rent requirement in cities to £6 and providing no relief for the country voters. It was ridiculed by the press and not taken seriously by Parliament. One of Parliament's main distractions from political reform at this time was its fixation on recent British imperialist activities, like the devastating second Opium Wars (1856–60) and the ghastly Indian Mutiny of 1857. British sales of opium produced in India were a huge contributor to China's massive number of addictions and the increasing wealth of British merchants.

Despite having enticed Russell's return to Parliament with the prospect of assembling a new reform bill, Palmerston remained opposed to any such thing. It was clear that this new bill stood no chance of passing. Undaunted, Lord Russell determined to drive a Reform Bill through in 1865–6, his first session as Prime Minister after Palmerston's death.

## 113 Short Time Come Again No More

Vaughn Williams Library: Broadside Collection of Cecil Sharp, 155 – Roud V17531

Tune: Hard Times Come Again No More; Stephen Foster, 1854

Let us pause in life's pleasures, and count its many tears,
While we all sup sorrow with the poor:
There's a song that will linger forever in our ears,
Oh short time come again no more

    CHORUS
    It's the song of the factory operatives
    Short time, short time, come again no more
    For we can't get our cotton from the old Kentucky shore,
    Oh, short time short time, come again no more.

Our wives and our children are pining day by day
Through the wars of America they say;
And we can't get them bread to ease them of their pain,
Oh short time, come again no more.

We are not constant beggars as you have seen before,
But poverty drives us from our homes;
And we can't procure bread as in the days of yore—
Oh short time, come again no more.

JT Kerrison, Printer, &c, market-place, Ashton-under-Lyme

This song, written to the tune of Stephen Foster's popular "Hard Times," was used to raise relief funds for the thousands of British workers affected by the so-called cotton famine due to embargoes during the American Civil War (1861–65). Unemployed cotton mill workers traveled to larger cities like Manchester to solicit assistance, or moved to areas where there was work, leaving major housing vacancies in factory towns.

Since the mill owners' outrageous lockouts in 1854 (as described in No. 109), cotton mill workers had enjoyed relatively stable employment, and their wages had been slightly higher than those of other factory operatives. Additional family members also employed in the cotton mills raised family income to a more, if still barely, livable level. Now suddenly, in late 1861, many mills either stopped production altogether or reduced workers' hours ("short time"). Cotton mill employment dropped from 533,950 in 1861 to 203,200 in 1862, then only gradually increased to 450,000 in 1865. (Brady: 1963, 156) This situation, affecting most of the Lancashire cotton mills throughout the American Civil War, was widely attributed to the Union Navy's blockade of the Confederate cotton ports, which created a major shortage of raw cotton.

The hardships caused by short time and unemployment during this crisis were well documented by Edwin Waugh, special correspondent of the *Manchester Examiner and Times.* He wrote of the "sad-looking singers and instrumental performers, in the work worn clothes of factory operatives, pleading for help in touching wails of simple song... These flocks of street musicians were a sad reminder of happier times." (Longmate: 1978, 113) Charitable contributions from all over the country came into Lancashire, but distribution systems were lacking, leading to unrest in towns like Stalybridge, Ashton, and Dukinfield in March of 1863. Local police relied on help from a troop of cavalry to stop the protests. Finally, at Chester Assizes, forty-two rioters were sent to prison for one to six months, "a surprisingly lenient outcome in all the circumstances." (Longmate: 1978, 202)

The discomfort dealt the cotton mill workers at this time was attributed to the American North's blockade of the South's cotton shipping ports, but Eugene Brady observes: "The so called Cotton Famine was not predominantly due to a shortage of cotton of the raw cotton input, but was in large measure the result of an excess supply of cotton yarn and textiles that resulted from over production during the years 1858 through 1861." (Brady: 1963, 156)

The enormous cotton crops of 1857–60 had filled Lancashire warehouses and were sufficient to last through 1862. By 1863 adequate amounts of cotton could be obtained from India, Egypt, and from migrant capitalists from the Northern U.S. paying to harvest cotton. (Freehling: 2002, 180) Mill owners even longed for an effective blockade to relieve the glut of the market. It seems that the suffering of the workers was not due to lack of cotton; it was due to overproduction.

## 114 Great Naval Action Between *The Kearsarge* and *The Alabama*

Bodleian Library: Firth Collection, c.12(76) – Roud V7049

*Tune: Pretty Little Polly Perkins of Paddington Green; Harry Clifton, 1865*

Come all you gal-lant he-ro's of high and low de - gree
And lis-ten to the glo-rious fight, was fought up-on the sea;
The A-la-ba-ma and the Kear-sarge not far from the French Shore
Met on the nine-teenth day of June, eight-een hun-dred and six-ty-four.

CHORUS It was a glo-ri-ous bat-tle, the crews fought man-ful-ly,
In the A-la-ba-ma and Kear-sarge, That day up-on the sea.

Come all you gallant hero's of high and low degree
And listen to the glorious fight, was fought upon the sea;
The Alabama and the Kearsarge not far from the French Shore
Met on the nineteenth day of June, eighteen hundred and sixty four.

It was a glorious battle, the crews fought manfully
In the Alabama and Kearsarge, That day upon the sea.

The English Yacht Deerhound, was all the time quite near,
She belonged to Squire Lancaster, Of Wigan in Lancashire
And many a gallant seaman so nobly did save
Who when the Alabama sunk would have met a watery grave.

About nine miles from Cherbourg this gallant fight took place,
The noted Alabama She did the Kearsarge chase.
The Alabama's guns did rattle, and captain Semmes believed
That he would win the battle but he was much deceived.

The men did fight like hero's, and round the decks did run,
Each ship did shake and no mistake as they fired their powerful guns
Brave Captain Semmes did loudly call, as he on the deck did stand,
Don't move or flinch a single inch, "Do your duty every man."

But alas! the Alabama, began to feel affright
Her side were dreadful shaken and she could no longer fight
The Kearsarge was chain plated, and her guns were fired so free,
She beat the Alabama, and sunk her in the sea.

The Deerhound was in readiness the conquered to receive;
And rendered great assistance, my friends you may believe.
When the battle it was over the conquered void of fear,
Safe in the steam Yacht Deerhound, did to Southampton steer.

Now to conclude this gallant fight undaunted brave and bold,
A great and glorious battle as ever yet was told,
To the seamen and the officers, we drink with three times three,
Who did their duty manfully that day upon the sea.

This song tells the front story of a famous sea battle of the American Civil War, fought off the coast of France. Known as the Battle of Cherbourg, it involved two schooner-rigged steamships: The Confederate *Alabama* and the Union *Kearsarge*. The back story is that the *Alabama* had been built clandestinely as "ship hull number 290" in the yard of John Laird in Birkenhead, across the mouth of the river Mersey from Liverpool. Its funding, arranged by James Bulloch, an agent for the Confederate Navy, came from profits managed by the cotton brokerage firm Fraser Trenholm Company, the only Confederate funding source that remained functional through the Civil War. Beside the combination of steam engine and schooner rigging, for disguise the *Alabama* was equipped with a system to retract and conceal its funnel. In addition, her propeller could be disengaged and lifted aboard to lessen drag while under sail. (Merli: 2004, 124) The *Alabama* slipped out to sea after its launching under the name of *Enrica* and headed to the Azores where she rendezvoused with Confederate supply ships and was rigged out as a commerce raider for the Confederate States of America. She was commissioned on August 24, 1862 in nearby international waters as the *Alabama*. Her subsequent two-year cruise made her the most successful commerce-destroyer of all times. This Confederate raider never visited a port in the Confederacy. At least two other commerce raiders, the *Florida* and the *Shenandoah*, were also acquired from Britain and deployed to destroy Union commercial vessels.

Early in the Civil War, the Union Navy sent vessels to blockade Confederate ports. But the South believed that Britain needed continuing shipments of American cotton and would soon be economically compelled to break the North's blockade. Some industries and a substantial number of British members of Parliament held the same opinion, but the 1860 crop had been so large that the mills had surplus stocks. It was not until the winter of 1861–2 that destitution faced the workers as one mill after another came to a standstill. (Wood: 1960, 243) By 1863, ships were more frequently able to break through the blockade and supplies from the East became more available, bringing the British mills back to life.

The Kearsarge and The Alabama

## 115  Working Men of England

*Tune: Plymouth Sound; Broadside, 1777-1844*

Oh! Working men of England, we labour for the great
We toil away both night and day to keep the church and state,
In every part, in every clime, our commerce and our toil,
Adds luster to the genius of Great Britain's native isle;
On every fort on every tower, The British flag's unfurl'd;
Which tells the strength of Britain's power in all parts of the world,
Our hardy tars that plow the deep our glory to expand
With the produce of our labouring men, the pride of Britain's land.

  CHORUS
  Oh! the working men of England will never cease to be
  The prop of this great nation and they ever should be free;
  They toil without a murmur when good wages they command
  And bring honour, glory, and renown to Britain's happy land,

Oh the working men of England when they get reform
What merry joy without alloy their happy brows adorn;
They care not for whig or tory, but to labour and be paid,
With honour to good masters & the founders of free trade.

And should a foreign foe ere threat to tread upon our shore,
Our working men would fly to arms as they have done before,
There's not a Briton in this isle but boldly forth would stand,
In defense of wife and kindred, his queen and native land.

Oh! the working men of England what progress they have made,
In iron, cotton, wool, and coals, the staple of our trade;
The morning bells that ring for toil oft fills them with delight,
In hopes of joyous plenty on a glorious Saturday night;
And may kind providence divine their humble efforts aid
And freedoms sons forever shine on commerce and free trade,
Contentment is the workmen's lot he'll toil by night or day,
But give him plenty in his cot with freedom and fair play.

T. Pearson Printer, 6 Chadderton-Street.<br>off Oldham Road, Manchester

This song was used to enlist workingmen's support for pending reforms. It thanks workers for what they do, advocates for reform, and makes the case for retaining the loyalty of the working man. The point needed emphasis during ongoing frictions between Gladstone and Palmerston over reform. Gladstone had committed himself to reform in a speech: "I venture to say that every man who is not presumably incapacitated by some consideration of personal unfitness or political danger, is morally entitled to come within the pale of the constitution." (Wood: 1960, 252) However, Palmerston and most Members of Parliament continued to oppose furthering enfranchisement.

Two major organizations emerged at this time promoting reform. In April 1864 a predominantly middle class National Reform Union formed as an offshoot of the remnants of Leeds Manhood Suffrage Association. The guiding light of this new association was one of the great Parliamentary orators of the time: John Bright, MP for Birmingham. Organized by Radical politicians and Lancashire merchants and manufacturers, the Union was attempting to repeat the success of the 1840s under the leadership of George Wilson, Bright's lieutenant in the anti-Corn Law agitation. (Cowling: 1967, 242)

In February of 1865, Edmond Beales, renowned public speaker and lawyer, formed the Reform League in London advocating household enfranchisement. The Reform League, with its working class membership including trade unionists and former chartists, had a larger profile than the Reform Union. Beales made whirlwind tours around the country, speaking before growing crowds on the importance and the value of the working man. He had been involved in recent campaigns supporting the Italian freedom fighter Garibaldi and freedom movements in Poland and Central Europe. On the original sheet for this song was also printed a song commemorating a public meeting in 1863 for Garibaldi which attracted 100,000 to Hyde Park.

Both the Union and the League had strong support from some members of Parliament, including William Gladstone, John Bright, and Richard Cobden. But Prime Minister Palmerston and others in the Liberal party held firm in their opposition. In July 1865 a special election increased the Liberal Party's majority, but on October 18 of that year the re-elected Prime Minister Palmerston died. Earl Russell replaced him and wasted no time in having Gladstone, his Chancellor of the Exchequer, submit a new reform bill early in 1866. Desire for working class enfranchisement was high; people were attending mass meetings and demonstrations in numbers not seen since the height of the Chartist period of the 1840s.

Cotton mill workers and idle factories

## 116 The Reform Battle in Hyde Park

Sir Frederick Madden's Collection of Broadside Ballads, 7/4813 – Roud V6591

*Tune: Oh Dear, What Can the Matter Be; The British Lyre, 1792*

Oh dear, What can the mat - ter be

I don't think for some time for re - form we shall fat - ter be,

All our hopes on that head for some time they will scat-tered be,

And all through the row in Hyde Park.

Oh dear! what can the matter be
I don't think for some time for reform we shall fatter be,
All our hopes on that head for some time they will scattered be,
And all through the row in Hyde Park.

On the 23rd of July I have you to inform, sir,
Was to be the great meeting of England's reform, sir,
They declared in procession they intended to form, sir,
And march like true bricks to Hyde Park.

Oh dear! what a fuss and a bother!
From one end of England there is to the other,
In every mouth it is the talk all over,
Concerning the fray in Hyde Park.

From all parts of London great bodies, they marching were,
Their feelings upon reform for to declare,
But the Government coves said they had no business there,
And they should not meet up in Hyde Park.

So W__ he sent for his friend Dicky M__, sir,
Says he, my friend Dicky, you must bear the blame, sir
For the people to ask for their rights it's a shame, sir
So you must not let them meet in Hyde Park.

Then Dicky he lifted his head from his shoulders,
And said he to his blues, get ready, brave soldiers,
The rolling pin you can use well I am told, sirs,
So onward, my boys to Hyde Park

The Park gates were closed, and the people could not get in,
So they said one and all it's no time to be thinking,
So down with the rails, come on and win,
For in we will go to Hyde Park,

To pull down the rails, they went in at it quite stiff, sir,
The stones they gave way the mortar and bricks, sir,
And they tore down the trees, just like walking sticks, sir,
For they expected a row in Hyde Park,

The sticks and the stones, and the brickbats about they flew,
And Each in the fray found he had enough to do,
It equaled Donnybrook Fair, or even famed Peterloo,
Did the battle they had in Hyde Park.

Now the blues by their General, naughty Dick, they were led,
Till a brick gave poor Dicky a nasty pain in the head,
So says he, I think I'd better toddle off to bed,
Oh! bad luck to the fray in Hyde Park.

He called his friend H__, saying tell me, where are you now,
Says he, I am in a sad plight, but I can't tell you how,
But I am all over nasty stuff left here by the cows,
Oh, I wish I'd not come to Hyde Park!

An old lady who was just about eighty-four, sir,
She run for her life as she had ne'er run before, sir.
Jump'd over Wellington statue, and was never seen more, sir.
And all through the row in Hyde Park.

A Bobby laid hold of a boy, saying, out you go,
You have no business here, and that I will let you know,
But, says he, I am as good those swells down in Rotten Row,
So I am bless'd if I budge for the Park.

So now, my good friends, my ditty is ended,
And I hope that no one around me is offended,
It's but to amuse is what I've intended,
To tell of the fray in Hyde Park.

There is no good, they tell me, without there's an evil,
And as at all times I can't afford to be civil,
I would pitch naughty Dicky head long to the lions
For causing the row in Hyde Park.

H. Disley, Printer, 57, High Street, St. Giles, London.

When Gladstone introduced his moderate 1866 version of the Reform Bill on March 18, neither the Reform Union nor the Reform League organized major gatherings in its support. Even though the 1866 Bill was not remotely radical, most members of Parliament resisted any sort of change. The main beneficiaries were to be professionals and business people working in the cities, many of whom were loyal Liberal voters. (Evans: 2000, 47) The Reform Union could see the likelihood of increases to the middle class electorate, but the Reform League was working to gain universal manhood suffrage; this modest Bill was far too meager to satisfy the demands of the working classes.

The temper of the discourse changed when Liberal member Robert Lowe delivered his inflammatory view of enfranchising. Here was new impetus to rally people together. The Tory government with Derby as prime minister had been formed for only two weeks in June 1866 when the Reform League, which had already secured the right to hold meetings in Trafalgar Square, made plans to hold a monster meeting in Hyde Park on July 23. The new Cabinet insisted that Home Secretary Walpole not permit a meeting in this space that was so much enjoyed by the "haves." Sir Richard Mayne, London's Chief of Police, banned the gathering from Hyde Park and assigned thousands of police to keep the "have-nots" out. Huge numbers of working people marched with Edmond Beales to Hyde Park, arriving at its locked gates shortly after 7PM.

After registering their complaint to the authorities at the gates of the park, the leaders turned away to hold the meeting in nearby Trafalgar Square; but the great crowd pressing against the railings that surrounded the park found them insecure and easily beaten down. The result was a large scale scuffle with the police in which a few people were injured and some damage was done to the flower beds. (Conacher: 1971, 70)

Forty or fifty persons were taken into police custody. Later, Bright met with Walpole and agreed that further meetings could be held in Hyde Park; two more meetings were held there without incident. Had the original Hyde Park scuffle actually been directed by either Beales or Bright it would have been blamed on the Reform movement, but it was seen as more of a warning about the working man's powerful commitment to achieving enfranchisement. Perhaps a similar situation could stir the fear of the riots that preceded the passage of the 1832 Reform Bill.

Reform League demonstration in Hyde Park

## 117 The Great Reform Meeting December 3rd 1866

Charles Hindley, Curiosities of Street Literature (1893): 107 – Roud V5910

*Tune: I Have Fruit, I Have Flowers; Edward Riley, 1826*

You true friends of Reform,
Just listen to my song,
And some truth in these verses shall be found:
It's the talk throughout the nation,
About the monster demonstration,
Announced to take place in Ashburnham Grounds.

CHORUS
Then cheer for Reform and on be marching!
And you will find you'll weather the storm;
For depend on what I say you will sure to gain the day.
If you will lend a willing shoulder to reform.

Now when the Tory's found
That in Ashburnham Grounds,
England's sons were to meet now only mark,
At their dirty work they got,
And determined they should not,
Do if they wished another scene like Hyde Park

But my lads do not despair,
There is the pure and open air,
Which belong to the great and the small,
And though our foes they make a fuss,
There our rights we can discuss,
For the song says "There's room enough for all."

Shall our liberties be crushed,
And be trampled to the dust,
By men who never earnt a penny in their lives?
And yet we must not meet,
Nor for our rights dare speak,
But if we cannot win boys, we must try!

Now the Tories they do say,
If we will only wait some day
They will give us Reform upon their plan;
But their kindness it comes slow,
And the quarters they would show,
Would be the sort the wolf he shows the lamb.

So England's working men,
The Rights they still defend,
Of the mightiest nation in the world;
And thousands will be found,
Who will gladly rally round,
So the banner of Reform we'll keep unfurled.

Then send the Adullamite crew,
And the pals the Tories too,
Headlong to Old Nick altogether,
But for men like Beale and Bright,
Let's shout with all our might,
Here's the good cause, Reform, ever!

This song was written to encourage attendance at the planned massive demonstration to be held on December 3, 1866 in the West End of London, organized cooperatively by the Reform League and the Reform Union.

Similar meetings had been held in major cities throughout the country in support of broadening Britain's electorate. Proceedings usually consisted of a large, well-marshaled march through the community, with Union representation, Coop Membership, Temperance Societies, and Friendly Societies proudly showing their banners. The parade usually ended in a large outdoor gathering with several speaker stands where identical resolutions were proposed and acted upon. After each big rally a large indoor meeting was held, which frequently featured John Bright, who would speak, taking care to give copies of the speech to the press reporters. This formula was repeated, with numbers well over 100,000 in cities like Birmingham (August 27), Manchester (September 24), Leeds (October 8), Glasgow (October 16), and Dublin (November 2).

The London rally was scheduled as the climax of the National Reform efforts to keep the heat on Parliament for increased enfranchisement. It was planned for West London, marching from St. James Park to the grounds of Beaufort Gardens in Old Brompton. The song says the march will end in Ashburnham Grounds, but according to the printed organization sheet, Lord Ranelagh had offered Beaufort Gardens for the rally when the government refused Hyde Park. (Cowling: 1967, 247) Beaufort Gardens are an ideal location in Old Brompton. 250,000 or more were expected, but a dreadful rainstorm reduced the turnout to as few as 25,000. "You will find that you'll weather the storm" was seemingly prescient. Nevertheless, it took the column over an hour to pass Carlton Club, the Conservative Party club in St James. The demonstration impressed onlookers with its high seriousness and good order; 10,000 of the marchers were voluntary marshals. (Smith: 1966, 143)

March in the rain from Whitehall to Beaufort House December 3, 1866

## 118  The Great Battle For Freedom and Reform

Sir Frederick Madden's Collection of Broadside Ballads,  7/4761 – Roud V5908

*Tune: The Girl I Left Behind Me; Maurice Hime, 1810*

You working men of England,
Who live by daily toil;
Speak of your rights bold Englishmen,
All through Britain's isle
The titled Tories keep you down
Which you cannot endure
And the reason I tell, am bound
You're but working men — and poor

With Gladstone, Russell, Beales, and Bright
We shall weather through the storm,
To give the working man his rights,
And gain the — Bill Reform.

If the Hyde Park meeting had been allowed
No disturbance would have been
Long life, they cried to the Prince of Wales
And god bless England's Queen!
Why should the banks be ever closed,
Against the poor who for them pay
Work with a will for equality,
And you will gain the day.

We want no Tory government.
The poor man to oppress,
They never try to do you good,
The truth you will confess.
The Liberals are the poor man's friend,
To forward all they try,
They'll beat their foes you may depend
And never will say, die.

Great meetings are held in high parts,
In country and in town,
The names of Beales and Gladstone,
With working man resound
Riches are but worthless dross,
Without our working brother
Which proves that in our national cause
We could help each other.

God praise is due to the Reform League
They have generous hearts and minds,
For the Prisoners taken in Hyde Park,
They intend to pay the fines
At the Agricultural hall they met,
With band and flags so gay,
And when they meet at Lincoln's-Inn-fields
Give them a loud huzza!

The vote for manhood suffrage,
And the ballot too, likewise,
For freedom of opinion,
All English men doth prize:
And why should not a working man
Have power to give his vote,
To one that is the poor man's friend
Tho' he wears a ragged coat

If public Parks of London
Are only one class,
They ought to put this notice up:
The poor they cannot pass.
It's time our laws they altered were,
You'll say it is a bore,
That one law should be for the rich
And another for the poor.

An Englishman is not a slave,
For that was never sent
Then give the working man his rights,
You'll find he is content;
Give us the ballot and franchise,
It's the only boon we ask,
Then shouts will rend the skies,
For that will end our task.

The winter of 1866–67 was bitingly cold, and it took a popular song like this to keep up the spirits of the un-enfranchised and unemployed workers. But events of 1867 soon brought issues to a head. In February, when Queen Victoria opened Parliament for the first time since the death of Prince Albert, she demanded that Parliament consider the question of representation. The new Tory government of Derby and Disraeli, with Majestic and street pressure, took up the issue, but Disraeli's early concil-iatory statements regarding reform were not well received by Parliament or the people. John Bright wrote in his diary on February 11, 1867: "Disraeli's speech on his Reform Resolutions. Speech very bad in every respect; much unfavorable comment, and nothing satisfactory as to Reform." (Walling: 1931, 295) The Reform League sponsored a rally in Trafalgar Square for March 18th, the day that Disraeli was to present the bill. The bill still need-ed some major amendments that the League relied on the Liberals to push for. It was hoped that 100,000 would attend the rally, but as few as 20,000 people were there, reflecting the working men's low expectations of any bill that the Tories would draft. They were right, as Disraeli's bill, although more encompassing of household suffrage in the boroughs than the Russell/ Gladstone Bill had been, was full of special clauses to limit the expansion of franchise. However, the new Bill was estimated to cause an increase of the borough electorate to over 1,000,000, and with reduction of county requirements and fancy franchises, an additional 309,000 would be added. (Smith: 1966, 168)

Seeing that it was essential to keep pressure on Parliament to force amendments to increase the franchise and improve the bill, a delegation of Reform and League Union leaders met with Disraeli on a hot April Fool's Day to air their complaints about the bill's shortcomings. Then on April 16 Birmingham held a vast reform rally with speaker George Nuttall's speech heavily quoted in the *Morning Star*: "The people should rise in their might and majesty. If like the raging sea they should sweep on in their righteous indignation, every barrier set up against them... the aristocracy... itself might be swept into oblivion forever." (Foot: 2005, 154)

## 119 The Reform Demonstration in Hyde Park, May 6th, 1867

Bodleian Library: Harding Collection, B 14(321) and Madden 7/4813 – Roud V6583

*Tune: Flying Trapeze; George Leybourne, 1868*

Good people come listen I'll tell you a lark,
That happened on Monday the 6th in Hyde Park,
For brave Edmund Beales and his friends they did start,
To meet the working men there.
They reached there at six o'clock gallant and right,
And when in so boldly did shout,
We're here me brave boys, and we'll show them this night
We'll speak, and they shan't turn us out.

    CHORUS
    So remember me boys, 'twas a glorious sight,
    In Hyde Park on the 6th, it was right against might
    With Beales for our leader, we beat them that night,
    At last working men they are free

Now Dicky Mayne to his friend Walley said,
If you go to Hyde Park pray mind your poor head,
And I'm sure I expect to be taken home dead
And for me it will not be a lark.
Now don't go says Walley, to you I declare,
Against us you know they've a spite
The people mean business, so I shan't go there
Not in Hyde Park, on that Monday night.

In buses the poleaxes hurried along,
And when they arrived they were five thousand strong,
But during the night you couldn't see one,
Interfere with our friends in Hyde Park.
I heard that one said to his mate, "Bill I say,
If they have a row, I'll be off quick,
For I got in a bother last reform day,
And they measured my head with a brick."

Now government frightened on Monday they were,
Some constables special in then they did swear,
Their staffs they did hide, when in the park there,
They thought that they would have to fight.
One went home enraged, says "I'll have a row
Since to Hyde Park I've been on the march,
I am almost a boiling we have been I vow,
Like dummies stuck on the Marble Arch"

So the Franchise forever we've beat them, hurra!
Long life to brave Beales and Reformers, I say,
United let's be and we'll yet gain the day,
And always remember Hyde Park.
We don't want special duty to be done,
Our rights! it is all that we ask,
To meet with each other when labour is done
And speak our minds in the Park.

Henry Disley, Printer, 57, High Street, St Giles, London: W.C.

Meetings and demonstrations for reform escalated throughout the country, climaxing during Parliament's 1867 Easter break when another meeting was scheduled by the combined Reform League and Union for May 6, which was to coincide with the return of Parliament after its Easter recess. Placards went up all over the country announcing this mass demonstration for universal manhood suffrage. On May 1, seeking to avoid an embarrassing repeat of the government's inability to control the meeting the year

before, Home Secretary Walpole reluctantly issued the following proclamation:

> Whereas it has been publicly announced that a meeting will be held
> in Hyde Park on Monday the sixth day of May next for the purpose
> of political discussion: and whereas the use of the Park for the pur-
> pose aforesaid is illegal, and interferes with the enjoyment of the
> Park by the people, and is calculated to endanger the public peace,
> now all persons are hereby warned and admonished that they will
> attend any such meeting at their peril, and all her Majesty's loyal
> and faithful subjects are required to abstain from attending, aiding
> or taking part in any such meeting, or from entering the Park with
> a view to attend, aid or take part in any such meeting. (Foot: 2005,
> 154–55)

The announcement was posted all over the city and presented to activist Charles Bradlaugh as he spoke at an earlier large demonstration in
Trafalgar Square. Bradlaugh ridiculed the prohibition proclamation, to the
delight of those attending the rally. Large numbers of people were plainly
ready to defy this law, and the Government responded at first as though
it were facing another Peterloo. Troops of Hussars were summoned up
and held in waiting round the Park. Thousands of special constables were
sworn in and Woolwich Arsenal worked overtime making staves and even
pikes. A mighty confrontation seemed inevitable. Yet long before 6PM on
May 6, Walpole and his advisers backed away. There were so many demonstrators and so many gates to the park that the crowds were impossible to
control. "This was the first time that any political organization representing
the working class had openly defied the law of the masters, and the effect
on the masters was catastrophic." (Foot: 2005, 15) In spite of Walpole's
threats, the meeting was held at Hyde Park and police or armed forces did
nothing to stop it. In part it is from this peaceful event that the free speech
area in Hyde Park remains to this day.

The Bill was then in the second reading stage under scrutiny and review of
proposed amendments. Surprisingly, Disraeli accepted many amendments
from both sides of the House, but he was not willing to accept recommen-
dations from Gladstone or Bright. Then, less than a week after the Hyde
Park demonstration, Disraeli sought a back bench member of the Liberal
Party, Grosvenor Hodgkinson, for help with the issue of renters who would
not be eligible to vote because their rates were paid by their landlords.
Hodgkinson's amendment would actually end the practice of compound
rate paying. With this addition it was now clear that all male householders
who paid rates were to be franchised. To achieve passage, Disraeli then
accepted amendments to correct most of the Liberal criticisms of the initial
Bill. The Bill was also changed from £15 to all £12 rate payers when Locke
King submitted his amendment, which he had submitted in eight successive
sessions to extend the £10 franchise to the county constituencies. Disraeli

offered to accept it at £12, and Locke King accepted it without a division. The final Bill reduced the two-year residence requirement to one year and dropped the remaining fancy franchise and the dual vote that allowed property owners to vote in both town and country. When the highly amended Bill was brought up for its third reading, it immediately passed without a division. "Jauntily, the Tories shook hands among themselves. While the Liberals gave a tired cheer..." (Smith: 1966, 209) Why did Disraeli accept all of the amendments that turned this bill into a truly democratic document? Paul Foot suggests:

> The explanation lies outside Parliament, in the great wave of agitation that arose quite suddenly after the defeat of the Liberal Bill in 1866 and in the blatant defiance of attempts by the Government to suppress the agitation by force. Even the Parliamentary debates themselves bear witness to the sense of panic that was shattering the solidarity and confidence of an unrepresentative assembly. (Foot: 2005, 158)

Meeting at the Reform Tree in Hyde Park

**120** The Great Liberal Majority of 110:
The Tories are Froze out and got no Work to do

Charles Hindley, Curiosities of Street Literature (1893): 110 – Roud V15923

Tune: Fathom the Bowl; S. Baring-Gould, 1794

Draw near all you true Li-be-rals, And lis-ten for a while,

While I a dit-ty sing to you That will cause you for to smile;

It's con-cern-ing of the poor To-ries Who are in a pre-cious stew,

They are out of a job so-help-my-bob, And got no work to do.

CHORUS
For the Li-be-rals have gained you see, One hun-dred and ten ma-jo-ri-ty,

And the To-ries they are all froze out And got no work to do.

Draw near all you true Liberals,
And listen for a while,
While I a ditty sing to you
That will cause you for to smile;
It's concerning of the poor Tories
Who are in a precious stew,
They are out of a job so-help-my-bob,
And got no work to do.

    CHORUS
    For the Liberals have gained you see,
    One hundred and ten majority,
    And the Tories they are all froze out
    And got no work to do

Through England and Ireland,
Scotland, and Wales they cry,
Give us the brave Liberals,
And let their colours fly;
For you may see by the returns,
The Tories they have cause to mourn,
They are in disgrace and out place,
And got no work to do;
They are a selfish crew, oo-oo,
And their noses look quite blue oo-oo,
Their day is past done brown at last,

Now there is the Irish Bishops,
Must spout their shovel hat and wigs,
They will get no rent in shape of tenths,
Nor get no nice tithe pigs:
And the little boys will them get at
I say old boy I'll have your hat;
You have lost yours and serve you right,
You will have no work to do.
Yes, they will be licked clean off their perch,
If they capsize the Irish Church,
For Gladstone will give them the sack,
They'll have no work to do.

Ben Dizzy he is lamenting,
For he is in a dreadful fix,
And from St Stevens cabinet-works,
He has had to cut his stick;
He is grieving for the loaves and fishes,
He may say his grace to empty dishes,
For Gladstone he will cut his comb
Oh dear what will he do?
His hopes are up the flue oo-oo
But I pity him don't you oo-oo
He is all the way from Buckinghamshire
And got no work to do.

Now the Tories boast in Westminster,
They have gained a victory,
But how John Mill he has turned out,
You all may plainly see;
And there are more in the same state,
Who have been fishing with a golden bait,

But it is all of no use, we have cooked their goose,
They'll have no work to do,
They dirty tricks can do, oo-oo
What I tell you is quite true, oo-oo
In St Stephen's Hall they will sing small,
We have got no work to do oo-oo.

Now the working men of England,
May chance get their rights,
While they have their champion Gladstone,
Their battles for to fight;
For that he is a brick you'll say I am right,
And so is that old cock Johnny Bright,
And the Tories them to affright,
Will have their work to do.
Then for reform give three huzzas!
The Liberals have gained the day,
And the Tories they in grief do say,
We have got no work to do.

Winning a 116-seat Liberal majority in Parliament with the 1868 election was a major step for the working man toward achieving democratic representative government in Britain. That is, provided you were a man, that you lived in an electoral borough, and you were willing to reveal how you voted at the husting. It must be remembered that this breakthrough in 1867 only added 7.9% more of the men over 21 years old to the voting register, but still only 8.25% of the population of Britain could vote. Perhaps most amazing was the efficiency with which the revised district system was implemented. The entire process, from passing the Scottish and Irish Representation of the People Acts in June 1868 to holding the national election, took less than six months. Such efficiency had also been seen after the passage of the first Reform bill.

This song celebrates the achievement of a Liberal majority of 110 after the 1868 election, which actually was only an increase of 30 seats over the previous government. The government that passed the Second Reform Bill was a Tory minority government that had been elected in 1865 with a Liberal majority of 80. The Liberal majority included many old Whigs, as well as most of the committed radical reformers and the "Abdullah cave dwellers." Robert Lowe became the new Chancellor of the Exchequer. The social composition of the Commons in 1869 was 51.1% aristocracy and landed gentry, 24.4% business men, 13.2% lawyers, and 5.2% miscellaneous. (Jenkins: 1996, 104)

As soon as this Reform Bill of 1867 was passed, the Liberals were in a position to reunite. "At least as important as the story of the session of 1867, but much less studied, is that of the session of 1867–8, during which

Gladstone again took command of his party and fashioned it into a new progressive instrument." (Beales: 1969, 208) Remarkable changes included passage of the Compulsory Church Rate Abolition Act of 1868, ending mandatory rates charged all parish residents regardless of church membership, and the beginnings of the disestablishment of the Irish Protestant Church.

There were some disappointments in this election for the reformers. Ernest Jones was unsuccessful, by a small margin, in his quest to fill the third seat given to Manchester; John Stuart Mill was defeated in his bid to regain his seat for Westminster; and Gladstone's campaign for the Lancashire seat was unsuccessful. However, as was common in those days, Gladstone had also sought and obtained a seat in Greenwich. Of course, much more work remained to achieve a fair and equitable government system; meanwhile, the era of street ballads was coming to a close. However, the second Reform Bill brought Britain closer to democratic representation than it had been in 1768.

Now the working men of England,
May chance get their rights,
While they have their champion Gladstone,
Their battles for to fight;
For that he is a brick you'll say I am right,
And so is that old cock Johnny Bright,
And the Tories them to affright,
Will have their work to do.
Then for reform give three huzzas!
The Liberals have gained the day,
And the Tories they in grief do say,
We have got no work to do.

Victory for Liberals in Leeds, December 1868

# Epilogue

With passage of the second reform Bill, radical thinkers were still needed to achieve a better democracy. Over the years those who sought to achieve the objectives of democracy continued to be called Radical by those who felt the need to hold the line.

Many labeled as radicals are still chipping away throughout the world to occasionally achieve human progress. In the long hard struggle, Britain can now look back on:

**1872  The Ballot Act**
required Parliamentary and local elections to use secret ballots

**1884  Representation of the People Act**
enabled uniform franchise for county and Borough. Two thirds of men could vote.

**1911  Parliament Act**
Members of Parliament were to be paid and the power of the House of Lords was reduced.

**1918  Representation of the People Act**
Women over age 30 that met property requirements could vote. All men over 21 could vote regardless of property ownership.

**1928  Representation of the People Act**
All women and men over 21 could vote.

**1949  Parliament Act**
Along with the 1911 Act, became part of the constitution and greatly reduced the power of the House of Lords.

**1969** Representation of the People Act
Reduced the voting age to 18.

**1981** Representation of the People Act
A representative detained for more than a year must vacate their seat.

**1983** Representation of the People Act
Limited candidates' and parties' conduct and expenditure during elections.

**1985** Representation of the People Act
Enabled British citizens to vote overseas up to 5 years.

**1989** Representation of the People Act
Extended eligibility of overseas voting to 20 years.

**1990** Representation of the People Act
Enabled absentee ballot

**2000** Representation of the People Act
Removed restrictions for most voters with disabilities.

**2006** Electoral Administration Act
Lowered the age for candidacy for office to 18.

Despite all of these amendments, gaps persist. For example, voting districts are not equal in population. This is particularly true in Greater London and Northern Ireland.

The work continues.

# Illustrations

*Unless noted, all illustrations are reproduced from images that were originally printed as multiples and are now in the public domain.*

CHAPTER 3: PAINE

CHAPTER 4: INSURRECTION

CHAPTER 9: CHARTER

CHAPTER 10: REFORM

# Bibliography

Ashton, John. *Modern Street Ballads*, 1888. Benjamin Bloom, 1968.

Barrell, John. *Imagining the King's Death: Figurative Treason, Fantasies of Regicide 1793–1796*. Oxford University Press, 2000.

Barrell, John. *The Spirit of Despotism, Invasion of Privacy in the 1790s*. Oxford University Press, 2006.

Bartel, Roland, editor. *Liberty and Terror In England: Reactions to the French Revolution*. D. C. Heath and Co., 1965.

Bartlett, Thomas. *Revolutionary Dublin, 1795–1801: The Letters of Francis Higgins to Dublin Castle*. Four Courts Press, 2004.

Beales, Derek. *From Castlereagh to Gladstone 1815–1885*. W. W. Norton & Co, 1969.

Belchem, John. *'Orator' Hunt: Henry Hunt and English Working-class Radicalism*. Clarenden Press Oxford, 1985.

Bennett, Betty T., ed. *British War Poetry In the Age of Romanticism: 1793–1815*. Garland Publishing, 1976.

Berresford Ellis, Peter & Mac A'Ghobhainn, Seamus. *The Scottish Insurrection of 1820*. Pluto Press, 1989.

Bewley, Christina. *Muir of Huntershill*. Oxford University Press, 1981.

Bewley, Christina and David. *Gentleman Radical, A Life of John Horne Tooke*. I. B. Tauris Academic Studies, 1998.

Brady, Eugene A. A Reconsideration of the Lancashire "Cotton Famine." *Agricultural History,* Vol 37 No 3, July 1963.

Brown, Roly. Number 20: Transports. *Musical Traditions Internet Magazine* Artical 176, 2005.

Chase, Malcolm. *Chartism: A New History*. Manchester University Press, 2007.

Chase, Malcolm. 1820, *Disorder and Stability in the United Kingdom*. Manchester University Press, 2013.

Chase, Malcolm. *The Chartists Perspectives and Legacies*. Merlin Press, 2015.

Chappell, William. *Popular Music of the Olden Time*. Chappell and Co, 1857.

Cobbett, William. *Political Register*, December 4, 1819.

Cole, G. D. H. *The Life of William Cobbett*. Harcourt, Brace, and Company, 1924.

Cole, G. D. H. and Postgate, Raymond. *The Common People 1746–1938*. Methuen & Co. Ltd., 1971.

Cole, G. D. H. *Chartist Portraits*. Cassell Publishers, 1941.

Cone, Carl B. *The English Jacobins*. Scribner, 1968.

Conner, Clifford D. *Colonel Despard: The Life and Times of an Anglo-Irish Rebel*. Combined Publishing, 2000.

Conway, Stephen. *The British Isles and the War of American Independence*. Oxford University Press, 2000.

Cowling, Maurice. *Disraeli, Gladstone and Revolution: The passing of the Second Reform Bill*. Cambridge University Press, 1967.

Cox, Jeffrey N. *Poetry and Politics In the Cockney School*. Cambridge University Press, 2004.

Curtin, Nancy J. *The United Irishmen: Popular Politics in Ulster and Dublin*. Clarendon Press Oxford, 1994.

Dickinson, H. T. *Britain and the French Revolution, 1789–1815*. Macmillan Education, 1989.

Dinwiddy, J. R. "Sir Francis Burdett and Burdettite Radicalism." *HISTORY, Journal of the Historical Association*, vol. 65, 1980.

Dinwiddy, J. R. *From Luddism to the First Reform Bill*. Basil Blackwell Ltd., 1986.

Dodds, John, W. *The Age of Paradox: A Biography of England, 1841–1851*. Rinehart and Company, 1952.

Dugan, James. *The Great Mutiny*. New York: Putnam & Sons, 1965.

Durant, Will and Ariel. *The Age of Napoleon*. Simon & Schuster, 1975.

Dyck, Ian. *William Cobbett and Rural Popular Culture*. Cambridge University Press, 1992.

Edsall, Nicholas C. *Anti-Poor Law Movement, 1834–44*. Manchester University Press, 1971.

Elliott, Marianne. *Wolfe Tone: Prophet of Irish Independence*. Yale University Press, 1989.

Engels, Friedrich. *The Condition of the Working Class in England*. Reprint of 1845 edition, Stanford University Press, 1958.

Evans, Eric J. *Parliamentary Reform, c. 1770–1918*. Pearson Education Limited, 2000.

Firth, C. H. *Naval Songs and Ballads.* Navy Records Society, 1908.

Foot, Paul. *The Vote: How It Was Won And How It Was Undermined.* Penguin Books, 2005.

Fraser, Antonia. *Perilous Question: The Drama of the Great Reform Bill of 1832.* Public Affairs, 2013.

Fraser, Flora. *The Unruly Queen: The Life Of Queen Caroline.* Alfred A. Knopf Inc., 1996.

Freehling, William W. *The South vs. the South: How Anti-Confederate Southerners Shaped the Course of the Civil War.* Oxford University Press, 2002.

George, Dorothy. *English Political Caricature, 1793–1832.* Oxford, 1959.

Gill, Conrad. *The Naval Mutinies of 1797.* Manchester University Press, 1913.

Hague, William. *William Pitt the Younger.* Harper Collins, 2004.

Halévy, Elié. *The Liberal Awakening (1815–1830).* Barnes & Noble University Paperbacks, 1961.

Hammersley, Rachel. "Jean-Paul Marat's The Chains of Slavery In Britain and France, 1774–1833" *The Historical Journal*, 48:3. Cambridge University Press, 2005.

Harland, John. *Ballads and Songs of Lancashire.* Scribner, 1865.

Hayes, Edward. *The Ballads of Ireland, Vol. 1.* James Duffy, 1856.

Haythornthwaite, Philip J. *Who Was Who in The Napoleonic Wars.* Arms and Armour Press, 1998.

Hepburn, James. *A Book of Scattered Leaves: Poetry of Poverty in Broadside Ballads of Nineteenth-Century England, Vol. 1.* Associated University Presses, 2000.

Hibbert, Christopher. *King Mob.* Dorset, 1958.

Himmelfarb, Gertrude. *The Idea of Poverty: England in the Early Industrial Age.* Knopf, 1984.

Hindley, Charles. *Curiosities of Street Literature.* London: Reeves and Turner, 1893.

Hobsbawm, Eric. *Uncommon People, Resistance, Rebellion, and Jazz.* Weidenfeld & Nicolson, 1999.

Hobsbawm, Eric and Rudé, George. *Captain Swing.* New York & London: W. W. Norton Co., 1975.

Hochschild, Adam. *Bury the Chains: Prophets and Rebels in the Fight to Free an Empire's Slaves.* Houghton Mifflin, 2005.

Holloway, John and Black, Joan. *Later English Broadside Ballads, Vol. 2.* London: Routledge & Kegan Paul, 1975

Hughes, Robert. *The Fatal Shore: The Epic of Australia's Founding.* Knopf, 1988.

Hugill, Stan. *Shanties From the Seven Seas.* Routledge & Kegan Paul, 1961.

Huntington, G. *Songs the Whalemen Sang.* Barre Publishers, 1964.

Jenkins, Roy. *Gladstone.* Macmillan, 1996.

Jensen, Oskar Cox. *Napoleon and British Song, 1797–1822.* Oxford: Palgrave Macmillan, 2015.

Jones, E. H. Stuart. *An Invasion That Failed.* Oxford: Basil Blackwell, 1950.

Jones, W. *Biographical Sketches of the Reform Ministers, Vol. 2* (1835). Kessinger Publishing, 2010.

Kee, Robert. *The Green Flag, Vol. 1.* Quartet, 1976.

Kovalev, Y. V. *Anthology of Chartist Literature.* Moskva, 1956.

Lang, Sean. *Parliamentary Reform, 1785–1928.* Routledge, 1999.

Lean, E. Tangye. *The Napoleonists: A Study in Political Disaffection, 1760–1960.* Oxford University, 1970.

Longmate, Norman. *Hungry Mills: The Story of the Lancashire Cotton Famine, 1861–5.* Temple Smith, London, 1978.

MacManus, Seumas. *The Story of the Irish Race, 1921.* Random House, 1990.

Manwaring, G. and Dobrée, B. *The Floating Republic.* Frank Cass and Co. Ltd., 1935.

Marlow, Joyce. *The Tolpuddle Martyrs.* Panther Books, 1971.

Marlow, Joyce. *The Peterloo Massacre.* Readers Union, 1970.

McCullough, David. *John Adams.* Simon and Schuster, 2001.

McCullough, David. *1776.* Simon and Schuster, 2005.

Merli, Frank J. *Great Britain and the Confederate Navy, 1861–1865.* Indiana University Press, 2004.

Moore, Frank. *Songs and Ballads of the American Revolution.* D. Appleton & Co., 1855. Kennikat Press, 1964.

Morton, A. L. *A People's History of England,* 1938. Lawrence and Wishart Ltd., 1979.

Moylan, Terry. *The Age of Revolution in the Irish Song Tradition, 1776 to 1815.* Lilliput Press Ltd, 2001

Mulcahy, M & Fitzgibbon, M. *The Voice of the People: Songs and History of Ireland.* O'Brien Press, 1982.

Nelson, Craig. *Thomas Paine: Enlightenment, Revolution, and the Birth of Modern Nations.* Penguin Books, 2006.

Paine, Thomas. *The Rights of Man.* Reprint of 1791 edition, Doubleday and Co., 1961.

Palmer, Roy. *Songs of the Midlands.* EP Publishing Ltd, 1972.

Palmer, Roy. *A Touch On the Times.* Penguin Books, 1974.

Palmer, Roy. *The Oxford Book of Sea Songs.* Oxford, 1986.

Palmer, Roy. *The Sound of History*. Oxford, 1988.

Parry, Jonathan. *The Rise and Fall of Liberal Government in Victorian Britain*. Yale University Press, 1993.

Patton, W. F. Thesis: *Political Expression Through Song and Verse*. University of Belfast, 1983.

Pearce, Edward. *Reform! The Fight for the 1832 Reform Act*. Jonathan Cape, 2003.

Pearce, Robert and Stearn, Roger. *Government and Reform 1815 to 1918*. Hodder & Stoughton, 1994.

Pelling, Henry Mathison. *A History of British Trade Unionism*. Penguin Books, 1963.

Pivca, Otto V. *Navies of the Napoleonic Era*. Hippocrene Books, 1980.

Pocock, Tom. *The Terror Before Trafalgar*. W.W. Norton, 2002.

Pybus, Cassandra. *Epic Journeys of Freedom: Runaway Slaves of the American Revolution and Their Global Quest for Liberty*. Beacon Press, UK, 2006.

Robins, Jane. *Rebel Queen: How the Trial of Caroline Brought England to the Brink of Revolution*. Simon & Shuster, 2006.

Roud, Steve, and Bishop, Julia. *The New Penguin Book of English Folk Songs*. Penguin Classics, 2012.

Roud, Steve. *Folk Song in England*. Faber and Faber, 2017.

Royle, Edward. *Chartism*. Longman Press, 1980.

Royle, Trevor. *Crimea: The Great Crimean War, 1854–1856*. Palgrave MacMillan, 2000.

Rudé, George. *Wilkes and Liberty: A Social Study*. John Wiley & Sons, 1962.

Schama, Simon. *Rough Crossings: Britain, the Slaves, and the American Revolution*. Harper Collins, 2006.

Scheckner, Peter. *An Anthology of Chartist Poetry: Poetry of the British Working Class, 1830s–1850s*. Associated University Presses, 1989.

Schom, Alan. *Napoleon Bonaparte*. Harper Collins, 1997.

Scott, John A. *The Ballad of America*. Grosset & Dunlap, 1967.

Seymour, Charles. *Electoral Reform in England and Wales*. Yale University Press, 1915.

Shenton, Caroline. *The Day Parliament Burned Down*. Oxford University Press, 2012.

Smith, F. B. *The Making of the Second Reform Bill*. Cambridge University Press, 1966.

Sparling, H. Halliday. *Irish Minstrelsy*. Walter Scott Publishing, 1890.

Thomas, Hugh. *The Slave Trade: The Story of the Atlantic Slave Trade, 1440–1870*. Simon and Schuster, 1997.

Thomas, J. E. *Britain's Last Invasion: Fishguard 1797.* Tempus, 2007.

Thompson, David. *Weavers of Dreams.* Center for Cooperatives, University of California, 1994.

Thompson, Dorothy. *The Chartists: Popular Politics In The Industrial Revolution.* Pantheon Books, 1984.

Thompson, E. P. *The Making of the English Working Class.* Vintage Books, 1966.

Thompson, Neal. *The Real Rights of Man.* Sutton Publishing, 1998.

Trevelyan, George M. *The Life of John Bright.* Constable and Co. Ltd, 1913.

Turner, Michael J. *The Age of Unease: Government and Reform in Britain, 1782–1832.* Sutton Publishing, 2000.

Walling, John. *The Diaries of John Bright.* Barnes & Noble, 1931

Ward, J. T. *Chartism.* Batsford, 1973.

Weber, Paul. *On The Road To Rebellion: The United Irishmen and Hamburg 1796–1803.* Four Courts Press, 1997.

Wells, Roger. *Insurrection: The British Experience, 1795–1803.* Alan Sutton, 1983.

Wells, Roger. *Wretched Faces: Famine in War Time, 1793–1801.* New York: St. Martin's Press, 1988.

Wilson, David A. *Paine and Cobbett: The Transatlantic Connection.* Sheffield: McGill-Queen's University Press, 1988.

Wilson, John. *The Songs of Joseph Mather. To which are added a Memoir of Mather and Miscellaneous Songs relating to Sheffield.* Reprint of 1862 edition, Kessinger Press, 2010.

Wilson, Kathleen. *The Sense of the People: Politics, Culture and Imperialism in England 1715 1785.* Cambridge University Press, 1995.

Wilson, R. *Paddy's Resource: Being a Select Collection of Original and Modern Patriotic Songs.* Evans Early American Imprint Collection, 1798.

Wise, Steven, M. *Though The Heavens May Fall: The Landmark Trial That Led to the End Of Slavery.* Da Capo Press, 2005.

Wood, Anthony. *Nineteenth Century Britain, 1815–1914.* Martins the Printers, 1960.

Wood, Peter. *The Green Linnet.* Martins the Printers, 2015.

Woodbridge, George. *The Reform Bill of 1832.* Thomas Crowell Company, 1970.

Woodham-Smith, Cecil. *The Reason Why: The Story of the Fatal Charge of the Light Brigade.* Penguin, 1953.

Young, A. F. and Ashton, E. T. *British Social Work in the Nineteenth Century.* Routledge and Kegan Paul, 1956.

Zimmermann, George Denis. *Songs of Irish Rebellion.* Folklore Associates, 1967.

# Index of Song Titles

# Index of First Lines

# Index

Lightning Source UK Ltd.
Milton Keynes UK
UKHW020620260122
397727UK00003B/247